CW01650806

**ALL ABOUT CRYSTALS**
Connie Islin
ISBN 965-494-111-2

**ALL ABOUT TAROT**
Hali Morag
ISBN 965-494-062-0

**ALL ABOUT THE WICCA OF LOVE**
Tabatha Jennings
ISBN 965-494-110-4

**ALL ABOUT THE SIXTH SENSE**
Tom Pearson
ISBN 965-494-138-4

**ALL ABOUT NUMEROLOGY**
Lia Robin
ISBN 965-494-109-0

**ALL ABOUT PALMISTRY**
Batia Shorek
ISBN 965-494-094-9

**ALL ABOUT DREAMS**
Eili Goldberg
ISBN 965-494-061-2

**ALL ABOUT PREDICTING THE FUTURE**
Sarah Zehavi
ISBN 965-494-093-0

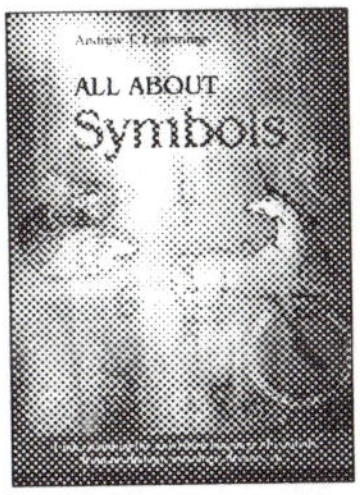


**ALL ABOUT SYMBOLS**
Andrew T. Cummings
ISBN 965-494-139-2

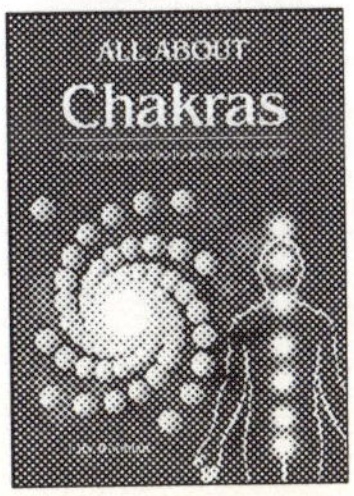


**ALL ABOUT CHAKRAS**
Lily Rooman
ISBN 965-494-149-X

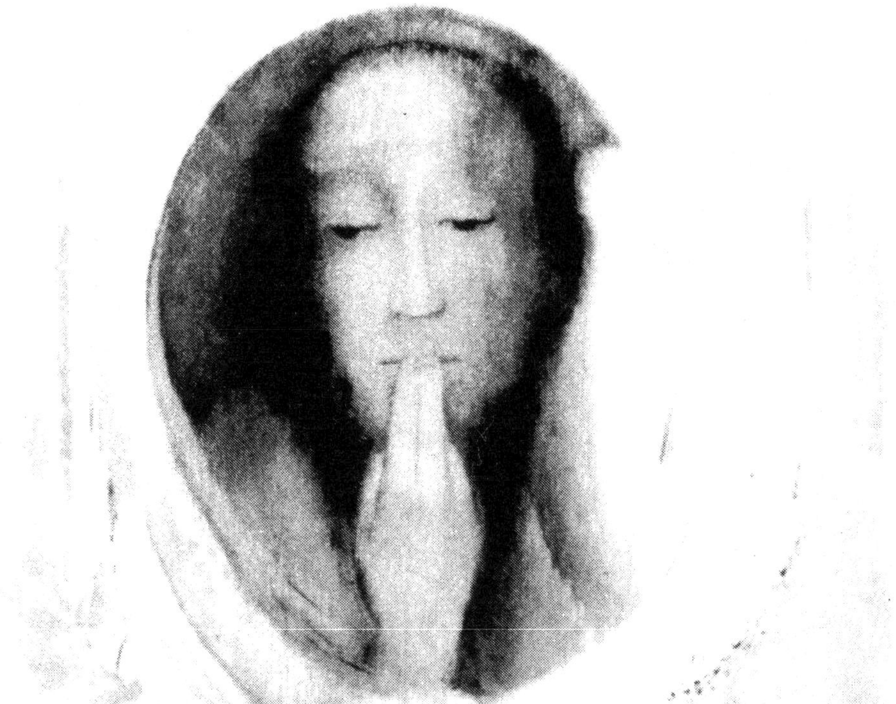

# ALL ABOUT THE SIXTH SENSE

**Tom Pearson**

Astrolog Publishing House Ltd.

Cover design: Na'ama Yaffe

© Astrolog Publishing House 2003

ISBN 965-494-138-4

All rights reserved to Astrolog Publishing House Ltd.

P. O. Box 1123, Hod Hasharon 45111, Israel

Tel: 972-9-7412044

Fax: 972-9-7442714

E-Mail: info@astrolog.co.il

Astrolog Web Site: www.astrolog.co.il

All rights reserved. No part of this publication may be reproduced, stored in a retrieval system, or transmitted, in any form or by any means, electronic, mechanical, photocopying, recording or otherwise, without the prior permission of the publisher.

Published by Astrolog Publishing House 2003

10 9 8 7 6 5 4 3 2 1

contents

# About extrasensory phenomena

One of the scientists who is involved in the study of extrasensory phenomena as well as in other branches of sciences, made an interesting observation. He related that every time he was asked for information about some kind of scientific matter, his words were accepted as gospel truth. He could give genuine information or invent "facts" that were the fruit of his imagination – and yet his words were always received seriously, and were related to as solid facts, even if they were not substantiated by any scientific proof. Conversely, the moment he began to speak about extrasensory phenomena, many people simply refused to believe him!

The sciences of extrasensory phenomena have already come out of the closet. After man reached outer space, the ordinary "man in the street" was compelled to broaden and develop his consciousness beyond the known physical laws as a result of the new reality, which was ostensibly taken from science fiction books that had begun to materialize in front of his eyes.

*Extrasensory phenomena?! Truth or stories, fairy-tales, and superstitions?*

While some of us wonder, find it difficult to believe, and try to understand how things that are invisible to the eye exist and contradict every basic scientific law, healers, channelers, wizards and witches do what they wish with enchanted energies, cast spells, and spin enchantments. Research institutes in which the top scientists from several well-known world powers conduct in-depth studies on the phenomena that we will discuss in this book – today it is already known, verified, and authorized information – make use of some of the phenomena that we have not yet decided whether to believe or not.

Today, there is a wave of great awareness, the "New Age" current, extrasensory phenomena. We will try to understand, as much as possible, the way some of them work and appear, and we will present true, verified stories that describe their occurrence. In the first part of the book, we will talk a bit about the extrasensory phenomena themselves, how they were revealed, what research has been conducted on them, and what explanations were given for some of them. It must be admitted that many of them still lack explanations that can be accepted as "unequivocal," and many of the attempts to explain "how" are only hypotheses.

We will attempt to describe the philosophical side that relates to the fact of the person's having extrasensory powers and his ability to activate them, several holistic philosophies that accompany the ability to have extrasensory powers, and also things to be watched out for and avoided. Although this part is conceptual information, it constitutes an essential basis for developing extrasensory abilities and for learning how to use them. Without assimilating these ideas, "playing" with the world beyond the senses and in the range of energies and phenomena that exist in it is liable to be useless, arbitrary and unpleasant at best, and dangerous at worst. Already by means of reading, assimilating and applying the ideas that appear in this part of the book, you may naturally discover your innate extrasensory powers – because they are inside you, you don't acquire them from anyone – you just open up and use what already exists in you. Nothing is "new" to you. You simply recall what you always knew, and when your consciousness "remembers," physical action begins to manifest itself actively, your world-view changes, and, with this change, your personal and concrete world also changes and opens up.

We will present several practical tools, techniques, ideas for meditation and simple exercises for practicing and training our innate abilities, so that we can feel and use them (to good ends for ourselves and the world!). Although we have selected relatively simple exercises, some of which may even be familiar, they are good and very powerful. Power is a wonderful thing – if we know how to use it wisely. If not, it is very dangerous and unhealthy. Therefore, if after reading the second part of the book, you feel that you are still far from spiritual cleanliness and are dominated by material interests and passions instead of dominating them, you should perhaps make do with the interesting stories that appear in the first part and in the ideas presented in the second part, and leave the practical exercises for times when your emotional, mental or spiritual balance is more stable.

The spiritual world is fast, strong, and dynamic. Your extrasensory ability is an energetic boomerang that always returns to you. Throw it into the air with love, and it will return directly to your hand and drench you with pleasant blooming fragrances. Throw it with rage, self-interest or fear, and it is liable to come back and knock your head off.

For this reason, caution – caution that derives from self-knowledge – is mandatory when we set about using our innate extrasensory powers.

"Innate extrasensory powers? I don't know of any 'innate extrasensory power' in me. What on earth are you talking about? Not everyone has innate extrasensory powers."

Our point of departure, which we learned from observation and experience (from personal experience and from the experience of others), is that every one of us has a certain degree of extrasensory abilities, just as we are all able to use, to a greater or lesser extent, our five physical senses. This natural ability may vary from person to person, both in its expression and in the level and intensity of the expression. However, everyone has the capacity to develop his extrasensory abilities and to bring them to a higher plane than he started out with. Many people tend to discover a certain extrasensory ability in their youth, but since they don't know how to define it, they are forced to repress it, both because of the reaction of the people around them and because of their inner fears about what they perceive as different and weird. If, when you were a child, you were able to see auras or could sense other people's feelings without them describing them to you, or you knew who would be at the other end of the telephone line before picking up the receiver, these properties have not disappeared. They were either repressed or simply "faded" from lack of use. Even if you do not remember experiencing these phenomena in your childhood, it is possible that after doing some of the exercises in this book, you will enjoy new revelations and surprising insights regarding your abilities.

Everyone has a "sixth sense." The trick is knowing where it is, how to use it, and how to be a loving and spiritually clean human being.

Beyond that, everything is possible.

# Extrasensory phenomena – pioneers of research

What are "extrasensory phenomena" and "extrasensory abilities"? Are these abilities and senses obvious and perceivable like sight, hearing, and the other senses, senses that are at the disposal of most human beings, or are they perhaps unique phenomena that are granted to a privileged few? Are they "genuine" phenomena that can be subjected to research and scientific study, or are they "superstitions" employed by man in order to escape from irksome everyday reality? Is the belief in natural abilities advancing and constituting an additional step toward the New Age and the technologies of the new millennium, or is it a primitive belief that curtails human progress?

These questions, and many others, inspired many scientists to try to understand the nature of extrasensory phenomena.

While in certain cultures, people with extrasensory abilities were highly esteemed, used their abilities for the benefit (or destruction) of other people, and enjoyed the general support of the culture in which they lived, other cultures considered involvement of any kind in the extrasensory to be dangerous, "dark," and a kind of witchcraft that contradicted religion and sometimes normative "common sense." (Every era has its particular norms of "common sense.") In the Middle Ages, when the involvement in the extrasensory actually flourished and alchemists investigated it in depth, people who were suspected of engaging in this type of activity were severely tortured, excommunicated, or burned at the stake. Abilities that we are more amenable to accepting and trying to comprehend today were thought to derive from contact with "Satan" or "demons." Mind-reading, telepathy, telekinesis (the influence of thought on objects), future prediction and so on had to be conducted clandestinely for fear of the church authorities and extreme social reactions.

However, despite all the attempts to quash them, those actions and abilities have not only survived to this day, but are blooming and flourishing. Having said that, it is not unusual to meet people for whom any hint of extrasensory activity sparks fierce opposition or trepidation. In the past, as in the present, there were people who felt that there was more to the world than what we can perceive with our five basic senses, and, with great courage, and sometimes under a torrent of withering social or scientific criticism, decided to go with their truth to the bitter end and investigate the extrasensory world. Their efforts were not in vain, since today these fields are being investigated scientifically, and the greatest "enemy" of understanding the world beyond the senses, namely science, is beginning to remove the barriers and the protective walls and relate seriously and scientifically to the possibility of the existence of these phenomena. This is an attempt to gain a scientific understanding of how they occur and to comprehend the way the universe works.

Before reviewing the broad range of existing extrasensory phenomena and presenting numerous ways of improving and perfecting the extrasensory abilities that exist in every single one of us, we will briefly review the bumpy paths along which the study of extrasensory phenomena and its first pioneers advanced.

## John Dee

The Welshman, Dr. John Dee, was born in 1527. His father was a secretary in the court of King Henry VIII. While John Dee was studying at Trinity College, Cambridge, he already stood out as a person with creative powers, inspiration, and extraordinary will power.

Upon completing his studies, Dee set out to see the world beyond the borders of England. During one of his voyages, he encountered the famous Flemish cartographer, Gerhardus Mercator, from whom he learned a great deal about mapping and astronomy. When he returned to England, he became a highly esteemed expert on mapping and navigation as a result of this knowledge.

An important milestone in his life occurred in the middle of the $16^{th}$ century, when he came across Agrippa's book, *The Philosophy of Occultism*. The serious and scientific attitude (according to the standards of those days) toward occultism that he found in Agrippa's book inspired John Dee to begin to investigate and become involved in the supernatural, and he concentrated mainly on soothsaying. He crystallized and perfected his knowledge of alchemy, astrology and mathematics, and began to engage in the prediction of the future by means of a crystal ball, linking the "modern" knowledge of those times to predicting the future. He managed to turn the prediction of the future using a crystal ball into a profession, and was so successful and sought after that he was compelled to employ several assistants. Out of a sense of obligation to his inner truth and scientific integrity, John Dee investigated the subject and obtained every serious book about it that he could lay his hands on. His library consisted of some 4,000 rare books, most of which contained valuable information about various ways of predicting the future and about the wisdom of the occult.

When he became renowned for predicting the future, he became acquainted with Edward Kelly, who was a magician and a medium who had not enjoyed the same degree of esteem as Dee. His activities were defined as witchcraft, and he was accused of being a fraud and a phony. Through Kelly, John Dee began to make contact with the world of spirits, which he called "angels." The messages he received from those spirits did not fit the conventional perception of angels, since they occasionally contradicted the basic rules of morality, which, in those days, were iron-clad. By means of mirrors made of black glass, Kelly and Dee managed to get in touch with the spirits, which spoke to them in a special language. Sometimes the spirits relayed important information, either general or personal, or taught them various bewitching techniques and technical tricks for doing magic. At other times, the spirits "joked" and suggested things like wife-swapping.

Whether or not these were messages from angels or from dead spirits, John Dee's reputation spread far and wide, and his fame attracted Queen Elizabeth I. She visited him in his home in order to see for herself how he used his magic to predict the future.

*John Dee and Edward Kelly, standing in a magic circle in a graveyard, invoke a spirit.*

After this encounter, the road to the royal court was open to John Dee. He became a close associate of the queen and her sister, Mary, and became the royal family's astrologer and soothsayer. After he succeeded in pinpointing the day of Elizabeth's coronation by means of astrological calculations, she appointed him her personal advisor. She saw his great potential for assisting her reign, and sent him on special missions to Europe, as an ambassador. In fact, his role was that of political spy.

In 1583, during his sojourn in Europe, a mob broke into Dee's home and destroyed his library, which contained extremely valuable information about occult wisdom.

This was the first hint of John Dee's end. Not long after that, Dee was accused of exhuming the corpse of a nobleman and forcing it to speak to him. He addressed a passionate plea to King James I to clear his name, but the king ignored it. In 1608, John Dee died in abject poverty.

Despite his ignominious end, John Dee earned a great deal of respect after his death, and as time passed, he was acknowledged as one of the greatest soothsayers and wizards in Europe. The discoveries and conclusions he reached in his research on the extrasensory world match many of the discoveries of contemporary parapsychologists.

## Franz Anton Mesmer

Dr. Anton Mesmer was born in 1735 in Baden, Germany. Mesmer studied medicine in Vienna, and in his doctoral dissertation, it was already possible to identify his attraction to the link between science and the supernatural. The topic of his dissertation was "The Effect of the Planets on Human Health." Mesmer believed that the human body contained an essential fluid that was affected by the planets and could also be affected by magnetic action. He considered this fluid to be responsible for the body's health and illnesses. In 1773, Mesmer met a woman who believed that he could cure her stomach-aches by means of treatment with magnets. He began to treat her and other patients with magnets, and attained substantial success.

While he was treating his patients and trying out his method on them, there was another advance in his theory of magnets. One day, when he was drawing blood from one of his patients, he noticed that when he came close to the patient, the bleeding increased, and when he moved away from him, the bleeding decreased. This phenomenon caused Mesmer to conclude that he himself operated as a kind of magnet, and he called it "animal magnetism" – magnetic forces that were emitted by the living body.

He developed a healing technique that he called "magnetized water." He asked a group of patients to stand around a large metal container of water in which he had placed iron rods. Each of the patients had to stand next to the container, grasp one of the rods, and aim it at the diseased organ in his body. The treatment was accompanied by music, and the patients had to move to its sounds, while Mesmer moved among them dressed in an impressive robe, employing his magnetic powers on them. In general, the patients would go into a state of trance at a certain point. Although the treatment was quite weird, it turned out that many patients actually recovered as a result of it.

Today, the success of this method of treatment, Mesmerism, is explained by autosuggestion and by hypnotic activity. It is possible that many of Mesmer's patients suffered from psychosomatic diseases, and he, without understanding this consciously, used autosuggestion in order to assist their recovery.

In 1778, Mesmer moved to Paris. His success was dazzling. His enormous fame evoked suspicion in the French government, which appointed a special committee to investigate his treatment methods. The conclusions of the committee's report were that in spite of Mesmer's good results, his methods were "patently immoral." After the report was published, his good reputation was ruined, and he encountered many difficulties in his later activities and research.

Mesmer died in 1815, but his work constitutes the basis of hypnotism and the use of suggestions for healing purposes. These techniques are used to this day for curing patients with psychosomatic diseases and diseases resulting from physical or mental shock or trauma. Moreover, his research and activities alerted many parapsychologists to the use of hypnotism as a "springboard" to the attainment and stimulation of supernatural abilities.

*Anton Mesmer treating a patient.*

# Categories of supernatural abilities

Before describing the various categories of supernatural abilities, we must differentiate between extrasensory abilities and mediumistic abilities. A person with extrasensory abilities receives information personally and individually, via various means. The medium, in contrast, channels with spirits and other entities in order to receive information or messages or to perform unusual actions. The medium must know how to differentiate between his personal knowledge or thoughts and the messages he receives from the spirit or entity with whom he is in contact. Many mediums have extrasensory abilities, but not everybody who has extrasensory abilities has mediumistic abilities.

Among the categories of extrasensory abilities, I will mention the most widespread ones. Most of them will be examined in depth in the following chapters:

**Clairvoyance, Remote Viewing** – The meaning of the word *clairvoyance* is "seeing clearly." This is the ability to see through the third eye, to see symbols, scenes, names and so on via the extrasensory sense of sight. Various parapsychologists call the person who has clairvoyance a *visionary*.

**Clairsentience** – This means "feeling clearly," extrasensory feeling. It is a person's ability to sense messages or information, as well as the feelings of other people who are either far away from him or near to him. Various parapsychologists call the person who has clairsentience a *feeler*.

**Clairaudience** – This means "hearing clearly." A person with this ability can hear verbal or sound messages without the interference of his own passive thinking. This ability is also called *audio*.

**Clairagustine** – This means "tasting clearly." It is the ability to sense a certain taste with the mouth and tongue without any contact with the food or beverage, and by means of this the person receives a message that is linked to this taste. "Smelling clearly" is also generally included in this category – this is the ability to smell something that does not necessarily exist independently in the inhaled air, but rather comes in order to transmit a message that is linked to smell.

**Psychometry** – This word means "measuring the soul." A person with this extrasensory ability can read the energetic frequencies that a certain object emits, and this enables him to read the personality of the object or the events it has gone through.

**Medical intuition** – This is the ability to pick up the energy surrounding the person's energetic bodies and describe how the person's thoughts are realized in substance.

**Telepathy** – This is the ability to receive messages and information transmitted without words or body language. The extrasensory phenomena include a certain degree of telepathy, and people with extrasensory abilities generally develop telepathic abilities to some or other extent.

**Aura-reading** – Aura-reading is generally an ability that is added to one or more of the above-mentioned extrasensory abilities, in accordance with the person's reinforced extrasensory sense (sight, feeling, etc.). Some people sense the aura by moving their hands over it or with an inner feeling; others see the shape of the aura and its colors around the person with their eyes open; still others see them with their "third eye," with their eyes closed. Some people receive information about the state of the aura intuitively, without seeing or feeling. Aura-reading is often an ability that is included in medical intuition or is added to it, or can be developed into useful medical intuition.

**Receiving intuitive messages** – This is inner knowledge of a certain message, event, or information, without seeing, hearing or feeling. This is a profound knowledge that can be considered as a "prophecy" when it reaches very high levels.

**Channeling and medium** – This is making contact with other dimensions or entities, and transmitting messages from them via the person who is channeling or the medium.

**Radiesthesia** – This is the use of a pendulum or a dowsing rod for a broad range of purposes, such as finding mines, locating lost people, receiving Yes/No answers, and so on.

**Telekinesis** – This is the ability to influence matter with the power of thought, such as bending teaspoons, lifting objects, stopping clocks, and so on, without physical contact.

# Telepathy

The word *telepathy* originates from the Greek terms "tele" – distance, and "pathe" – event or feeling. The term *telepathy* was coined in 1882 by the French researcher, Frederic Mayers, the founder of the "Society for Parapsychological Research" (SPR).

Telepathy is one of the most common extrasensory modes of channeling. It is very easy to develop, and most people can discern its presence in their everyday lives. Furthermore, it has been extensively investigated by scientists, and today there is hardly any scientific dissent regarding its existence.

Telepathy is a channeling phenomenon between two brains. It includes the transmitting of information such as thoughts, ideas, feelings, and mental pictures. While in so-called "advanced" societies telepathy is considered to be a "sixth sense," a unique supernatural ability that is the gift of people with extraordinary extrasensory ability, older cultures, such as the Aborigines in Australia, see it as a natural ability belonging to the whole of mankind. As we will see in the chapter on supernatural abilities in animals, animals are also gifted with powerful telepathic abilities.

The research interest in telepathy began with the development of mesmerism and the interest in magnetism. The champions of magnetism discovered that they could sometimes transmit instructions or thoughts to their patients. Psychologists and psychiatrists quickly began to identify phenomena of this type in their patients. Freud discerned telepathic activities so often that he eventually had to relate to them in his writings. He defined telepathy as an ancient, primitive ability that had gotten lost during the course of evolution, but could still emerge under certain conditions. Karl Jung related to it as an important phenomenon, while the psychologist and philosopher William James was extremely enthusiastic about telepathy and encouraged its study.

In 1884, the "Society for Parapsychological Research" (SPR) was founded in Europe, and subsequently the American Society for Parapsychological Research (ASPR) was founded in 1885. Telepathy was the first extrasensory phenomenon to be investigated scientifically by these societies. The first telepathic tests were simple. The "transmitting" subject had to transmit a certain taste, two-digit number or visual picture from one side of the room to the "receiving" subject sitting on the other side of the room.

The interest in telepathy increased at the beginning of World War I, when many people who had lost close relatives turned to spiritualism (of which telepathy was thought to be a part) in order to attempt to make contact with their dead loved ones. Telepathy in Britain and the United States at the time became so popular that it engendered a party game. During that period, scientific and amateur research on telepathy began to flourish.

The findings of this research revealed that telepathy generally occurs spontaneously in certain cases of crises. When a friend or relative was injured or wounded, the person sensed telepathically that something had happened to him, and could sense that he was threatened by danger or experience a bad feeling. The telepathic feeling could occur in different ways – as a feeling that "something bad" had happened, in dreams, in mental pictures, in visions, in fantasies, in clear inner knowledge, and sometimes even by hearing or by words that pop into the receiver's thoughts. Frequently, the information that reaches the receiver causes him to alter his actions or plans, or simply to contact the person about whose welfare he is concerned. Moreover, many cases of telepathy between people and animals were discovered.

Another finding that emerged from the studies was that telepathy has a significant link with the emotional state of both the receiver and the transmitter of the message. The studies showed that most of the people with telepathic ability were women. One of the hypotheses regarding this finding was that women tend to be more in touch with their emotions and to listen more closely to their inner feelings. Having said that, it is possible that if these studies were performed today, the results concerning this particular issue would be different. Another interesting finding revealed that telepathy is very common in the elderly and geriatric age groups. The researchers' hypothesis states that the deterioration in the other senses may sharpen telepathic ability or lead to a better ability to listen to telepathic messages. The researchers discovered that in many cases, some kind of biological changes occur in the transmitter and the receiver of telepathic messages: changes occur in the transmitter's blood volume, while changes in the receiver's brainwaves occur in order to match the transmitter's brainwaves. Certain drugs, such as caffeine, are detrimental to the ability to transmit and receive telepathically.

Prof. J. B. Rhine was one of the researchers who promoted the study of the extrasensory in the most significant way. He established a research laboratory for studying extrasensory perception (ESP) at Duke University in North Carolina in the USA and conducted an in-depth study of the phenomenon of telepathy.

The main problem facing Prof. Rhine was finding the tools with which to examine and measure the extrasensory phenomena he was studying so that he could show findings that were as scientific and unequivocal as possible. Rhine reached the conclusion that accepted symbols, such as numbers from 1 to 9, are not suitable for examining telepathic abilities, since biases and prejudices were liable to cause most people to choose a certain number such as 7 more frequently than a less "popular" number such as 8. Together with Dr. Zener, another researcher in the field, Prof. Rhine developed the Zener cards, which have been used to this day for examining telepathic abilities. The Zener cards include five types of cards, each of which has a different shape on it – a circle, a star, three parallel wavy lines, a cross and a square. He chose these signs because they do not evoke any emotional or symbolic associations in most people. There are 25 cards in the pack, five of each kind. The subject must stare at the cards that are placed face down, and guess which of the five forms will appear when the card is turned over. In principle, the person will guess five cards out of the 25 correctly, on average. When the number of guesses exceeds five or is lower than five over a length of time, this attests to the fact that it is not random guessing, but rather the ability to guess more or less than the average. Levels of guessing that exceed the average attest to an extraordinary ability – the ability to see what is hidden.

After checking the efficacy of the cards, Rhine began a series of tests with the help of students who volunteered for the task. Initially, Rhine examined the subjects' abilities while they stared at the inverted cards. Then he began to ask them to answer without seeing the cards. The subject sat at one end of the room with a screen concealing the cards that Rhine turned over. Rhine soon found a group of subjects whose results were higher than average. One of the subjects, Pierce, astonished Rhine with his results. Pierce could guess about 10 out of the 25 cards – that is, a 40% level of accuracy (as opposed to the average level of accuracy of 20%).

Zener *cards*.

When he was so inclined, Pierce was able to guess only two out of the 25 cards – in other words, a lower than average result. Pierce's unique ability was reflected in the fact that before each test he was able to guess the number of cards Rhine decided that he would guess in that particular test. Even more amazing was his ability to guess the cards in a pack without them being spread out face down on the table in front of him. Pierce succeeded in making a list of the 25 cards and guessing eight of them correctly – far above the reasonable average. After this success, Rhine decided to make his experiments even more sophisticated. He began to increase the distance between himself and the subject. He and Pierce synchronized their watches and began to perform the test with

Rhine initially in another room, and later on, in another building. At a certain moment, which had been agreed upon beforehand, Rhine would begin to turn the cards over, and Pierce, who was in a nearby building, began to write down the signs. Even in the distance telepathy experiment, Pierce's guesses were about 40% accurate.

In 1934, Rhine published a book based on the results of his tests. The book was not welcomed with open arms by the scientific community. It is possible that if Rhine had not made his name as a "serious" scientist prior to publishing the book, it would have received very harsh reactions.

In response to the publication of the book, Prof. Bernard Riess decided to repeat Rhine's experiments with the aim of refuting them as unscientific. Riess found himself changing from an opponent to a fervent supporter after a young girl who had participated in his tests succeeded in attaining an astonishing level of 70% correct answers! Once he had witnessed the phenomenon of telepathy with his own two eyes, Riess also began to investigate it. Prof. s was also one of the first researchers to examine the phenomenon scientifically. In his laboratory, he tested a person by the name of Shackleton, who claimed that he had supernatural powers.Shackleton was extraordinarily gifted – he could guess, with great accuracy, the sign on the card that would be revealed *after* the card revealed by the examiner.

After conducting his extensive research, Rhine reached the conclusion that it was not possible to make a sweeping separation in definition between telepathic abilities, clairvoyance, or precognitive clairvoyance – foresight or prediction. He concluded that telepathy and clairvoyance are the same extrasensory abilities that manifest themselves in different ways. In addition, he reached the conclusion that telepathy is not affected by distances or obstacles between the transmitter and the receiver.

A telepathic experiment that was conducted in 1971 after the launch of Apollo 14 proved that distance is not an obstacle to telepathic transmission and reception. The experiment was not authorized by NASA, and was not publicized until after the Apollo 14 mission was completed. The astronaut, Edgar Mitchell, conducted the experiment together with four "receivers" on earth, about 250,000 kilometers below the transmitter – Mitchell himself, who was in the spacecraft. Mitchell performed 200 sequences; guessing 40 of them would be a very reasonable average. Two of the receivers guessed 51 sequences accurately. The success of the experiment went way beyond Mitchell's expectations.

The numerous telepathic tests that were performed during the 1930s proved the existence of unexplained extrasensory phenomena to the scientific community, as well as to the general public, as well as the need for research on the subject. Over time, test means and methods improved in order to ensure that there would be no biases in the tests. Machines for shuffling the cards were invented, as were electric machines that linked examiner with subject and prevented eye contact or body language that could affect the results, and even machines that changed the place of the cards and projected the signs onto a screen by random choice of the order of the cards.

Among the general conclusions reached by the researchers, we will mention the four that are still considered valid after thousands of studies on the topic were conducted:

In tests of the Zener card type, there were people who could consistently achieve significantly higher or lower than average results, as they decided, throughout long sets of tests.

The ability to consistently achieve higher or lower than average results in accordance with the test subject's decision is rare and variable, and is affected by the subject's general mood. When the subject is in a depressed mood and his level of concentration is low, he achieves results that are not statistically significant.

Some of the subjects with high telepathic ability were able to define the level of accuracy of their guesses prior to beginning the test, and determine whether they would achieve a significantly higher or lower than average result. When they were asked to concentrate and make a greater effort, and also when they were offered some kind of "incentive" (such as a sum of money), the results they achieved were higher than their personal average.

Mental factors such as stress, agitation, fatigue and depression significantly lowered the accuracy of the guesses of the people with unique abilities.

Other scientists reached Rhine's conclusion that the test results involve telepathic abilities, clairvoyance and predictive abilities. For this reason, the scientists attempted to isolate each of these properties and examine them separately. A transmitter and a receiver were set up to perform telepathic tests. The transmitter gazed at a picture, while the receiver tried to pick up what the transmitter was seeing. In clairvoyance tests, the subject had to gaze at the face-down cards when no one in the room, including the examiner, knew what was on the right side of the card. In prediction tests, the subject had to guess which sign would soon appear on the screen – just like Shackleton, who was able to guess which card would follow the one the examiner had revealed.

# Prophecies and premonitions

On May 3, 1812, a British citizen awoke from a shocking nightmare. In his dream, he saw the prime minister of Britain, Spencer Perceval, in the lobby of the House of Lords, and a man dressed in brown attacking him suddenly and assassinating him. In his dream, he saw Perceval dressed in various shades of blue. For some reason, the colors of both the assassin's and the victim's clothes were etched in his memory.

Eight days after the dream, the British prime minister, Spencer Perceval, wearing a blue suit, was shot by a man in a brown overcoat.

In April 1974, a visitor to the Tower of London heard the screams of young children. He looked around carefully, but there were no children in the vicinity. It seemed to him that he had heard the screams, which were so clear and blood-chilling, in his head. The experience was so weird that he told several people about it in an attempt to understand what it meant. A few weeks later, a terrorist bomb injured over a dozen children in exactly that place.

We have just seen two examples of premonitions. The premonition is one of the most widespread extrasensory manifestations. At one time or another in our lives – and sometimes regularly – many of us experience a premonition or foreknowledge about what is going to happen in the future. Although this phenomenon is so widespread, the scientists who were studying extrasensory phenomena encountered many difficulties investigating it and proving its existence. One of the most obvious difficulties in investigating premonitions is caused by the fact that they are generally recognized as such only after the occurrence of the predicted event. Premonitions appear in many guises. They can occur as vague feelings, as knowledge that is accompanied by a certain degree of certainty (like telepathic knowledge, when the person knows who will be at the other end of the telephone line), as an odor that evokes some kind of feeling, as a voice or sound, as a sight or as a dream. The appearance of foreknowledge in a dream is not rare. Foreknowledge is generally clearer and sharper than a feeling. In contrast, the nature of the feeling tends to be more difficult to define precisely or even almost precisely. For this reason, the person may feel uncertainty about his feeling and about the manner and time of its realization. This vagueness in the person's own ability to define the nature of his premonition or of foreknowledge constitutes an additional obstacle for the researchers who are investigating such feelings. Of course, their spontaneity and their occurrence in the context of a particular event also make their investigation more difficult.

People sometimes tend to dream about various occurrences – disasters such as fires, explosions, accidents and so on. In spite of the irksome feeling that accompanies dreams of this type, many dreamers do not attribute great importance to them. Sometimes, even when the event troubles them, they are afraid to tell others about their dream. At times, they let it slip out of their consciousness and interpret it as "another of those scary dreams…" Only after the event occurs does the person grasp the truth of his dream or of his premonition. That is what happened in the case of John Dune, a Scottish citizen who saw a train becoming derailed in a particular place in Scotland. In spite of the bad feeling caused by the dream, Dune tried to attribute it to subconscious elements, interpreting it as a meaningless dream. Only after the accident actually happened in that very part of Scotland, exactly as Dune had seen it in his dream, did he understand that his dream had been a prophetic dream and a premonition.

For these reasons, the study of premonitions became almost impossible. It is very difficult for researchers to discover whether the information that reaches them after the event is genuine, or whether it is just some fictitious story invented by someone for reasons of his own after the event.

Important, in-depth research about premonitions was conducted following the fatal slag slide in the Welsh coal-mining village of Aberfen. It was an important step toward solving problems in researching the topic. On October 21, 1966, a fatal slag slide killed over 140 people in the Welsh village of Aberfen. Many people claimed that they had seen and sensed the fatal slide before it occurred. A psychiatrist by the name of Dr. John

Barker decided to investigate the phenomenon. He interrogated 76 of the people who claimed that they had had dreams or premonitions about the tragedy. Some of their forecasts were somewhat vague. One person dreamed that the village school disappeared, which is what actually happened during the slide. A woman who perished in the slide told her mother a few days beforehand that she felt her death approaching. Although it is not possible to prove that these forecasts actually preceded the disaster, Barker discovered several interesting points. None of the people who experienced premonitions saw the event in its entirety, but rather only parts of it. Moreover, the premonitions began about three weeks prior to the disaster, and were most widespread on the day before it. Patterns of this type were also revealed in other studies on premonitions.

However, dreams and premonitions do not only accompany disasters and traumatic events. Cases of good fortune may also be accompanied by foreknowledge, which permits the person to intervene actively in improving his situation. This was the case for John Goodly, a British student, who had a dream that is the secret dream of many people. Which of us would not like to go to bed at night and dream about receiving all the correct lottery numbers? A dream of this type changed Goodly's life. In March 1946, Goodly was a student at Oxford University, and, like many students, did not have a penny to spare – until the night he had a strange and unusual dream. In his dream, Goodly saw the names of two racehorses. When he woke up the next morning and remembered his special dream clearly, he discovered that both horses were running in a race that day. He quickly went to place bets on the two horses. To his astonishment, both horses won! During the subsequent twelve years, Goodly had many dreams like that, and won a fortune.

The case of John Goodly blurs the line between foreknowledge and prophecy. Although the border between the two extrasensory perceptions is not clear and unequivocal, it is possible to find several basic differences between premonitions and prophecies.

# Prophecies

## The writer who prophesied the sinking of the *Titanic*

The *Titanic* was the largest and most luxurious ship of its time. Its builders constructed it as a kind of floating palace intended for a pleasure cruise that combined refinement and elegant luxury with the most up-to-date maritime engineering and design techniques. The owners of the *Titanic* and its captain all declared unequivocally that the ship was unsinkable. As we know, this careless optimism cost many people dearly.

Fourteen years prior to its maiden voyage to New York, the writer Morgan Robertson wrote a book entitled *Futility*, in which he described the story of a luxury liner called... the *Titan*! In his story, the ship was equipped with an inadequate number of lifeboats, and he described how it was ripped apart under the water after colliding with a gigantic iceberg, and sank with tremendous loss of life.

On April 10, 1912, 14 years after the book was written, the *Titanic* sank below the waves on its maiden voyage. Its fate was identical to the fate of the *Titan* in Robertson's story.

This kind of story provides a classic and concrete example of a premonition, which, in this case, because it predicted such a massive disaster, could definitely be seen as a prophecy. In his story, Robertson focused on exactly the same points that we are familiar with from the *Titanic* – the lack of lifeboats, the collision with the iceberg, the splendor and luxury of the ship. However, above all, the name of the ship in the story – the *Titan* – leaves no room for doubt.

What is the difference between a prophecy and a premonition? In a field that is so delicate and so difficult to research, we cannot draw hard and fast lines between the two extrasensory experiences. Nevertheless, we can define premonitions as lighter and more elusive feelings that are not clear and that the person who experiences them generally does so "by chance" and is not certain about them. In most cases, premonitions are simply "feelings" – a feeling that something good or bad is going to happen. In general, the feeling is not accompanied by many precise details, such as the exact location of the event, the reason for it, and the exact manner of its occurrence.

Another example of a premonition came from an elderly lady in the United States. She related that a couple she knew, who had been going out for several years, told her with great excitement that they were going to be married. While the girl was an old friend of hers, she only knew the young man superficially. When they told her the good news of their plans to marry, she found that for some reason, intuitively, she found it difficult to share their joy. An uneasy feeling gripped her at that moment, and the only thing she could say in response to the joyful news was, "Oh, well." A few moments later, her premonition was clearer to her: this couple was not going to get married. Since this was a feeling that was uncertain and unsubstantiated by details, insights, or clear and absolute knowledge, she said nothing to the young woman. A short time later, the man was sent to Vietnam and the marriage did not take place.

Because premonitions are sometimes "vague," people who experience them find it difficult to talk about them with authorities on such matters. Since premonitions frequently occur in connection with blatantly unpleasant matters, such as death, disaster or failure, many people simply prefer not to say anything.

Prophecy, in contrast, is characterized by a relatively clear picture of the details. As in Robertson's story of the *Titan*, the details may be numerous and very similar to the actual event. In general, the prophecy makes the person feel very certain about what he is saying, and he often experiences an urgent need to communicate the prophecy to other people. Another characteristic difference between a prophecy and a premonition is their range.

Many premonitions concern more personal matters, such as deaths in the family, marriage or divorce, personal accidents, and so on. Prophecies, in contrast, relate to more extensive events, events that have the potential to change the world – political topics, terrible disasters, new inventions, and so on.

Prophecies and premonitions have occurred since the dawn of time, and many of them were fulfilled with exceptional regularity.

One of the most renowned historic prophecies was that of the soothsayer, Vastritius Saporina. He was a well-known prophet in the Roman Empire, and his words were generally taken very seriously. Saporina was the person who whispered the immortal words into Julius Caesar's ear in 44 BCE: "Beware the ides of March" ("ides" was the name given to the $13^{th}$ or $15^{th}$ of the month). Indeed, in the middle of March, Julius Caesar was murdered by conspirators while he was walking in the Forum Romanum.

One of the most famous soothsayers in Britain was "Mother" Shripton, a carpenter's wife who lived in Yorkshire from 1488 to 1561. She made many accurate prophecies, among them the arrest of Cardinal Wolsey on charges of treason, the rule of Queen Elizabeth I, and the beheading of Mary Queen of Scots.

"Mother" Shripton was in the habit of rhyming her prophecies and writing them in the form of poems. One of the poems she wrote was astounding if we take into account the fact that it was written in the $16^{th}$ century. Originally, the poem was written in rhyme:

*Around the world, thoughts will fly – in the wink of an eye.*
*Below the water, people will walk, ride, sleep and even talk.*
*Horseless carriages will go, and accidents will fill the world with fear,*
*In water, iron will float, lightly, as if it were a wooden boat.*

Many researchers attribute the first line to the invention of the telephone, television, satellites, and the Internet – all of which are means of "thoughts flying in the wink of an eye," of communicating quickly without limitations of distance – things that were difficult to imagine in Shripton's day. Moreover, some people claim that this line of the prophetic poem is even more far-reaching, and prophesies the development of telepathic and thought communications media by means of which we will be able to communicate rapidly – in the wink of an eye. Today, of course, people walk under the sea, and submarines, as well as underwater research laboratories, are inventions that enable people to "sleep and even talk" under the sea. Horseless carriages are, without doubt, a prophecy of automobiles, and the other part of the sentence – "and accidents will fill with world with fear" – aptly describes the situation nowadays. Heavy metal ships and submarines are already a part of our world, but during Shripton's era, they were only figments of the imagination.

Shripton's prophecies, as we can see from her prophetic poem, exemplify the difference between a prophecy and a premonition. Prophecies are clear, detailed, and, above all, they concern the future of the whole of humanity.

Many prophets, both in ancient and more recent times, excited and astonished the world. The most famous of all, however, was the Frenchman, Nostradamus, who was born Michel de Nostre-Dame in south-western France at the beginning of the 16th century. He was born a Jew, but was brought up as a Catholic. He changed his name to Nostradamus when he was a medical student, and quickly became renowned as a successful physician. Although he was a sought-after and marvelous physician, his true love was the field of extrasensory phenomena, clairvoyance, and astrology. When the Black Plague broke out, his wife and two children perished. Broken, Nostradamus quit his lucrative and respectable job as a physician and began to roam the streets. He traveled throughout Europe, spreading prophecies that mostly came true with astounding accuracy.

During his travels through Italy, Nostradamus fell to the ground at the feet of a young monk who was approaching him along the path. The monk thought he was crazy, but Nostradamus passionately declared that one day, this young monk would be a great and important man in the Catholic church. Fifty years later, the monk, Felice Peretti, became Pope Sixtus V.

In 1547, Nostradamus settled in Provence, remarried, and began to write his major and most famous book of prophecies. He wrote enigmatic and vague rhyming riddles that were full of symbols, engendering many interpretations for almost all of them. However, Nostradamus had two reasons for writing his prophecies in this form, which was loaded with meaning and difficult to decipher: first, so that it would not be possible to accuse him of witchcraft (an accusation that was very common in those days, and did not spare respected and accepted members of the community); second, in order to entertain the reader a bit and to avert the threat contained in a prophecy that related to the distant future.

When we read these things, we ask the inevitable question: Most of the topics that Nostradamus related to were disasters, wars, assassinations of important people in various countries. Why should the information be so vague that only after the actual occurrence of the event is it possible to understand more or less unequivocally the meaning of the prophecy? Perhaps Nostradamus did not consider his prophecies to be an instrument for preventing the events that were "inscribed" by the pen of fate. Whether this supposition is correct or not, his prophecies prove one thing: the ability of human beings, even of one gifted person among them, to predict the future.

*The young lion will overcome the old lion,*
*As on the battlefield, in a duel*
*In a golden cage, he will tear out his eye*
*Two wounds in one, he will suffer a cruel death.*

That is what Nostradamus wrote. In 1559, the king of France, Henry II, was wounded in his throat and eye during a duel – two wounds in one, and died in agony ten days later. The golden cage was the king's helmet, which did not protect him.

*The Great Plague in the maritime city will not cease*
*Until death has avenged the blood of the innocent, oppressed and condemned,*
*Even though innocents, and the great lady, will be harmed by imposter saints.*

Historians have interpreted this prophecy as a prophecy of the Black

Plague that attacked London in 1665. The great lady is St. Paul's Cathedral, whose French name was "The Church of Our Lady." The term, "the innocent," apparently refers to King Charles I, who was beheaded in 1649. "Imposter saints" refers to the Puritans of the time.

One of his most accurate prophecies predicted the Great Fire of London in 1666. In this prophecy, too, Nostradamus calls St. Paul's Cathedral "the lady."

*The blood of the innocent will be demanded by London,*
*Burning with fire in three times twenty plus six*
*The old lady will fall from the heights of her throne,*
*And many palaces with the same ... will be destroyed.*

Three times twenty is 60, plus six is 66 – the year of the event. Apparently, Nostradamus provided a clue as to the year in which the event would occur because of the uniqueness of the year with its three sixes.

*Nostradamus, the prophet of the New Age.*

Nostradamus' prophecies covered a period of many centuries. He predicted the rise of Napoleon, the outbreak of the civil war in France, as well as many prophecies that seem easier to decipher today, after their occurrence (but are still no less mysterious and intriguing). One of the especially shocking prophecies was the one that predicted Hitler's rise to power. In his prophecy, Nostradamus called him "Hister":

*A leader of Germany*
*Who will come to offer assistance that is nothing but false*
*Will stretch Germany's borders,*
*And cause France to divide into two parts.*
*Live fire and death concealed in globes will break out, terrible and horrifying,*
*At night, the enemy will reduce cities to dust.*

The "globes" in which death is concealed apparently refer to the bombs that were dropped on large cities such as London during the night. As we know, France was divided into two parts during the war, and Germany's borders expanded. Of course, Hitler offered "false" assistance – instead of helping with the rehabilitation of Germany after World War I, he caused even greater destruction.

One of the most disturbing of Nostradamus' prophecies was deciphered by researchers as referring to the year 1999. According to their interpretation, the "yellow race" would invade Europe in 1999, and "blood and corpses" would cover the ground. According to Nostradamus, it would be the war to end all wars, and it would end in 1999 and seven months, when the "great king of horror" emerged from the sky – the atom bomb, apparently.

Well, if you look at your calendar, you will see that we passed that date uneventfully. Let's hope that the researchers, or perhaps Nostradamus, were mistaken with the entire prophecy (even prophets can make mistakes; researchers certainly do), and that this is not simply a matter of a wrong date. Having said that, according to the principle of "all is foreseen, but freedom of choice is given," who knows? Perhaps this prophecy was part of history that we, human beings, have succeeded in changing.

A similar prophecy was uttered by the American clairvoyant, Jeane Dixon in the 50s. She prophesied a "great war" that was supposed to break out at the end of the 80s and terminate at the end of 1999.

Later on, Nostradamus collected his many prophecies and published them in a series of books. He claimed that some of the prophecies had already been fulfilled while others would come true in the future. The prophecies were written in verse, and complex imagery appears in many of them. For this reason, it is not easy to understand them in order to confirm them, and many of them were interpreted in several different ways. Others were so vague that they could be related to many events. For instance, we can take the prophecy that states "Next to the port and in two cities, two calamities of a type that has never been seen before will appear." Many people interpret this prophecy as referring to the atomic bombs that were dropped on Hiroshima and Nagasaki, both of them large port cities, in 1945. Conversely, other people claim that the prophecy is so vague that it could relate to a broad range of calamities.

From reading Nostradamus' prophecies, it seems that he was gifted with unique powers in several areas of extrasensory perception. Receiving a prophecy is not like reading it in a book. It can come as a clear piece of information – when the person's intuitive ability is very developed. In this case, the person simply "knows." Mediums and people who are involved in parapsychology call this ability "intuitive." Extrasensory ability can occur as a vision (a person with this ability is called a visionary) – and he sees events that are sometimes clear and sometimes blurred in front of his eyes. From many of Nostradamus' visions, it seems that he saw many things – and he might not have known what to call them, since they did not exist in his day. For instance, he described the pilots of the German army as people who "resembled pigs" – and indeed, when we look at the gas masks worn by the German soldiers, they look like pigs. It is possible that he used other aids in order to explain the visions he saw, such as kabbalistic or gnostic names (to which the scholars of those times had access), astrological and numerological maps, channeling crystals and other ways of predicting. The mention of Hitler's name with a mistake in pronunciation – "Hister" – raises the hypothesis that Nostradamus also had audio abilities, that is, he could hear a voice "inside his head," which uttered names or dates.

Jeane Dixon, whom we mentioned in connection with the prophecy of the "great war," was a clairvoyant who became a celebrity in the USA because of her extraordinary ability to predict certain things regarding President John F. Kennedy. In 1952, Dixon claimed that she had had a vision in which she saw a "blue-eyed Democrat entering the White House." She said that he would be there in 1960 and that his life would end as a result of assassination. Both prophecies, as we know, came true.

Following her predictions, Dixon became famous in the USA, and many VIPs, among them movie stars, would consult with her. The movie actress Carole Lombard was one of the celebrities who were enchanted by Dixon's abilities. During one of their encounters, Dixon warned Carole Lombard not to fly in the following six weeks, since she predicted that this would be dangerous for her. Lombard insisted that because of the pressure of work she had to fly – she had no alternative. Three days after her meeting with Dixon, Carole Lombard was killed in a plane crash.

Jenny Dixon also predicted the murder of Kennedy in Dallas on the very day it occurred. She woke up on the morning of November 22 and announced: Today it's going to happen. And indeed, the assassination occurred that same day.

However, it seems that John F. Kennedy himself had a premonition about his assassination. He told his wife, "If somebody wants to shoot me with a rifle through a window, I have no way to stop him. So let's not worry about him." A rifle shot through a window is exactly how the president was murdered. Five years later, the premonition repeated itself when Kennedy's widow said about her brother-in-law, Robert, "I know that he will die in the same way as my husband did." And Robert Kennedy was, indeed, shot to death.

One of the most famous New Age prophets was the American, Edgar Casey, an esteemed prophet and mystic. Casey used his mystical and prophetic abilities for the benefit of mankind, for increasing people's awareness, and for healing. Some people call him "the old prophet," since he was in the habit of soothsaying and prophesying while sleeping or in a state of trance. Casey dedicated his special gift to people in the entire world, and was gifted with the special ability to diagnose and to recommend treatments – recommendations that mainly turned out to be extremely successful – without seeing the people who had requested his help in person. In his private hospital on the Virginia shore, he succeeded in curing incurable diseases.

Casey began predicting the future at the beginning of the 20th century and continued doing so until his death in 1945. During his last years, a complete turnabout occurred in his prophecies, and during a trance he began to prophesy important universal events. He prophesied the exact day on which World War II would end and the assassination of President Kennedy. His prophecies continued to the distant future of that time – our days, about which he predicted many natural disasters that would occur all over the world. Moreover, he predicted heavy destruction in California and New York.

Casey's powers did not only provide predictions for the future. As a firm believer in reincarnation, he saw himself in one of his previous lives on the lost continent of Atlantis, an advanced civilization that existed 12,000 years ago. Casey was able to "return" to those days and relate many wonders of the life and spiritual endeavors of the people of Atlantis.

Casey related that Atlantis was an amazingly advanced civilization from the technological point of view, and that its people developed aircraft, electrical appliances, and weapons of destruction. Casey said that one of their weapons was, as he called it, a "death ray" or a "super-cosmic ray," with properties similar to a laser or, according to some people, to nuclear weapons. According to Casey, this ray and its utilization were the reason for the destruction of Atlantis.

Casey prophesied that the western end of the lost continent, which sank below the sea, would begin to appear in 1968 or 1969. In 1968, divers made an archeological discovery that shook the entire academic world: they discovered remains that were attributed to prehistoric roads, walls and houses, near the Bimini shore. It is possible that those relatively sophisticated roads, although they were attributed to prehistoric times, were a part of the lost continent of Atlantis.

Many books describing Edgar Casey's prophecies have been published over the years, and are still popular and fascinating today.

# Psychokinesis

Psychokinesis is the ability to move objects or influence them or people with the power of thought. While various studies on telepathy and other extrasensory phenomena were conducted over the years and evoked a great deal of interest, the phenomena of telekinesis or psychokinesis were not formally investigated until the appearance of Uri Geller. In his performances, Geller turned these phenomena into phenomena whose existence could no longer be ignored. However, before we tell a few things about Uri Geller's astonishing feats, we will briefly survey the beginnings of the study of these phenomena in the Western world.

As early as 1853, the famous physician and chemist, Michael Farraday, investigated various psychokinetic phenomena. He reached his study topic indirectly. At that time, mediums were extremely fashionable, and the field of channeling with entities from the "other" world was expanding rapidly. Many mediums claimed that the spirits with whom they channeled caused various objects in the room to move –tables rising, objects floating, and so on. These claims made Michael Farraday wonder about the authenticity of the phenomena, and he began to study several mediums. Some of them turned out to be phonies who used diverse tricks in order to lift objects and create background noises that sounded like drumming or the rustle of spirits. However, Farraday discovered that some of the mediums actually did cause objects to move without any phony techniques. While Farraday could not determine unequivocally if it was spirits that moved the objects or the psychokinetic ability of the medium to move them with the power of thought, he was impressed by the fact that objects could in fact be moved by the power of thought, human or non-human. Michael Farraday was one of the first researchers to engage in the formal study of the phenomenon of psychokinesis.

After him, scientific interest in the phenomenon increased, even though it was still quite limited, since most broad-minded researchers who were interested in extrasensory phenomena focused mainly on the study of telepathic phenomena. When scientific interest in psychokinesis began, the investigating scientists tried to devise various tests that would enable them to examine the existence of the phenomenon in as controlled a way as possible. Ingo Swann, one of the most famous subjects, impressed scientists with his ability to affect the temperature of water in a container. He did this in a series of tests in which water was poured into two completely identical containers. A thermometer that was inserted into the water determined that the temperature of the water in both containers was absolutely identical. Swann concentrated, and ten minutes later, the water in one of the containers was ten degrees hotter than the water in the other container! In contrast to other subjects or actions of various mediums, Swann was able to repeat these amazing results in every one of the many tests he was asked to perform in the presence of a battery of various scientists and spectators. Swann reached the same astonishing result over and over again with the greatest of ease.

Another person who became famous for her unique abilities was Anna Rasmussen. In the tests she underwent, she had to influence the order of the illumination of light bulbs that were connected to a power source that conveyed an electrical current to the light bulbs in a completely random manner. The results were astounding. It transpired that Anna could influence the order in which the light bulbs lit up, sometimes to the point of 100% success.

The study of psychokinesis commenced officially with the work of the famous researcher, Prof. Joseph Rhine. In the 1930s, Rhine tried to examine scientifically the effect of thought on objects. Concurrently with his in-depth research of this topic, he was fortunate to receive unexpected help and acquire a fascinating research subject. Tom Beades, a young man and a gambler, approached him with the intention of demonstrating his telekinetic abilities – the way he influenced the die and directed it to show the number he wanted!

The best-known story about Tom Beades took place in the casino of a Las Vegas hotel. The place was crowded with excited, adrenaline-filled people gambling at the one-armed bandits and the gaming tables.

That day, young Tom Beades lost everything he owned – all the money he had saved up went down the drain. The lust for gambling had been too powerful and uncontrolled, and Tom had not managed to stop in time. Now he was penniless. Desperate, depressed, anguished and stunned, he walked to the bathroom, oblivious of the people around him. While he was washing his face, which was shining with the cold sweat of the anxiety that had gripped him when he had failed so dismally, he glimpsed a five-dollar chip lying under the sink. He picked it up. The chip was worth so little – what could he do with it? But in Tom's penniless situation, he saw the chip as a sign – a sign from heaven. He clutched it tightly in his fist, and strode with determination to the gaming tables. He stopped at one of the tables and waited impatiently for a place to come free so that he could place the bet. When a place came free, Tom placed the chip on number seven. The dice-thrower began to shake the dice in a special cup. Tom muttered to himself, "Seven. It must be seven now." The dice-thrower threw the dice onto the table, and the numbers three and four appeared in front of Tom's eyes. He swept up the chips he had won, and quickly placed them on another number. Once more, his lips moved in a kind of silent prayer, and his eyes stared at the dice, as if he were hypnotizing them. Again, the number he had gambled on came up. He continued gambling until his pocket contained a sum of money that not only covered all his losses, and but gave him huge profits as well. Astonished and admiring people watched him as he finally left the table, the expression on his face indifferent and not betraying what was going on in his heart. Two girls tried to attract his attention, clutching at his arms so that he would invite them to have a "good time," but Tom ignored them and slipped away quickly. He hurried over to a bank to deposit his winnings. Withdrawn and serious, he walked to his room in the modest hotel where he was staying. He extracted a pair of dice from among his belongings. Concentrating and silent, he began to roll them on the floor, staring at the numbers that came up.

Two weeks later, he arrived at Prof. Rhine's office at Duke University. Prof. Rhine, who was conducting many studies on telepathy at the time, was prepared to listen to the surprising words of the 30-year-old man who had come into his office. The quiet words uttered by the man were to have a tremendous effect on the development of the study of telekinesis. "I'm a gambler," said Tom Beades, "and I can influence the dice with the power of thought. The number I choose is the number that comes up when the die is cast."

From that day on, for ten fascinating years, Prof. Rhine investigated the astounding phenomenon that Tom Beades had presented to him. In his lengthy research, the professor studied the ability of certain people to convert thought energy into kinetic energy – the energy of movement – thereby influencing moving objects, such as dice, as they pleased.

Prof. Rhine performed many experiments with dice because they were very convenient for the aim of the research. When two dice are thrown, the resulting totals range between 2 and 12. There are 36 possible combinations. Prof. Rhine divided up the chances as follows: There are 15 possibilities of getting a total of 8 or more, 15 possibilities of getting a total of 6 or less, and 6 possibilities of getting a 7. After eliminating the parameter of the person's influence on the dice by using a special machine to cast the dice, it is possible to work out the proportion, in a large number of throws, between the results of 8 and above, 6 and below, and 7.

During the research, when a person throws the dice a certain number of times, and there is an upward or downward deviation from the above-mentioned proportion after checking the machine-cast dice, this means that somehow a certain influence was exerted on the dice, thereby changing the proportion between the various groups of results. How does this deviation occur? Is it possible that with the power of thought, or with strong will power, the person can influence the results of a throw of the dice? This was the question that bewitched and bothered Prof. Rhine, and he was determined to find an answer.

For ten years, with the help of students and his research team, Prof. Rhine performed numerous dice-throwing experiments. These studies showed that certain people, consistently and non-coincidentally, could direct the dice to show results of above or below 7 when throwing two dice. This ability disrupted the existing proportionality between the number of the various groups of results attained from machine-cast dice.

However, despite this impressive finding, Prof. Rhine still feared the objections of his scientific colleagues as well as the reaction of the public to his research. He felt that the results of his studies had to be even clearer and more unequivocal in order for them to be received with understanding rather than with an endless stream of rejection and opposition. He continued devising new tests for throwing the dice in order to investigate the influence of the subject's power of thought or will power on the results of the throw of the dice.

Another unique study was conducted by means of a unique machine, which cast the dice onto a board that was divided in two by a line along its length. The subject's aim was to try to influence the dice to roll further away from one side of the line than from the other. "Rationally" speaking, there is no any reason for the dice to roll further on one side of the divided board. There should not be any clear and non-random difference in the distances. But, surprisingly, it turned out that certain people, using their power of thought or will power, could get the dice to roll further on one of the sections of the board. The number of cases in which this unique phenomenon occurred and the consistency with which certain people could repeat the "trick" over and over again, removed any suspicion of coincidence.

During the course of his research, Prof. Rhine discovered that there were additional parameters that influenced the results of the experiments and their success. These parameters were dependent on the human factor – the urge that motivated the person to succeed in the test and the level of his personal interest, such as a tempting sum of money that he was offered if he succeeded in obtaining the desired result. This parameter turned out to be extremely important, since many of the people who were able to "control" the movement of the dice were far more successful when they had a clear personal motive to do so.

After ten years of experiments, discoveries and insights in the field of psychokinesis, Prof. Rhine decided to publish the results of his research and its procedure. Since they were in-depth and firmly based, they were received with great faith and with ever-increasing interest both by his scientific colleagues and the general public.

However, the person who brought the wonderful field of psychokinesis "out of the closet" was the renowned Uri Geller. Studies that appear in scientific journals or even in popular magazines exert a certain effect on the reader and arouse his interest. But when a person has the opportunity to see the results of psychokinesis with his own eyes, via his TV set, or even more than that – to feel the influence of the power of thought on objects in his home – the effect is far greater.

Even before his big public appearance on British television in 1973, Uri Geller was known for his telekinetic abilities. However, his appearance on the British TV program was stunning. During a live broadcast, Uri Geller bent forks and succeeded in reviving watches that had stopped working. Among other impressive feats that demonstrated his amazing telekinetic abilities, he stopped Big Ben, disrupted the computer system of a large German publishing network, and influenced objects in the homes of TV viewers – objects moved and floated, "dead" watches suddenly started working, and cutlery became bent and crooked. Uri Geller did all this in front of the TV cameras and in the presence of other people.

A close friend of mine told me about a personal experience that occurred at the end of the 1960s in Israel. Several curious friends suggested that she go with them to a performance by Uri Geller in Tel Aviv. She was not particularly impressed with Uri Geller and thought that he was a phony. She felt that the whole idea of telekinesis was a particularly successful magician's trick, a kind of illusion that had no bearing on reality. She was sure that Uri Geller "pulled strings" offstage, planted certain people in the audience, and used watches and forks that he had prepared beforehand, somehow making them easy to bend so that his "tricks" would succeed on stage. Despite the contempt she felt for "the Uri Geller phenomenon," she was quite happy to have a night out with her friends. While she was in the auditorium, she watched the performance with great skepticism, but she had to admit to herself that it was enjoyable and quite fascinating. Having said that, she could not keep her suspicions to herself, and every now and then insisted on bothering her friends with her ideas about how the guy she considered a charlatan succeeded in pulling the wool over the eyes of the audience. When Uri Geller requested a female volunteer who was wearing a ring that did not mean much to her come up onto the stage, her friends pushed her, pointed at her, and created a slight commotion, until she was forced to go up. Geller looked at the rings on her fingers and asked her if she was prepared to "sacrifice" one of them. He promised her that afterwards she would receive a sum of money equal to the value of the ring so that she could purchase a new one. Curious, the girl pointed at the gold ring she had bought recently. It was not an expensive or special ring, and she agreed to "risk" it. Deep inside, she thought that now the cat was out of the bag. She didn't believe that anything would happen to her ring. Geller asked her to take off the ring, hold it in her hand, and make a fist. She held the ring in her closed fist. Geller concentrated and made a few movements over her closed fist. She felt heat and a strange sensation in her hand. When he instructed her to open her hand, the ring was broken in two equal pieces. She knew very well that there was no way that she had broken her gold ring with the strength of her fist.

The amazing findings in the field of psychokinesis were not limited to psychology or entertainment only. As in the far-off days of Atlantis, when people had access to extrasensory knowledge and insights as well as a more developed ability to use those powers, there were people who searched for ways to exploit these findings for their personal benefit, even if this was generally considered manipulative and immoral.

In the USSR, researchers of psychokinesis took another step forward (and, we might add, from the point of view of mankind, a step backward...). Through simple logic, they reached the conclusion that if a person has the ability to influence objects with the power of thought, he can also influence various weapons – not to mention other people – with the power of thought. But before we become acquainted with the Soviet attempts to use the power of thought for bellicose and manipulative purposes, it is interesting to examine the experiment of the Czech researcher, Robert Pavelita, to use the thought inspiration ability on inanimate objects.

The fact that human beings can cause deviations in the results of die throws, turn on particular light bulbs in a device with a random electrical current, or bend teaspoons, inspired various theories among scientists. One of the theories stated that certain people can convert low-tension physical energy in their brains into high- tension psychic energy, and vice versa. Robert Pavelita began to work on the practical side of these theories. He built several small appliances that he called "psychotronic generators." The objective of these appliances was to store human mental energy and to release it for particular purposes. Actually, what Pavelita did was to charge various inanimate objects – paper, wood, wool, and so on – with energy that could serve a variety of purposes: curing and healing on the one hand and exterminating pests on the other!

Pest extermination was one of the topics on which Pavelita concentrated in his research. He focused on this topic because it had extensive applied and commercial potential, so that even if the scientific community rejected the results of his research, it could bear fruit commercially.

In the 1970s, the experimental tests in the field of pest extermination commenced, with the help of the psychotronic generators. It turned out that these generators really could exterminate pests in the fields! However, the side effects that accompanied the success of the experiments eliminated any possibility of marketing the generators for pest extermination.

It transpired that in addition to exterminating pests, the generators caused more serious phenomena among human beings – anxiety attacks, heart attacks, thought neutralization, strange and disturbing sensations, and more. Having said that, the Czech researchers attained considerable success in other fields with the activation of the generators, in which the results were not so dangerous as they had been with pest extermination. They managed to move various objects by means of the psychotronic generators, to move the hands of clocks, and so on.

The American government, well aware both of the similar experiments performed by the Soviets and the danger inherent in these abilities (for instance, the potential of the generators to activate warheads or explosives from a distance), wasted no time in becoming actively involved in these studies. With surprising frankness, one of the members of the American Atomic Energy Commission admitted that the US was deeply interested in topics such as securing nuclear weapons by extrasensory means and activating and deactivating missiles by means of telekinesis. Several years after the Czech group commenced its experiments in charging objects and telekinesis, American researchers sponsored by the government joined in.

A more beneficial and straightforward experiment in charging objects is being conducted nowadays by the parapsychologist, David Ashdown, and a small group of researchers in the field of physics. Following many years of research, this group succeeded in creating a unique method of charging various objects with energy for purposes of curing and healing. Prominent among the unique energetically-charged objects invented by the group are the prints called "vibrations." The vibrations are sheets of paper on which computer-processed printing appears. The energy-charged vibrations create opening, healing, soothing, or stimulating sensations. Moreover, every unique vibration has a particular range of shapes and colors, which have a mental and energetic effect on the person who looks at them and touches them. The success of the energy-charged vibrations has not yet been subjected to testing by a battery of scientists and researchers, but the recording of the results of the effect of the vibrations on a broad range of people indicates considerable success.

# Mental photography

Mental photography is one of the branches of psychokinesis, and affords an additional example of the influence of mental powers on matter. Mental photography, or "psychic photography," is the person's ability to imprint a certain picture on a photographic film without the use of a camera. With this astounding technique, the person can transmit a picture that is the fruit of his imagination to a film.

This technique is not new; it was used by many mediums and occultists in ancient times. In those days, they did not use a photographic film, of course. The pictures produced by the person appeared in a bowl of oil, on glass, or on copper bowls. However, with the development of the photographic plate, this phenomenon became known all over the world.

Both in regular photography and in mental photography, the photographic action stems from the activation of energetic radiation on the film – radiation that creates the resulting picture. The difference is that with mental photography, no use is made of a camera or any other photographic device.

Most of the modern mental photography experiments have been conducted in a darkroom equipped with a table upon which a photographic plate is placed, generally covered with silver paper or lead paper, or a Polaroid photographic plate holder. The person who is due to perform the mental photography decides in advance on the picture he is about to photograph, or receives instructions for photographing a particular picture from the researchers who are performing the experiment. The person concentrates, focuses his thought, and projects it onto the film. Certain "photographers" perform mental photography by placing their hand on the photographic plate, while others can perform mental photography from a distance, even a distance of several kilometers! The picture that appears on the film is often clear and identifiable, and sometimes has the good quality of an old photograph. In any event, it can be identified as the object agreed upon by the person and the researchers. One of the advantages of the mental photography method is the concrete proof of its existence – the picture itself.

One of the first mental photography experiments that was displayed publicly was that of a Japanese researcher who published a book containing pictures that had all been photographed by mental photography. That researcher also demonstrated the mental photography process to journalists by means of three girls who performed mental photography in his laboratory. Regrettably, it seems that the world at that time – the beginning of the 19th century – was not ready for this amazing discovery. The Japanese researcher was widely discredited and called a "phony," "con-man," and "fraud." In time-honored Japanese tradition, he burned his books and committed *seppuku* (ritual suicide). If he had only known that about 80 years later, Henry Talbot would perform experiments in mental photography that would be received with great understanding and interest by both the scientific community and the general public, he might have avoided such a sad end to his life.

William Henry Fox Talbot was one of the best-known photography pioneers, a man who was accorded a great deal of honor and esteem as a result of his achievements in developing the science of photography. At the end of the 19th century, he produced a series of photographs that had been taken without the use of lenses. Talbot instructed one of his assistants to look through a hollow box at a photographic plate and at the same time to think about certain topics. Talbot suggested that he think about women and about objects that had a particular significance for him. No doubt he knew his assistant, and intuitively, perhaps, understood that things that are near to a person's heart are likely to create a more powerful concentration of thought. Henry Talbot had no idea what the negatives of the pictures would reveal when they were developed. Even if he had heard of mental photography, there was no way to ensure that this experiment would actually work. However, like many other inventors and pioneers, he, too, out of intellectual curiosity, permitted himself to try. The results were surprising. The negatives revealed various pictures that matched the imaginings of the assistant, without any actual "photograph" of a particular object being taken! Talbot's estate still contains some of the pictures that he took using the mental photography technique.

*A mental photograph from the estate of Talbot, one of the pioneers of photography.*

Another person who was famous for his ability to produce mental photographs is Ted Serios, who became renowned in the US during the 1950s for his ability to project his thoughts in order to photograph any picture that came into his mind, or any picture that his examiners or his audience requested. Serios was subjected to many different tests, and was wildly successful every time.

One of the most difficult tests he underwent (difficult in the examiners' opinion, but, as we will see, not for Serios!) was conducted under strict laboratory conditions. Mental photography researchers placed eight photographic plates, which they themselves had examined and to which Serios was forbidden to have any access, in an opaque, lead-lined safe. The safe was placed at a distance of 1.5 kilometers from Serios. They gave Serios eight pictures of sites in the US and asked him to imprint them on the photographic plates.

When the safe was opened, the researchers were surprised to discover that seven of the photographed pictures that Serios had been asked to project onto the photographic plates were imprinted on the plates in the same order in which he had concentrated on the pictures, with great accuracy. Seven out of eight, in scientific terms, constituted irrefutable proof. In this case, the researchers knew very well that there was no possibility of fraud. Serios actually transmitted the exact pictures that lay on the table before him onto the photographic plates in the opaque safe that was located far away from him!

But this was not the sum total of Serios' marvelous abilities. In addition to the projection of an accurate picture onto a photographic plate, he could also create a photomontage from several pictures on a single photographic plate. In one of the tests he took, five different items were placed before him at 10-minute intervals. Serios projected the items one after the other onto the photographic plate, and after it was developed, it was possible to see each of the five items on the single plate.

In the 1970s, mental photography became even more famous when a Japanese woman called Ikoko Nagao became renowned for her ability to project precise Japanese writing onto a photographic plate. Ikoko would think of a word or sentence and project it onto a photographic plate that was located far away from her.

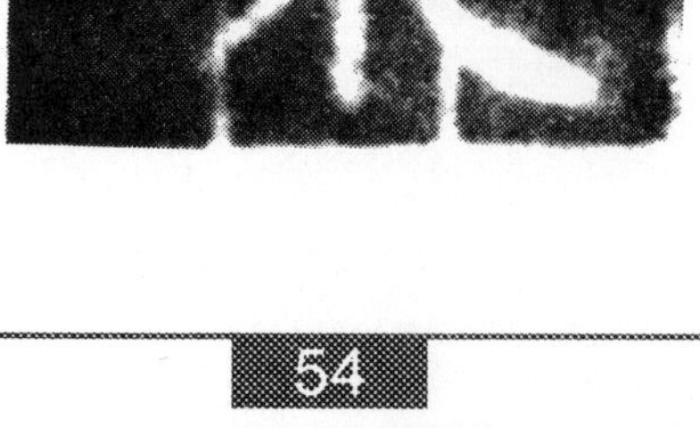

Soviet scientists tried their hand at this technique as well. During the 1980s, scientists examined over 30 mediums and "regular" people who excelled at mental photography. The Russian scientists divided mental photography into two groups. The first was defined as mental photography that involves contact. It transpired that certain people could create mental photographs only when they placed their hands on the photographic plate or made some other kind of physical contact with it. Others succeeded in creating clearer and more precise photographs if they made physical contact with the photographic plate. The second group included people who could create a mental photograph by projecting thought from a distance. Every mental photograph that was produced from a distance of over three meters was included in this group.

One of the most up-to-date studies in the field was conducted in Boston in 1994. This study was of great importance, since it included a group of some 2,000 subjects. A research group of this size is one of the guarantees for the accuracy of every scientific experiment. The uniqueness of the study lay in its focus on ostensibly "regular" people rather than on mediums or people with extraordinary spiritual powers. All of the subjects were asked to perform a simple exercise. Each one was given a small pendulum, which they had to hold over a film. As we will see in the chapter on pendulums, the pendulum itself is also activated by the person's energies, mental energies, and thought energy. The movement of the pendulum itself provides a clear example of psychokinesis, since almost everyone can move it merely with the power of thought along a path decided by him. (After reading the chapter on pendulums, you will be able to try this for yourself and see how easy it is to move the pendulum with power of thought only.) The subjects were asked to concentrate their thoughts on the pendulum and move it in a circular fashion either clockwise or anti-clockwise, or in a linear fashion above the film. The researchers recorded the movement of every subject's pendulum. After developing the negatives, a shining line that was an exact match of the movement of the pendulum could be seen in 17% of the photographs.

## Kirlian photography

If the veracity of mental photography was still in doubt after so many tests, it was because the idea behind it conflicted with the "simple" logic of many scientists who did not succeed in comprehending the nature of the phenomenon. However, with the discovery of Kirlian photography, mental photography also took a step forward, and became more accepted in scientific circles. Kirlian photography proved irrefutably that by means of radiation (the Kirlian photograph is taken by means of powerful electromagnetic radiation rather than by lenses) it is possible to take photographs.

The Kirlian photograph is without doubt one of the biggest breakthroughs in the field of documentation, clarification and proof of topics that, until its discovery, had been lumped into the category of "metaphysical topics" – topics whose source lay in faith, and which seemingly had no way of being proved.

Kirlian photography is named after the person who developed it, the Russian scientist S. D. Kirlian. He succeeded in developing a technique by means of which it was possible to document the energetic field surrounding live organisms on the negative of a photograph. Today, this technique is known as electrophotography, and it is used both for mental and medical diagnosis and for the study of phenomena that are connected with the emission of electromagnetic fields. Electrophotography exploits a phenomenon that is called "emission of the aura." The aura is a result of electronic emission in which millions of electrons are emitted and move to a special part of the camera which receives them, and, in accordance with the structure of the camera and the type of film, stunning and brilliantly colored pictures of energy emission patterns are created. In Kirlian photography, it is generally hands and feet that are photographed. The hands or feet are briefly exposed to high-frequency rays on the photographic plate, and the result is documented on photographic paper. After the film is developed, a breathtaking picture of the electromagnetic field surrounding the hands or the feet is revealed. Every person and every organ in his body and every fingertip photographed has a unique energetic radiation!

When Kirlian photography first appeared, it supported many different fields of holistic medicine. It turned out that when the Kirlian photograph shows that a certain region of the foot has a weak aura or an aura with blockages, holes and so on, the meridian or the reflex area (in reflexology) connected to that point is at the height of a state of imbalance, and is suffering from a lack or excess of energy or from some kind of physical/psychosomatic problem. Of course, the Kirlian photograph served as a stable and factual support for the various theories related to electromagnetic fields – the auras. With the help of Kirlian photography, it was possible to prove the influence of thoughts and emotions on the human aura. Experiments revealed that the negative thoughts and emotions that the researchers evoked in the subjects in various ways created a blocking effect that was manifested in the photograph as weaker radiation, blocked radiation, or radiation with "holes." Conversely, positive thoughts and emotions created a reinforcing and strengthening effect on the electromagnetic field that was manifested in the photograph as a broad, strong and more perfect aura.

In fields of medicine, too, Kirlian photography led to new insights. One of the fields that had been considered a "mystery" by many researchers and scientists was the phantom effect. The phantom effect is a situation in which an amputee still feels the physical existence of the amputated organ, an organ that no longer exists physically. The person may feel the "weight" of the amputated organ, or itching, stinging and even pain in the organ that no longer exists! While performing experiments with Kirlian photography, it was discovered that when a leaf is cut in two, and each half is photographed by Kirlian photography, a photograph of the whole electromagnetic field of the entire leaf is revealed! After this discovery, the researchers began to photograph amputees using this technique. Although they had already witnessed the amazing phenomenon that occurred when photographing the cut leaf, they were unable to conceal their astonishment when they discovered that by photographing amputees, it was possible to see the electromagnetic field outlining the shape of the amputated limb. Even when the amputated limb no longer exists, its electromagnetic field continues to exist.

Kirlian photography, which was accorded a great deal of recognition and esteem by the scientific community, marked the beginning of a new era. The ancient topic of the aura, which appears both in ancient writings (such as *The Book of the Zohar*) and in the traditions of many cultures, always belonged to the metaphysical field, a field that science was afraid to touch or experience. After the existence of the electromagnetic field was irrefutably proved and was accepted as a concrete fact by scientists all over the world, many psychological and conceptual barriers from which the philosophy of science had suffered were torn down. At the same time, the research of supernatural phenomena was promoted and the subject that was considered "beyond the pale" by first-class scientists for so many years was developed.

# Dreams

In a state of full consciousness, there are many emotional and rational barriers, most of which are unconscious, that block the reception of telepathic emissions or the recognition of extrasensory phenomena that may occur in everyday life. The inner "chatting" processes that accompany many people are generally normal processes. They include a "replay" of conversations, events, and situations that we experience, have experienced, or want to experience, "staged" conversations between the person and people who play a part in his life (sometimes, even in the street, we can see people holding conversations of this kind with themselves; their lips sometimes move slightly and their body language hints that they are involved in some kind of "conversation" with themselves), imaginings, daydreams, plans, and sometimes just everyday stress that is linked to routine chores. These processes are completely natural and familiar to most people. However, in a person who is not especially attuned to and aware of subconscious and extrasensory processes, they are liable to block the reception of extrasensory messages or prevent him from understanding the messages concealed behind seemingly ordinary everyday phenomena. In the chapter on telepathy, we mentioned the fact that all of humankind is connected in a broad telepathic net that seemingly enables us (if we know how to use this "net") to pick up many messages, especially from people who are close to us, but also from people to whom we are connected and linked in a stronger way. However, because of the emotional and rational occupations during the day, many of these messages evade our consciousness. This is not the case when we sleep.

Because of the unique state of awareness that occurs when we dream, the dream constitutes a broad cushion for picking up various cosmic messages. These may be telepathic messages that reach us in various guises, in a certain translation, or even directly, prophetic dreams, symbolic dreams, and even dreams whose objective is to process and review various impressions that emerge from our subconscious. They may be impressions that were absorbed during the day, or even in past years, and are "published" when the state of consciousness enables them to manifest themselves.

Since the dream state is a different state of consciousness, in which imagination and reality, past, present and future as well as various images and situations are all mixed up without the limitations of the recognized laws of reality, dreams have always evoked a great deal of interest – both in ancient times and cultures and in the modern era. Because of the mysterious covering that accompanies many dreams, various mystical contexts, superstitions, and even prophetic contexts have been attributed to dreams. In contrast, the many processes of rationalization that appeared in the 18th, 19th and 20th centuries contributed to the creation of psychological theories that attempted to explain the nature and meaning of dreams.

Attempts to understand the dream states were already made in ancient times. Especially famous is the story of one of the wise men of the Mishnah who got into a conversation about dreams with a Greek general who was in the Land of Israel at the time. Speaking from a profound psychological understanding, the wise man told the general that he would dream of being assassinated that night. He elaborated on the details of the dream that the general would allegedly dream. The next day, the general, upset and scared, admitted that his dream had been exactly as the rabbi said it would be. He was very surprised and assumed that the wise man could "see the future" and knew what he would dream. However, this was not the case. As the wise man explained to him afterwards, the act of "brainwashing," the persuasion and the suggestion, the manner of describing the dream to the general – all these things caused the dream to actually occur. In fact, many dreams are "vain speech" – that is, dreams that involve motives from everyday life that bother us when we are awake, bring to the conscious level conflicts and anxieties, hopes and sometimes even things that were read in newspapers or viewed on TV. At night, these things are released from the subconscious, sometimes as a way of relieving the tension that is created by unconscious conflicts or anxieties. Although these dreams are not essentially prophetic or telepathic, they are very important, since they can teach us a great deal about ourselves.

Some dreams occur in order to make us aware of various things – such as fears or hidden passions that are bothering us – which we do not allow to rise to the conscious level. When such a repressing mechanism is activated in daily life, a symbolic dream may occur, which describes the repressed feeling. The most widespread of this type of dream is the falling dream, the drowning dream, the fleeing dream, and so on, whose purpose is to describe a feeling to which the person does not related sufficiently in everyday life, but certainly bothers him unconsciously. Symbolic dreams are also very important, and the ability to remember them and process them consciously can contribute greatly to knowing oneself and developing one's personality.

Thus, when we deal with dreams in this book, we will relate to them on two planes – the symbolic dream, or the bridging dream (a dream that bridges between the repressing conscious and the subconscious, in which the repressed situation is alive and active), and the telepathic and prophetic dream.

Understanding symbolic dreams and bridging dreams is very important in the practical training of extrasensory ability. The ability to be aware of what is going on around us but does not reach us via the "conventional" senses (the senses of sight, hearing, and so on) is greatly dependent on our ability to introspect and be aware of what is happening inside us. The greater the amount of repressed inner content, and the more blocked the bridge between the conscious and the subconscious, the smaller the chance of developing extrasensory abilities or extrasensory perception (except for people with an "innate" ability, or an ability that is sparked suddenly following an extremely significant event). For this reason, it is very important to remember and understand dreams. Later on, we will present several methods for remembering dreams and for gaining insights concerning dreams whose meaning is not clear. Other very powerful tools for understanding and remembering dreams (in addition to self-awareness and intuition, of course) are the various crystals, because they are very effective and easy to use, and do not require extensive study, exhausting practice or exceptional talents.

As opposed to symbolic and bridging dreams, there are telepathic and prophetic dreams. Prophetic dreams are familiar to us from many stories and legends. The Bible is full of such dreams – Joseph's dreams, Pharaoh's dreams, Jacob's dream, and so on. The prophetic dream is a tool for receiving a cosmic message, and it served many prophets, visionaries, clairvoyants, as well as artists and scientists. Prophetic dreams dreamed by creators and researchers are known to be closely linked to the person's research topic or occupation. Since every person has a vocation in this world, people who have found their vocation or who delve deeply into a certain topic may receive many clues and insights regarding their field of occupation via dreams. Many people who are involved in religion, the humanities and the sciences used this kind of channeling dream and prophetic dream for their work. Although some of them were very rational people and some of them lived in eras when no importance was attributed to dreaming in its mystical sense, they knew how to use dreams for their own benefit. Sometimes, from a deep insight that the unique abilities they possessed in this world came from something "greater" than could be perceived and absorbed by the senses, these people knew, consciously or unconsciously, how to "order" dreams that would provide them with information or inspiration concerning the issues in which they were engaged. One of the most famous of these "dreamers" was Rabbi Jacob of Marvish, a Kabbalist and one of the greatest 12th-century French Hasids, who wrote a whole book about Halachic questions and responses based on information that came to him while he was dreaming! The field of the Halacha, which he dealt with, was widely considered to be a logical and rational field, in which one thing had to be deduced from another by means of logical reasoning and intellectual analysis. Having said that, however, the book he wrote, like his responses that became renowned among the Halachic sages, was accepted unequivocally. Rabbi Jacob of Marvish was in the habit of asking Halachic questions that had been addressed to him during prayer, while linking up to holy names and the names of angels, and he would receive the answers at night in his dreams!

Friedrich Kekule, a well-known German chemist who discovered the molecular structure of benzene, grappled with the problem for a long time without reaching the desired results. He received the answer to the question that had been irking him for days and nights via a dream while he was sleeping. He saw a snake biting its own tail. This vision joined up with all the information he had already discovered, thereby enabling him to discover the molecular structure he had been struggling to find for so long. Albert Einstein, too, admitted that some of the equations he solved had been revealed to him in dreams.

Prophetic dreams can occur during situations of distress or when disasters are about to befall the person himself or the people close to him. The sinking of the *Titanic*, for instance, sparked prophetic dreams in many relatives of people who perished in the disaster. Many of them related that they had received clues or visions in dreams prior to the sinking.

A fascinating story involving this kind of dream occurred in October 1965, in the Welsh village of Aberfen. A sudden collapse of a slag dump buried 128 children and teachers in the village school. A week before the event, a woman from Sidcup in Kent dreamed about the disaster. Another woman, from Aylesbury in Buckinghamshire, dreamed about the disaster two days before it occurred, and a day before the actual event, one of the children at the school told her mother that she had dreamed she was going to school, but instead of seeing the school building, all she saw was black stuff covering the entire school area.

History is full of reliable testimonies of seeing the future through dreams. The interesting thing is that in most cases, although the dream attempted to announce something and get the relevant parties to talk about their predictive dream – even when the dreamer dreamed about something that was liable to happen to himself – in some strange way, the disaster was not averted.

World War I began with the unexpected assassination of the Archduke Franz Ferdinand of the Austro-Hungarian Empire. In this case, the information reached a man who himself was of high standing – Bishop Joseph Lanay. In his dream, Lanay saw the archduke riding on his horse along a Sarajevo street, when he was suddenly slain by a bullet from a pistol. Taking no chances, Lanay hurried to send a telegram to the Archduke – but the latter was assassinated before the telegram reached its destination!

The American president, Abraham Lincoln, was assassinated by actor John Wilkes Booth while watching a play. A few days prior to the assassination, the president had a particularly disturbing dream. In his dream, he saw himself walking through the White House. When he reached the East Wing, his eyes espied a corpse lying on the funerary platform. In his dream, Lincoln asked the guards who the dead man was. They answered, "It's the president; he was murdered by an assassin." This dream did not prevent the actual event, either.

## Telepathic dreams

Telepathic dreams are another kind of extrasensory phenomenon that occurs in dreams. In various cultures, there is a belief that dreams originate in a "whisper" of the spirit of a dead person who is related or linked to the dreamer, or in a tie that is created between the dreamer and a certain figure that communicates with him, and transmits its messages to him via the dream.

Sometimes, telepathic dreams are dreamed simultaneously by two closely linked people.

There are many stories about telepathic dreams in which a person dreams about something that happens to someone close to him who is far away from him physically. Sometimes, the dream occurs at the same time as the event that concerns the person he dreamed about. Such dreams are not rare, and may occur in people whose ability to link up to their surroundings, that is, their ability for spiritual openness and reception, is especially high, consciously or unconsciously.

Modern studies have attempted to examine whether it is really possible to convey telepathic messages to the dreamer while he is asleep. One of the most common ways for conducting these studies was to transmit telepathic messages to the sleeper while he was asleep. Generally speaking, the transmitter received a picture and began to concentrate on it, while the receiver was sleeping and linked up to electrodes that measured his brainwaves. The researchers waited until the measurement of the brainwaves and of the rapid eye movements signaled that the sleeping receiver was dreaming, and woke him up immediately after the dream. Frequently, the dreamer was able to describe the picture that the transmitter concentrated on as a part of his dream, as a picture, or as a detail that got mixed up in his dream. Several scientists claimed that this experiment was not reliable, and there was a chance that the dreamer could guess what the transmitter had transmitted to him. In order to make the experiment more reliable, the researchers used five Zener cards or five animal cards that are used in telepathic experiments.

By using these cards, the chance of a random guess was one out of five, that is, a 20% chance of a correct guess. In experiments performed in France, the level of guessing the cards reached 55%, far beyond any possibility of a random guess. Later on, we will describe an easy method for conducting these experiments at home, with a partner.

*Animal cards used in telepathic experiments.*

However, beyond the scientific experiments for telepathic revelation while dreaming, the stories about unique telepathic messages received by sleeping people from relatives are especially fascinating. Like prophetic dreams, many of these telepathic messages occurred when a person close to the dreamer was in some kind of danger.

Another amazing story linked to the sinking of the *Titanic* tells of the brother of one of the ship's sailors. The brother woke up in the middle of the night, sweating and shaken, having seen his brother drowning in the ocean. The brother, who was on the deck of the *Titanic*, was fighting the waves exactly at the time when his brother saw him drowning in his dream!

Telepathic occurrences between siblings in dreams are not rare. The blood ties and the link between the souls that causes two people to be born as siblings in this incarnation are so powerful that the distress of one of the siblings can appear in the dreams of the other siblings.

The author, Mark Twain, told of a shocking nightmare he had had. In his dream, he saw a large hall containing a metal coffin that was lying on two chairs. When he approached and peeped inside the coffin, he saw the body of his brother. On his dead brother's chest was a bunch of white flowers, among which there was a single red flower.

At the time, Mark Twain's brother was serving on the ship, the *Pennsylvania*.

Mark Twain was aware of the power of dreams. Various parts of his books, as well as his ideas for writing, occurred more than once in his dreams. He had a hard time forgetting the dream the next day, and his heart presaged bad news. And so it was. That same day, he was informed that an explosion on the deck of the *Pennsylvania* caused the death of 150 crewmen – among them his brother.

In pain and sorrow, Mark Twain noticed, on the day of the funeral, how similar the image of the coffin in his dream was to the real coffin in which his brother was lying. Everything was so similar – only the bunch of flowers he had seen in his dream was missing. Suddenly, a woman entered the funeral parlor, holding a bunch of white flowers, with a single red flower in the middle!

The famous Prof. Rhine, who conducted extensive research on extrasensory phenomena, told a story that he had heard from one of his professors when he himself was a young student. The professor related an event that had occurred during his childhood. One night, the professor's family woke up in a fright to the sound of loud banging on the door. One of their neighbors, panicked and terrified, burst in and begged them to lend her their carriage. They tried to calm the frightened woman down – she looked as if she had just woken up. Her hair was wild, and her eyes were full of fear. But she would not calm down, and demanded that they make their carriage available to her, since she had just awoken from a terrible dream. She saw her brother, on another farm, committing suicide in the barn. Immediately, they prepared the carriage for her, and she set out for her brother's farm. When she returned, broken and grieving, she told them that when she went into the barn, she found her brother lying dead in a pool of his own blood after shooting himself.

As we have said, dreams are an extremely important tool for developing awareness and extrasensory perception. Since some of them are messages from other dimensions, even when they occur as a result of things that happen in the subconscious world, they develop our ability to listen to messages from dimensions other than the physical-concrete dimension in which we live. The first step toward developing the ability to dream and the ability to receive messages in dreams is, of course, the ability to remember dreams.

# Levitation

Levitation is one of the most mysterious aspects of extrasensory phenomena. It is a rare occurrence, and many people believe that it is not possible. Others, in contrast, spend days, years, and sometimes even a lifetime, attempting to achieve this state. Levitation is the ability to concentrate a prodigious amount of mental energy and express it as a clear and tangible physical force that causes objects to move through the air, to lift them and to move them without manual contact. However, the most fascinating form of levitation is the ability to activate this energy on one's own body. Despite the fact that the likelihood of any person floating in the air without any kind of technical assistance or sleight of hand is liable to appear completely impossible, two people at least have proved it to be possible.

The first was Colin Evans, who lived in London at the beginning of the 20th century. In the 1930s, he became famous for his mediumistic abilities. In 1938, Evans took his audience's breath away when he appeared in a small London club. After meditating profoundly for several minutes, his body rose into the air and remained standing in the air for a few long moments! The audience was agitated and perturbed, and some people were deeply afraid. Some of the spectators at the astonishing show rushed to examine the space around Evans' floating body, to touch him, to try to see how he had done this amazing "trick," but Evens was not hooked up to anything, nor was anything propping him up in the air, other than his incredible powers.

Colin Evans levitated for about five minutes, with his eyes closed and his feet about half a meter from the floor. Photographers who attended the event hurried to photograph him. About five minutes later, Colin Evans slowly descended to the floor, and landed with a slight bump. The first sentence he uttered when he opened his eyes was: "Now I know that Daniel was right!"

*Colin Evans levitating.*

Daniel Home has always been considered one of the most impressive figures in the world of extrasensory phenomena. He operated in London (two streets away from the club where Colin Evans performed his levitation!) about 70 years before Evans' levitation. In matters of levitation, Daniel Home's name is an inseparable part of this astounding phenomenon.

Daniel Home was a medium of Anglo-Scottish origins. He appeared mainly in the United States during the second half of the 19th century, and became renowned for his marvelous mediumistic powers. His performances attracted thousands of people because he could cause objects to move through the air and dance, he could play a trumpet that was 10 meters away from him without touching it, and he would hold a "request program" for his audience, in which they asked him to do various things. He raised dead spirits, passed his hands through fire without any subsequent sign of a burn, and once, in a Boston hotel, he even caused a powerful earthquake that left cracks in the walls of the building. In contrast to many other mediums, Daniel Home fearlessly exposed himself to scrutiny and criticism, thereby proving that his abilities were not sleight of hand. However, above all, he astonished his spectators with his levitational abilities. At the request of the audience, he would levitate, rise up to the ceiling, turn around, and turn left or right according to the spectators' instructions. Sometimes, he would sometimes perform a somersault in the air. The rumors about his amazing abilities provoked various criticisms, and he was asked to prove his levitational ability in front of a kind of test committee composed of journalists, researchers, religious figures, judges, lawyers, scientists, illustrators, and two people from the British royal establishment.

The day he performed his fantastic levitation in the presence of all these astute critics signaled an important landmark in the annals of the history of the extrasensory.

*Daniel* Home.

It was a cloudy but pleasant fall day in London of 1868. A procession of carriages, some of them impressive and luxurious, halted in front of one of the city's edifices, and their passengers alighted. They included several renowned public figures, famous journalists, a priest, and several people who were less known to the general public, but well known among their professional peers – scientists and investigators of extrasensory phenomena. The dignitaries all went in to watch a unique performance given by Daniel Home in his home. They assembled in a large room, devoid of furniture and rather dark and gloomy, sat down, the newspaper illustrators crowding together in a place that would afford them a good view of the performance, and whispered among themselves. What could he be planning this time, they wondered. Even the skeptics among them found it difficult to contain their excitement.

But the whispering and chatting ceased abruptly when Home, a handsome man with a thin mustache of about 35, strode into the room. He smiled at the assembled guests, briefly greeted his acquaintances, cleared his throat, and requested his audience's attention. Home asked them to assemble next to one of the walls and to try and maintain absolute silence. He approached the broad window, which was covered with a curtain, drew the curtain, and opened the window wide. Daylight penetrated the room and illuminated its gloom slightly. Home looked down briefly from the window of his home on the third floor of the apartment block. The spectators had a hard time containing their curiosity. They knew that Home put on marvelous performances. But to gather the *crème de la crème* of the lay and scientific community – no doubt what they were going to see would be even more amazing and stunning than his usual performances.

Home returned to the center of the room and stared at the wall. The spectators waited silently. Suddenly, with astonishing slowness, almost motionlessly, his feet detached themselves from the floor and he began to rise, his body erect and tense. It rose slowly upward until his head touched the ceiling and bumped against it lightly. It moved slightly downward, as if seeking the appropriate angle of movement and preparing itself for another occurrence, and then turned around and began to levitate toward the wide-open window. Home went out the window, his heels scraping the windowsill lightly. Several stunned spectators rushed over to the window and looked down, upset and frightened. They expected to see his crushed body on the sidewalk, but all they saw was their waiting carriages next to the sidewalk! When they looked to both sides, amazed, they saw Home's body going through the next window, which was also open – the window of one of the other rooms in his apartment. Moments later, Home entered the large room, a triumphant smile on his lips. The reliable spectators could do no more than admit that Home had succeeded in doing the impossible: overcoming the limitations of gravity, of one of the most clear-cut physical laws, and of the human body.

Daniel Home wrote his memoirs in a series of books in which he himself attempted to comprehend the secret of his special and mysterious power. The numerous contemporary accounts according to which he actually performed all these marvelous feats, including levitation, are important documents in the research and proof of extrasensory phenomena.

Another fascinating story about Home occurred in the 1950s. Because of his incredible and documented extrasensory abilities, certain researchers wanted to examine his body and perform an autopsy on it in order to see whether it would reveal anything that could shed light on the meaning of those marvelous phenomena. When they exhumed his body, however, all they found was the body of a child!

Daniel Home and Colin Evans were not the only ones who succeeded in performing genuine levitation, however. Stories of religious figures and saints who managed to levitate, such as the wonderful story of Jesus walking on the water (that is also a kind of levitation) were common throughout the world. In Hebrew writings, as well as in Biblical interpretations and Kabbalistic writings, a similar matter called "a miraculous abridgement of a journey" is mentioned. In one of the interpretations, the rapid arrival of Eliezer, Abraham's slave, at the well where Abraham met Rebecca, Isaac's future wife, is described as "a miraculous abridgement of a journey," as the arrival at a particular place without walking in the usual time-consuming way. Having said that, some people interpret the matter of "a miraculous abridgement of a journey" as concerning time – a kind of "fold" in time, which enables the person to reach his destination not in his usual manner. The "miraculous abridgement of a journey" is attributed to several Hebrew religious figures, and is described in Kabbalistic books as being possible, especially when angels' names and various spells are used.

One of the famous stories about the levitation of saints tells about the Christian saint, Joseph Copertino, who lived in the 17th century. Copertino lived a life of asceticism, abstinence and prayer. Several strange occurrences are attributed to him, such as an ability to eat food that was inedible to other human beings. It is told that he would mix a bitter powder into his food. When several other monks in his monastery tasted his food, they all became desperately ill from the powder, while Copertino ate it every day without any ill effects. It is further told about him that he would crush pebbles between his teeth while praying and flagellate himself until he drew blood. Suddenly, one day, while praying, Joseph Copertino's body began to rise up in the air. Several agitated monks rushed to grab hold of his body – and immediately rose up as well as a result of their grasp on his ascending body! From that day on, Copertino would levitate on a daily basis. This story would sound like just another legend of the saints had it not created extensive ripples and attracted hundreds of dignitaries from all over Europe, who arrived to witness Copertino's levitation with their own eyes. An especially reliable testimony is that of the well-known philosopher Leibniz, who saw Copertin's marvelous levitation with his own two eyes and watched it, fascinated, for a whole week.

A 19th-century European traveler wrote about a fantastic vision he had seen in Tibet in his travel journal. The Tibetan monks were in the habit of performing levitation, sometimes to great heights, which was called *long gom* – walking while in a trance. This technique of levitation was learned (and may still be learned and applied) in special Tibetan monasteries. This is what the European traveler wrote upon seeing the levitation of the Tibetan monks for himself: "Two novices sat in the lotus position that is familiar to Yoga practitioners. They took slow breaths, and it was possible to see their chests rising and falling like a bellows. Suddenly, without changing their sitting position, their bodies began to rise up into the air, and they began to move away from us, the spectators, toward the mountain-peak. I could not believe my eyes. I began to pinch myself until I injured myself with my fingernails, and when I realized that it was not a dream, my entire body trembled with terror and fear!"

# Teleportation and disappearance

Peter Stuart Ney was a French teacher in Florence, South Carolina. He was considered to be a quiet, well-liked and respected member of the community, a modest man, whose name was unsullied by anything unusual or out of the ordinary. However, when he was on his deathbed in 1846, his words engendered astonishment in the members of the community. In a weak voice, Peter Stuart Ney declared: "I am the French Marshal Ney."

Marshal Michel Ney was one of Napoleon's generals. He was executed by firing squad 31 years before this strange declaration, in 1815, after Napoleon's defeat at Waterloo.

Nobody believed the dying teacher. Some of the members of the community reckoned that on his deathbed, his reason had deserted him, and he was saying meaningless things, or was delusional – until a physician who was examining the scars on Stuart Ney's body compared them to the information in Marshal Ney's medical files, in which the war injuries of the marshal were described in detail. The scars on Ney's body were in exactly the same places as those of Marshal Ney in his battles. Later, the famous New York graphologist, David Carballo, compared the documents that were written by the general with the teacher's handwriting. He declared that they had all been written by the same person!

Ney, as the researchers who studied the phenomenon believe, is a person who underwent one of the strangest phenomena in the extrasensory realm – the phenomenon that is known as "disappearance" or "teleportation."

The name "disappearance" is given to phenomena and incidents in which people simply disappear without any explanation, without leaving any traces. Until today, the only explanation that has been provided for this phenomenon is that those people fell victim to a kind of time loop, which conveyed their bodies at a tremendous, inconceivable speed somewhere out into ethereal space, without a trace, never to be seen again.

One of the strangest of these cases is that of an elderly disabled man called Owen Parfitt, who disappeared from the front of his home in 1769. Owen Parfitt was sitting next to the front door of his home in Somerset. Since he had been disabled by a stroke, he was unable to move. His niece went into the house for a moment, and when she returned, she saw Parfitt's robe lying on his chair, but Parfitt himself had disappeared! There was no one in the vicinity of the isolated house, and although she knew that her paralyzed uncle could not move, she combed the area surrounding the house in a state of shock and horror – to no avail. Old Parfitt had simply disappeared!

The most famous case of disappearance ever was that of the British diplomat, Benjamin Bathurst in 1809. Bathurst was in the middle of a trip back to Hamburg after being sent to Austria on a diplomatic mission. He stopped for lunch at an inn in the town of Perlberg. After the meal, he and his entourage returned to the carriage that was waiting for them outside. Bathurst's friend saw him go to the front of the carriage to see how the horses were faring – and from that moment was not seen again. In front of the very eyes of his astonished friend, Benjamin Bathurst disappeared, never to be seen again.

Although these events occurred a long time ago, they are not legends. The people who disappeared left shocked relatives and friends and anxious employers behind – as in the case of Bathurst, who was a diplomat (just imagine some of the members of our federal administration in such a situation!) – and sparked horrified articles in the newspapers. However, in much more recent times, the following type of weird events occurred:

In 1975, Jackson Wright, an American, was driving from New Jersey to New York with his wife Martha. After they had driven through the Lincoln Tunnel, Jackson got out to clean the front windshield while his wife went to clean the back windshield. When he was through a few minutes later, he looked around, and there was no trace of Martha Wright. She had disappeared!

The most dramatic case of disappearance in history was reported by three former soldiers who were already elderly people when they reported the incident (50 years after its occurrence). Over the years, they had kept the incident to themselves as if it were a military secret, and it haunted them like a nightmare, giving them no rest, until they decided to report it. The terrifying disappearance occurred during the fateful battle at Gallipoli during World War I. The three, who were members of the New Zealand Field Battalion, related that from a clear vantage point, they watched the Royal Norfolk Regiment marching up the hill in the Bay of Suela, in Turkey, on August 12, 1915. They were quietly watching them climbing up the hill, when suddenly they noticed that the English soldiers were approaching a strange, small, and low-lying cloud on their march.

When they reached the cloud, they marched straight into it without the slightest hesitation, but no one emerged from the other side. About an hour later, after the last ranks had disappeared behind the cloud, it slowly rose up from the ground and began to move upward, until it regained the rest of the low-lying clouds over the mountain.

After the Turkish surrender in 1918, Britain demanded that the regiment be returned – the prevailing opinion being that the entire regiment had been captured. The Turks, however, replied that their soldiers had never come into contact with this regiment, and had certainly not captured it. In fact, they knew nothing about its existence. That is what the war veterans related.

Although those are memories from 50 years after the incident, and it is possible that the memory of the veteran soldiers was not so clear, the disappearance of the regiment following the last communication with them on August 12 is a concrete fact. Only a few bodies of soldiers in the regiment were found, but the vast majority disappeared without trace.

One of the theories explaining the phenomenon of disappearance states that the universe contains strange cosmic whirlpools that pull people into them without permitting them to resist or fight back, and transfer them to some place on the planet, or perhaps hurl them into some completely different dimension…

On November 24, 1971, a man hijacked an American airliner on a domestic flight. After threatening to blow up the plane, he received $200,000 and a parachute. When the Boeing 727 was drifting above the Cascade Mountains, the man jumped. In spite of the exhaustive search conducted by hundreds of skilled search parties, nothing was found – no money, no parachute, and no body.

The mysterious disappearance of Emilia Earhart, a woman who was considered to be a national heroine in the United States after she broke numerous aviation records, has also been described as an unsolved disappearance phenomenon by several researchers. In 1937, Emilia took off for a flight around the world, a flight that was covered thoroughly by all the media. She took off from New Guinea on June 30 of that year, but she never reached her destination. Neither her body nor the plane has ever been found.

Not only human beings disappear, however. Objects – much bigger and heavier – also do, and it is even more difficult to explain their disappearance. The 12,000-ton American freighter, *The Poet*, disappeared in October 1981 while it was approaching Egypt. Its crew sent no distress signal before the disappearance. Even a 300,000-square-mile search, both above the sea and below it, did not bring the ship to light, and to this day its remains have not been found. How can the remains of such a large ship disappear like that?

As opposed to disappearance, researchers attribute teleportation to the person's own will, which is not necessarily activated by the person consciously. They claim that at times of life-threatening danger, of tremendous pressure and of fear of the danger of death that reaches almost supernatural proportions, as happened in the case of Ney, the person can disappear – and reappear later on far from the place of his disappearance.

# Cursed objects – jinxes

Can objects become cursed by a certain power, by the evil eye, or by curses from beyond the grave? Cursed in such a manner that everyone who comes into contact with them suffers ill fortune, accidents, illnesses, and even strange demises? What makes a car or a ship, which was manufactured in exactly the same way as thousands of other similar machines, become cursed, bringing bad luck and sometimes even worse than that?

Are all the stories about the evil eye or "jinxes" (cursed objects) that have been passed down over many generations and attributed to various objects simply a figment of a fertile imagination, or is there an element of truth in them? Can a force from beyond the grave use objects to affect the world of the living?

Among all the cursed objects, few have caused so much suffering as "the cursed car" of the Austrian Habsberg dynasty.

It was an open limousine, impressive in its beauty, which was given as a gift to Archduke Franz Ferdinand, heir to the Austrian throne. In 1914, Franz Ferdinand paid an official visit to Sarajevo in Bosnia Herzogovina, which was part of the Austro-Hungarian Empire at the time. On that fateful day, the car was conveying the archduke and his wife, Archduchess Sophie, the general of the Austrian army Potiorc, three other dignitaries, and the chauffeur. A hot-tempered nationalist fanatic, Gabriello Princip, strode to the front of the car and shot the archduke and his wife. This incident sparked World War I.

General Potiorc became the new owner of the car. A few weeks after the beginning of the war, the general's armies suffered from many dangerous riots in Serbia, and the general was recalled to Vienna by the emperor, Franz Joseph I. In the capital, he not only lost his good name and reputation, but gradually lost his mind in a peculiar manner until he finally died after his long and honorable career had came to naught.

One of the general's staff members took the cursed car. Nine days later, in a horrifying accident, he killed two farmers at a crossroads. As he veered off the road, he collided with a tree and was killed instantly.

After the war, the ruler of independent Yugoslavia appropriated the luxurious vehicle, which had undergone numerous repairs until its gleaming and seductive appearance was restored. The ruler of Yugoslavia did not escape the curse of the car, either. Within a short time, he too was involved in a chain of terrible accidents, one of which cost him his left arm.

The car was subsequently sold to a physician who was crushed to death when the car overturned and rolled into a canal. The next owner of the car was Simon Manthraides, a wealthy diamond merchant. Manthraides fell to his death from a high cliff. This, however, was not the end of the saga of the car that never brought happiness to any of its owners. It passed into the hands of a Swiss racing driver. He was someone who knew how to drive a car and assumed that there was no car that could "get the better" of him. During his life, he had driven many cars, some of them experimental racing cars. He always held the steering wheel firmly with both hands, and had never been involved in a serious or dangerous accident, despite the vagaries of the road and his fast driving. This was not the case with the cursed car. Shortly after purchasing it, he was killed while driving it.

The official car of the crown prince gradually passed into less and less high-ranking hands, as if it were going down in rank from one incident to the next. However, it did not lose any of the dangerous effect that, in a completely inexplicable way, destroyed the life of anyone who touched it. After the death of the racing driver, the car came into the possession of a rich Serbian farmer. Although the amount the farmer paid for the beautiful vehicle that had already amassed such historical value was unknown, it was estimated to be a fortune. Like the people before him, he too fell under the mystical spell of the car's beauty and prestige, as well as the famous hands that had driven it. However, for some reason, like all the other victims, he also ignored the bitter fate that had pursued every single one of the car's previous owners.

He drove it for some time, puffed up with satisfaction every time he got into the beautiful car, and attracted excited glances wherever he went. It seemed as if everything was going just fine. Perhaps in the hands of a farmer, a simple man, albeit wealthy, the car could rest and its curse would calm down.

Not for long. One morning, when the farmer tried to start the car, the engine showed no sign of life. He tried to start it a few times, and then called one of his farmhands to help him. Since they did not succeed in starting it, he asked the farmhand to tow it, with him sitting in the car, using a horse and cart. Regrettably, the owner of the car forgot to turn off the ignition, and the engine sputtered and suddenly ignited, causing the car to shoot forward onto the cart that was towing it, overturning the cart, and bringing the life of the unfortunate farmer to an abrupt end.

Finally, a garage owner lost his life in the car while returning from a wedding. He tried to overtake a long line of cars, but was killed when the car suddenly went out of control and ran amok on the road.

Now the cursed car rests in a safe place where, let's hope, it won't cause any more strange deaths and terrible accidents: in the Vienna Museum. Since it was placed in the museum, nobody has dared to take it out on the road again.

Many people are inclined to scoff at the phenomenon of cursed objects. But what can we say about such a case, in which anybody who drove the car died in it?

Was it a cursed object or the "evil eye" that caused one single woman to be on board ship during three shipwrecks, the worst that occurred during the 20th century? Or was it simply a matter of luck – luck that enabled her to survive the three most serious maritime disasters of the century?

In 1915, Mrs. Joan Murray boarded the *Lusitania*, a pleasant passenger liner. What was supposed to be a pleasure-filled cruise for the woman who, just a short while previously, had managed to recover from the treachery of the sea, became a severe trauma when the ship was torpedoed by the Germans off the coast of Ireland, with massive loss of life. Joan

Murray survived the terrible catastrophe, considering herself to be a fortunate woman, since this was not the first time she had survived one of the most famous maritime accidents in history, three years before – when she was on board the *Titanic*. In 1927, she received the gift of her life once more, when, as a guest on board ship, she survived a collision between two ships, the *Caltic* and the *Anaconda*.

An interesting, but "opposite" story, which concerns the fortune that pursues man and causes him to be involved over and over again in accidents or situations of a certain kind, is attributed to a Mexican man who survived four (!) railroad accidents within a period of a few months. He considered himself to be an extremely lucky man, of course, because many people were hurt in those accidents. This was true until the day, shortly after he survived the last accident, he tried to fix his son's electric train – and was killed by a fatal electrical short circuit.

Another person who was cursed or blessed – depending on the reader's perspective – was, of course, Wesley McIntyre, who got caught up in a chain of fatal situations just to discover that, by some divine miracle, he survived them time and time again just as he was looking death in the eye.

During World War II, he dived from an American warship moments before it was blown up, killing most of his shipmates. In 1950, he managed to steer his truck, which was racing at a crazy speed without brakes for almost three kilometers down a steeply sloping mountain road. Eventually Wesley succeeded in bringing it to a parking area by driving the truck in circles.

In 1959, Wesley was involved in an accident in a truck loaded with inflammable gas, which, for some reason, did not ignite after the serious accident.

In another accident, he was saved by a mattress that absorbed the full shock when the air tanks of the truck's brake system exploded.

Finally, he was the only survivor of a terrible disaster in which 35 people were killed. He was thrown into the water when a boat collided with the Sunshine Skyway Bridge at the entrance to the Tampa Bay in

Florida. "The good Lord must certainly be looking after me in a special way," said Wesley, as he was taken away on a gurney from the scene of the ghastly accident.

However, it is not only objects that are large and inherently dangerous, such as cars or ships, that bear a strange death-curse. Small, apparently non-dangerous objects, too, are liable to bring fatal misfortune to the people who come into contact with them…

In 1928, a middle-aged English couple, Charles and Mary Lambert, halted in front of a small souvenir store in Kobe, Japan. In the store window, their eyes were drawn to a small "good luck" charm with a miniature figure of an Oriental monk standing out on it. They hurried into the store to examine the object more closely. When they examined the image on the charm closely, the couple, who had some experience in assessing antiques and ornaments, noticed that the figure was made of excellent quality, flawless, milky and valuable ivory. Somewhat anxious about being charged a price that was "impossible" for their average means, the modest couple asked the price of the ornament. To their surprise, the storekeeper mentioned a price that was too good to be true… They quickly paid and got out of the store before the storekeeper changed his mind or discovered that he had underestimated the value of the exquisite jewel. They congratulated themselves on their good luck at finding such a valuable object at such a low price. The figure on the charm was that of Ho-Ti, a sixth-century Buddhist monk whose life was devoted to helping others, especially hapless children and orphans. At a later period, the monk was "promoted" to the rank of god, and it was still possible to purchase good luck charms bearing his smiling image in various parts of the Far East.

However, he did not bring any good luck to Mr. and Mrs. Lambert. On the contrary, he brought them a considerable amount of bad luck…

The chain of awful events began almost immediately after they had booked their passage on the ship that would take them back to England.

On the second day on board, as the ship was sailing in the direction of the port and permitted its passengers to disembark on the shores of Manila in the Philippines for a few hours, Mrs. Lambert doubled up with the pain of a terrible toothache. The medications administered by the ship's physician seemed to be completely ineffective in the face of the pain that was tormenting her.

When they reached Manila, the couple disembarked onto the shore with a high fever. Mrs. Lambert was rushed to a dentist in the city, who, in a "work accident," cut one of the nerves of the tooth, causing her even more ghastly pain. Mr. Lambert had not noticed that his wife had transferred the little charm from her suitcase to his while packing for the next leg of their journey, toward Australia. This time, it was Mr. Lambert who was taken off the boat with an abnormal toothache that wracked his entire body with pain. When he was rushed to a dentist in Sydney, Mr. Lambert, crazed with pain, instructed the dentist to extract all of his teeth, one after the other, until the pain subsided.

Their next stop was in Auckland, New Zealand. In Auckland, the couple parted with their baggage as part of the baggage procedure, and their toothache subsided. When their suitcases were returned to their cabin on the next ship on their journey, renewed agonizing bouts of toothache attacked them simultaneously.

While they were sailing on the Pacific Ocean, the couple lent their charm to a lady they knew on board ship. She took an interest in the charm and the figure on it, and asked them to lend it to her so that she could examine it. She kept the charm overnight, and returned it to them in the morning, telling them that she and her husband had had a sleepless night due to severe toothache. Perhaps if the nice couple had been in the habit of reading books like this one, they would have done a bit of "simple arithmetic," or at least surmised about the source of the terrible toothaches that had no visible physiological cause. However, it would seem that this did not occur to the naive couple, nor did they suspect anything.

When Mr. and Mrs. Lambert reached the United States, she with serious nerve problems in her jaw and he in urgent need of a set of perfect dentures, they thought that the charm would be a perfect gift for Mr. Lambert's elderly mother who lived there (I know a few grudge-bearing people who would be prepared to give a present like this to their mothersin-law…), after the old lady was enchanted by the figure of the smiling monk on the charm. She was so infatuated with the charm that they immediately gave it to her as a heartfelt gift.

When the curious old lady examined her new gift carefully, she noticed, at the base of the figure, a little hole that was neatly closed with a tiny ivory stopper. Finally, with a flash of healthy intuition, she told the couple quietly that she felt the touch of "black magic" in the charm, and rejected their generous gift. The couple did not in the least believe in "superstitions," as they were wont to call things like these. But the old lady's quiet and confident words, together with the most vivid memories of the excruciating agony that had suffered since the charm had come into their possession, caused them ultimately to understand that although they had owned a "good luck" charm, for some reason it had only brought them pain and suffering. For fear of even more serious events, the coupled rushed to sell the Ho-Ti charm to an antique dealer in London as soon as they returned to England. After a lengthy scrutiny of the charm, the antique dealer – who was known for his ability to assess the origin of antique decorative objects from the Far East – announced that beyond any shadow of a doubt, the small ivory figure had been extracted from a Buddhist temple by robbers. Perhaps the theft of the charm had released a vindictive curse when the figure of the Buddha had been removed from its sacred resting place on the walls of the temple.

This is not the only instance known to researchers of supernatural phenomena in which disturbing the rest of a special figure engendered bad luck that entailed pain and disaster. The most famous case of this kind in history is linked to the young Egyptian king, Tutankhamen.

## Tutankhamen's curse

Of the original large archeological delegation that was present at the opening of the ancient tomb of the Egyptian king, Tutankhamen, only one man reached a ripe old age. Was this a strange coincidence, or was it the realization of the curse that was transmitted from one person to the next over hundreds of years – a curse that was too evil, mysterious and fatal for people in the modern world to understand, a curse that exerts its blood-chilling effect to this day?

The last wall of the sealed burial chamber of the young pharaoh was breached for the first time in 3,000 years on February 17, 1923. The archeologist, Howard Carter, whispered in an excited, almost breathless manner, that he could see "things, wonderful things" when he peeped fearfully into the burial chamber, staring in wide-eyed astonishment at Tutankhamen's treasures.

When Carter, together with the Egyptologist, Lord Carnarvon, who was almost obsessed with opening the tomb, gazed at the golden treasures, the precious stones and the priceless ornaments lying in the pharaoh's burial chamber, they both ignored the frightening warning that had been written thousands of years before to warn off potential grave robbers. In ancient hieroglyphics above their heads was inscribed:

*"Death to those who dare disturb the repose of the pharaohs."*

The last blow of the excavators' pick-axes released the terrible curse of Tutankhamen.

Lord Carnarvon had never taken the ancient curses of the Egyptian priests lightly. In England, before his delegation set out for Egypt, he consulted with one of the most famous mystics of the time, Duke Hamon, who warned him: "Death will take its revenge on you in Egypt." Two additional visits to mediums in England were also fraught with prophecies concerning the fateful end that was approaching. But the human lust for honor can sometimes be more powerful than reason – more powerful even than the fear of death itself. After Carter and Carnarvon had invested so much money and effort in one of the biggest archeological discoveries in history – a discovery that would cover them with glory – they were not prepared to forgo it. When they stood in front of the opening of the tomb, everything they had heard about curses, death, disasters and so on evaporated from their memories in an instant. They could only see the stunning ancient treasures they had surmised to be in the tomb, and the magnificence of the discovery that would make Carter into one of the greatest archeologists ever, and Lord Carnarvon into a well-known and highly praised Egyptologist. When the burial chamber was exposed, they were overcome by tremendous exultation and the joy of triumph over what symbolized the end of the back-breaking searches and the difficult excavations.

The site of the tomb at Luxor had escaped the notice of the grave robbers, who had done their work so thoroughly over the centuries, and the burial chamber was packed with treasures that had not been touched by human hands since it had been sealed – fantastic treasures, whose value could not be compared to any other archeological finding. Archeologists, researchers, and Egyptologists heaped praise and glory on the two explorers and their team. Museums all over the world dispatched excited telegrams to them, among them the famed and respected museums of California and Cairo. Carnarvon bathed in glory the likes of which he had never known in his entire exhausting and sometimes frustrating career. He was hungry for this glory, since many archeological institutions had not accorded him the honor that he felt was his due for his many years of work. Finally his efforts had been rewarded. What he did not know was that he had less than two months to enjoy the fruits of his success.

On April 5, 1923, only 47 days after the breach of Tutankhamen's resting place, Lord Carnarvon, who was only 57 years old, died in agony from an infected mosquito bite. At the moment of his death, in the Continental Hotel in Cairo, the lights of the entire city all went out and remained extinguished for a few minutes. And if it is necessary to present more proof showing that a powerful and mysterious force was indeed at work during those moments, thousands of kilometers away, in Lord

Carnarvon's country house in England, his beloved dog began to howl and bark in a kind of blood-chilling lament that shocked the entire staff of the house in the middle of the night. The hair-raising howl continued until the agonized creature rolled over on its back and died.

The daily newspapers rushed to offer speculations that the horrible and strange events were the result of the mysterious curse, of an evil, hitherto unknown force that had been released into the world when the two explorers opened the grave. The sensational conclusion was substantiated when two days after Carnarvon's death, the mummified body of the pharaoh who had died a bloody death was examined. To the astonishment of the investigators, they discovered a kind of peculiar defect in the left cheek of the mummified corpse in exactly the same place and exactly the same shape as the fatal mosquito bite that had been visible on Lord Carnarvon's face!

This event might ultimately have been explained by cool-headed scientists as simply a coincidence. This would have been the case had it not been for the chain of strange deaths that occurred over the following days.

A short time after Lord Carnarvon's demise, another archeologist, Arthur Mace, one of the outstanding members of the delegation, went into a coma in the Continental Hotel where he was staying after complaining for some time about a peculiar fatigue. He died shortly afterwards, leaving the team's skilled physician and the local physicians astounded and confused.

The deaths continued. A close friend of Lord Carnarvon, George Gould, rushed to Egypt after hearing of his friend's fate. Before leaving the area and going on to do a bit of sightseeing in Cairo, he went to catch a glimpse of the burial chamber. The next day, he collapsed with a high fever, and 12 hours later, he was found lifeless in his hotel room.

The radiologist, Archibald Reid, an expert who used the most up-to-date X-ray techniques of those times in order to determine the age and possible cause of death of Tutankhamen, was sent back to England after he complained of severe exhaustion. He died a few hours after reaching England.

Carnarvon's personal secretary, Richard Bethell, was found dead in his bed as a result of heart failure four months after the discovery of the tomb.

The strange events did not cease. Joel Wall, a senior British industrialist of the time, visited the site and died a few months later of a fever that was incomprehensible to the specialists that examined him.

By the time six years had elapsed following the opening of the tomb, 12 of the people who had been present had met similar fates – they had all died one after the other during those six years. During the following seven years, only two of the original delegation to the tomb were still alive. Lord Carnarvon's half-brother apparently committed suicide in a bout of temporary insanity, and 21 other people who were somehow connected to the excavation of the tomb died in peculiar circumstances. Of the pioneers of the original delegation, only Howard Carter managed to reach a ripe old age and died a natural death in 1939.

While Egyptologists and many other academics tried to refute the legend of the curse and to claim that it was nothing but a myth or an empty superstition, more people continued to fall victim to the fatal influence. Muhammed Ibrahim, the director of the Antiquities Authority of Egypt, argued with his government in 1966, objecting to treasures from the tomb being exhibited in Paris. He petitioned the authorities to leave the items in Cairo because he had been suffering from terrible nightmares in which he dreamed of the ghastly things that would happen if these items were to leave Egypt. Ibrahim, exhausted from sleepless nights and from his serious dispute with the civil servants, left the government building and walked on that sunny day to what looked like an empty road, without any vehicle whatsoever in sight. Suddenly a car ran into him with tremendous force, and he was killed instantly.

Even more peculiar, perhaps, was the case of Richard Adamson, who, in 1969, was the only person from the 1923 delegation who was still alive. Adamson lost his wife within 24 hours of speaking disparagingly about the existence of the curse and claiming passionately that it was nothing but a myth! When he again claimed that the curse did not exist, and was nothing but a superstition, the plane in which his son was flying at the time crashed, causing his son to sustain a serious fracture in his back.

Still hard put to believe in the curse, Adamson, who had worked as a security guard for Lord Carnarvon, railed against the existence of the curse in a British television interview, during which he reiterated that he did not believe in it. Later that same evening, when he left the TV studio, he was thrown out of the taxi he was traveling in as a result of a sudden accident, and a truck that veered from its lane missed his head by a few centimeters. He was taken to the hospital with fractures and bruises. Only then was the skeptical 70-year-old Adamson compelled to admit: "Up to now, I had refrained from believing that the disasters that struck my family were somehow linked to the curse. But now I'm not so sure."

Even 50 years after the seal was removed from the curse of the pharaohs, the fatal force had still not died down. In 1972, when the treasures of the tomb were brought to London for a prestigious exhibition in the British Museum, the first victim was Dr. Jamal Ma'arj, the secretary of Muhammed Ibrahim in the Antiquitics Authority in Cairo. Ma'arj scoffed at the legend and claimed that he had spent his entire life researching Egyptian antiquities. According to him, all those peculiar deaths following the opening of the tomb were "simply coincidences." Ma'arj died just one night after supervising the packing of the items in preparation for their journey to England on a Royal Air Force jet. The crew of the plane suffered deaths, accidents, injuries, disasters and catastrophes in the years following the cursed flight with the treasures of King Tutankhamen in the hold. A captain in the British Air Force, Rick Lowry, a young man in perfect health, died four years after that flight, in 1976, from a heart attack. His wife declared: "It's the curse of Tutankhamen – the curse is what killed him!"

Ken Parkinson, a flight engineer who was among the plane's crew, had a heart attack every year on the same date from the day he was on the plane that brought the treasures from the tomb to England. The fixed date of his heart attacks was the date of the cursed flight! After a few heart attacks, he had a fatal heart attack in 1978. All the crew members of the plane had been examined before their flight to Egypt to bring the antiquities to Britain. They were examined by military specialists before their mission, and were all found to be fit and healthy. None of them suffered from any kind of cardiac or arterial problems, and they were declared to be fit and healthy by a battery of specialists.

During the flight, the chief technical officer, Ian Landsdowne, inadvertently kicked a crate containing the death mask of the young pharaoh. "It had to be one of the most valuable things in the world that I kicked by mistake," he remarked rather scathingly. Afterwards, as he was descending from the Royal Air Force plane after completing another mission, the staircase mysteriously collapsed under him, and he seriously fractured the leg that had inadvertently kicked the crate. His leg was in plaster for close to six months.

British Air Force captain Jim Webb, who had been on the plane during the flight to bring the items to Britain, lost all his property in a fire that destroyed his home. One of the stewards, Brian Rownsfall, admitted that he had played cards on Tutankhamen's sarcophagus on the way to Britain, and he too suffered two mysterious heart attacks. A female officer who had been on the flight was forced to quit the Air Force after undergoing serious surgery.

The mystery has not yet been solved. Were those wretched people who were somehow connected to Tutankhamen's tomb and its treasures simply victims of a huge chain of coincidental deaths over all the years since the tomb was opened? Or did the ancient dark curses of the priestly guards of the tombs really activate supernatural forces that caused so many disasters to befall those who had invaded the sacred tomb? Did they mete out the terrible punishments to those who plundered the treasure of their revered king?

Tutankhamen's curse engendered many hypotheses and theories. No case in history has consistently caused so many deaths – deaths that occurred after a clear and explicit threat was issued to the tomb robbers in the hieroglyphics at its entrance.

One of the most fascinating theories about the legend of the curse was propounded by the modern atomic scientist, Louis Bulgarini, in 1949. He wrote:

"It is certainly possible that the ancient Egyptians used atomic radiation in order to guard their holy places. The floor of the burial chamber was supposed to be covered with uranium. Moreover, it is possible that the tombs were sealed with radioactive stone. Rocks that contained both uranium and gold were quarried in Egypt. Radiation of this kind can be fatal to human beings up until this day."

# Psychometry

Psychometry is the ability to sense the vibrations that emanate from a particular object, thereby channeling or sensing the owner of the object. People with psychometric powers can grasp an object that belongs to a missing person, for instance, and, upon entering a meditative state or a trance, can see the things that befell the owner of the object by means of clairvoyance that is frequently combined with a supernatural sensory ability and intuitive knowledge. Many police forces throughout the world make use of people with these powers in order to locate missing persons, to reconstruct murders, or to obtain impressions and information about criminals who left some kind of personal object behind at the scene of the crime. This is one of the extrasensory abilities that is most widely used professionally, and generally speaking, the person with psychometric powers is consulted after all the other directions of investigation have reached a dead end. Although there are not many unequivocal scientific findings regarding psychometry because the topic has not yet been studied extensively, police detectives and investigators, as well as private individuals who face mysteries that cannot be solved in a conventional manner, do not hesitate to turn to these people.

*Eileen Grant, a medium.*

Arthur Young, the inventor of the helicopter rotor, tried to figure out what had caused the helicopter accident in which the pilot and copilot had been killed. Suffering severe guilt feelings, he searched in vain for the technical flaw that had caused the accident. Despite his prodigious technical knowledge, he did not find an answer. Finally, he brought a fragment of the helicopter's propeller to the famous medium, Eileen Grant. Grant held the fragment in her hands, and, using her psychometric abilities, tried to see what had occurred during the accident. She said that the accident had not been caused by a technical flaw, but rather by the pilot himself, who had been on the verge of a nervous breakdown at the time. She explained that the pilot had just decided to make a drastic change in his lifestyle – he was planning to enter a monastery. Young did not feel that he had the emotional strength to interrogate and question the grieving family of the deceased, and although the medium's words eased his conscience somewhat and provided him with a measure of relief, he could not be completely sure of their veracity. A year after that meeting, he met the director of the agency that had hired the pilot. During the meeting, the director told him in a low voice, as if he were revealing a deep secret, that the pilot had indeed been on the verge of a nervous breakdown and was considering entering a monastery.

The use of supernatural abilities for "detective work" is one of the most widespread ways of using these abilities. Gerard Kreust, the famous Dutch medium, became widely renowned as a result of cooperating with the police in numerous cases of locating missing and kidnapped persons.

## "The case of Liliane"

The following case was examined and endorsed by the French Metaphysical Institute, which is considered to be the highest authority on matters of the supernatural.

Liliane disappeared from her home in the suburbs of Paris without any prior notice or indication of her whereabouts. In the hopes of finding their daughter, her parents asked the medium, Raymond Riant, to meet with them. He agreed to help them, and they brought him a picture of Liliane and a dress that belonged to her in order to help him make contact with her.

During the first sitting, Riant saw Liliane safe and sound traveling in a train with a friend somewhere in northern France.

During the second sitting, Riant described what he saw: "Liliane is sitting on a bench in an old building that looks like a police building in Paris. A blonde girl is sitting next to her. Liliane is spending the night in what looks like a detention cell. I don't see her friend with her."

During the third sitting, Riant said: "The girls are hitching a ride. They are in a region of hills and valleys that looks a bit like Normandy. The girls want to get into a small motorboat. Liliane is wearing a black polo-neck sweater. The location I received by using a pendulum is the Helder district in Holland."

A few days later, Raymond Riant described Liliane's return to Paris, and followed her movements right up to the point when she returned to her parents' home.

After her parents told her what they had gone through during her absence, Liliane told them what had happened to her, and her father completed her sentences with the details he knew.

Liliane had run away from home in the direction of Paris with her friend Claudine. After wandering around for some time, she was arrested for attempting to steal jewelry. They had indeed hitchhiked to Amsterdam. That same day, they got into a small motorboat in order to get to north Amsterdam, to the Helder district. She was in fact wearing a polo-neck sweater that day, but it was beige, not black.

Liliane was astounded at the way her father described the events she had gone through, and although she tried to conceal her arrest, he told her confidently how she had spent the night in a detention cell, and demanded to know why. She was sure that her parents had hired detectives to follow her.

This case, which was investigated and documented, shows the amazing level of accuracy that a skilled and talented medium can reach. Riant could describe Liliane's activities, the places in which she was, and even whom she was with.

## "The Drummond case"

This case was presented in a book and its authenticity was confirmed by police investigators who participated in the investigation.

Mr. Drummond, a man who had passed middle age, went camping with his wife. He decided to take a short stroll, a brief hike after which he would return to their little camp. He was supposed to return within a half-hour to an hour, but he was absent for much longer. After a day of waiting, his anxious and worried wife turned to the local sheriff and asked him to help her locate her husband. The search began, and when there was no sign of Mr. Drummond, many people volunteered to join in. After two weeks of searching and over 300 people participating in the extensive search, there was still no sign of Mr. Drummond. Six months after the incident, when the police had already given up hope of finding him, Mrs. Drummond contacted Kathleen Rea, a medium who had become renowned for helping the police solve numerous cases. Kathleen Rea recorded a 40-minute cassette in which she described her feelings regarding Mr. Drummond's disappearance. She said that Mr. Drummond had completely lost his sense of direction, and had begun to walk in an easterly direction. She described a dirt road that went by a hut in the middle of a grove of trees. She went on to say that as soon as he had taken this road, he had had a heart attack, and had collapsed behind some large thorn-bushes in the grove. She claimed that his body was still there, and, surprisingly, was still completely intact. Mrs. Drummond brought the tape to the sheriff, who decided to try to find the place with the help of his deputy before organizing another search party. Kathleen Rea's descriptions were so accurate that the authorities located the avenue of trees next to the hut easily; behind a clump of tangled thorn-bushes lay Mr. Drummond's body. After that, the deputy sheriff declared that Kathleen Rea's descriptions on the 40-minute tape were almost completely accurate.

# Solving crimes using extrasensory abilities:

## The contribution of clairvoyance to the police resources

The crime-solving tools at the disposal of some of the police forces of the world today constitute an example of the "perfect" combination of the analytical human mind and the wonders of technology. New instruments for checking DNA, for creating computerized profiles of criminals, and so on, seem to have made the work of the detectives and the police investigators easier. Not necessarily, however. It is still true of well-documented cases that in this domain, too – which was considered to be conventional and narrow-minded regarding everything linked to the esoteric until quite recently – there is no substitute for that first spark of inspiration that passes through special people and produces sudden knowledge about what and how.

One of the most famous mystery writers, Sir Arthur Conan Doyle, the author of the "Sherlock Holmes" books, did not ignore this fact, perhaps subconsciously. The renowned Holmes used hallucinogenic drugs, had keen powers of observation, and was inclined to wait for that spark of intuitive "knowledge" that made him much more than "just another detective." It turned him into a person whose powers of observation and ability to solve crimes touched upon supernatural ability. When we read those books, we get the feeling that Holmes's power derives from more than regular analytical and logical power. Even though Doyle does not give any hints of this, and always makes sure to anchor Sherlock Holmes's findings in "elementary" facts and to tie up all the loose ends, we cannot ignore this feeling.

Among today's detectives, too, it is possible to discern that moment of "inspiration," that second when a gut feeling causes the detective to choose one particular direction when there are several possibilities. We tend to see this ability as a practical and useful tool of the veteran detective, a tool that comes from vast experience. Dr. Marcello Trozi calls these events "the blue sense" because of the color of police uniforms. It may seem odd that novice detectives, with their first glance at the scene of the crime or the murder victim, can sometimes also pick up a very significant "clue" when there are no facts to corroborate it as yet. Despite this, the detective often acts in accordance with that "gut feeling" and allows it to dictate the direction of the primary investigation. This type of intuitive flash is common throughout the history of the police, and can be found among pilots as well. No matter how advanced the instruments are, they pay great attention to "gut feelings," "clues," and signs that they create for themselves. Despite the study and training that, according to the skeptics, constitute the overriding reason for some of the exceptional qualities of certain detectives, many of the detectives and police officers confess that they wait for, anticipate, and wish for that "sixth sense" or "blue sense," as Dr. Marcello Trozi calls it. Sometimes, however, the department heads deny the search for "illumination."

In many places in the world, people with extrasensory powers are used both inside the police force and as external volunteers to assist in solving crimes. In research conducted by Dr. Trozi on the incidence of extrasensory assistance in police stations, he came up with an interesting finding. Some of the police precincts for which there was iron-clad evidence of the assistance of people with supernatural powers, denied having availed themselves of this assistance, and claimed that they had never sought the help of such people in solving crimes. Trozi discovered that it was generally small units that sought this kind of assistance, while it was less common in large stations and units. In another study, conducted by Dr. Raymond Waring in a crime-fighting unit in Montana, he discovered that approximately half of the departments that participated in the study used some kind of extrasensory assistance for solving crimes. Occasionally, the assistance was not external – some of the police officers and detectives themselves obtained information and "clues" that did not have a factual basis, but nevertheless led to the crime being solved. It was discovered that some of the police personnel who participated in the study had had extrasensory experiences even before joining the police force.

However, it is still a matter of "clues," "gut feelings," and so on. In contrast, there are people with extrasensory abilities, famous or anonymous, who offer to assist the police with their powers. These people usually receive neither payment nor publicity. Why do they do it? Perhaps they feel obligated to use the powers with which they have been blessed to help mankind.

These people can be divided up into several groups. There are people who read about a crime in the newspaper or see a report on TV. Although they have no personal connection to the event itself, they suddenly receive a flash of knowledge, a serious clue that helps the police get onto the tracks of the criminal or to come up with a direction of investigation that later turns out to be correct and useful. This group also includes people who, for some unknown reason, are "granted" dreams and nightmares about a crime that has occurred. In these dreams, they see what happened as well as the participants in the crime – sometimes during the course of the crime. The feeling of powerful knowledge or the terrible dream is sometimes so intense that the person puts his fears and doubts aside without any hesitation and simply phones the police to report what he dreamed or picked up intuitively. Sometimes the dreams occur a short time before the actual event. Although the police are very cautious and sometimes even skeptical about this information, they occasionally take the trouble to check it out – sometimes precisely because of the tone of certainty and knowledge in the caller's voice.

Another group consists of professional visionaries, the ones who use their supernatural talents professionally. In the past, there were cases in which a professional in the extrasensory domain received a powerful feeling about a crime that had been committed. He then told a friend, client, or family member who was somehow connected to the police about it, or simply phoned up and reported it, and the details were found to be correct. (Naturally, neither the clairvoyant nor his associate was involved in the crime.) A related group consists of the clairvoyants and visionaries who are presented to the police by the families of the victims. This is not rare in cases of searching for a missing relative, and more than once the information provided by the clairvoyant turns out to be useful.

The next group contains clairvoyants who have been known to the police for a long time. In various places in the world, there are departments that keep in close touch with a person with extrasensory powers, known or anonymous, whom they contact and generally invite to the crime scene, or present him with evidence he can actually touch in cases where he has psychometric powers. Peter Horcus, one of the best known of these people, has such a reputation for solving crimes that no police department is ashamed of admitting that it availed itself of his assistance. His successes are so significant that he is hired to help the police and he receives a fee for his assistance and discoveries. This group includes most of the visionaries who help solve cases of crimes. In most cases, they consider solving crimes to be only a part-time job, and they work as parapsychologists and visionaries for a large number of clients on a permanent basis. The interest of these people in their success with helping the police in solving crimes is understandable, since it enhances their reputation and attracts many clients.

The last group includes the people with extrasensory powers who do not turn their unique abilities into a profitable profession, but offer the police their assistance on a voluntary basis. Although many of them try to remain anonymous, their names are frequently leaked to the press after a shocking crime has been solved, in which the police did not have a single lead to solve the mystery. Dorothy Ellison, for instance, is such a person, as are many others in the PSI (extrasensory abilities) unit of the United States. This unit includes police officers on active duty and former police personnel, who have been especially trained to use and develop the extrasensory powers with which they are blessed, among them clairvoyance and remote viewing.

Remote viewing is described as the ability to use developed sensitivities in order to see beyond matter in time and space by means of the mind's eye. The authorities in both the former USSR and in the USA qualify people for these positions. Furthermore, there is information that such units have existed in China for a long time, and police personnel who have been qualified to use their innate extrasensory powers belong to them.

Among the especially gifted "professionals" in the field, sthe unit of Sri Lankan army personnel who serve as clairvoyants is prominent. Some of them, who are very successful in their jobs, are approached by the police force itself in order to work on serious crimes.

People from the two last groups are the most "popular" in the eyes of the police forces, and their help is very sought after in dead-end cases or when there is no lead to begin an investigation.

In one famous case, the chief of a medium-size police precinct in Belleville, Illinois, requested the help of Missouri's unit for investigators with extrasensory powers the day after the disappearance of a 14-year-old girl, Elizabeth West. After seeing and feeling the girl's clothes and photograph, the leader of the group of investigators immediately declared that she had been abducted, sexually abused and murdered, and her body had been dumped in a canal. He provided a description of her attacker, including his Elvis Presley sideburns, the information that his name began with B, and that he would be caught while committing an identical crime. This detailed information was presented to Chief of Police Bail, together with a map of the canals with a certain canal marked with an X, and the location of the murderer's hiding-place in the city. Certain numbers were included in the information the clairvoyant received, among them the number 5.

Two days later, on the fifth of the month, the girl's body was found in the exact place that had been marked with an X on the map, in a small hole beside a deep canal. After an identical case of the abduction and murder of another young woman (by the same murderer, as the unit for extrasensory powers had stated) had occurred, there was a third attempt. The murderer forced another young woman to get into his car. She succeeded in escaping and remembered important details about the abductor as well as his car registration number. After he had been sent to jail for attempted abduction, Bowman was eventually forced to confess to two murders, and was tried and convicted for the abduction and murder of Elizabeth West. The murderer with the narrow face did indeed have Elvis Presley sideburns and lived in Belleville in the same area that the clairvoyant detective had marked.

Large quantities of information have been provided to the police by the special unit of trained clairvoyants, and a large part of that information has been proved to be extraordinarily accurate.

Today, Chief of Police Barry Bail unhesitatingly recommends the assistance and training of detectives with extrasensory powers, declaring: "I believe that people with such an ability can help the police, and, in conjunction with the usual investigation techniques, can help bring the criminals to justice. I will not hesitate under any circumstances to use the services of this group again, if need be."

This is one of many stories about the cooperation between the police and people with extrasensory powers and clairvoyant abilities who are devoted to their work and use their powers in order to help the community, even though many of these stories do not make the headlines.

# Supernatural phenomena in animals: Instinct or extrasensory ability?

Richard Webster, who researches extrasensory phenomena in animals, tells the following story: One day, when he was a small child, his father woke up early in the morning to go to work. While he was walking through the dark hall, the father, who was a big, heavy man, accidentally trod on their pet cat. As a result, the cat died almost immediately. Since it was very early in the morning, and the father did not want to wake up the rest of the members of the household with the painful news, he took the body of the cat and buried it under an apple tree in one of the far corners of the spacious yard, and went to work.

A few hours later, the family's pet Labrador went over to the apple tree and lay down on the earth-covered grave of the cat. Webster mentions that the dog had never shown any interest in that particular corner of the yard before. However, ever since the death of the cat, he spent several hours every day lying on his friend's grave. Webster asks: How did the dog – who had been sleeping in the house at the time of the cat's death and burial – know about the cat's burial place? He went over to lie on the exact spot even before the father came home from work and told the family about the sad event.

We can propound various logical hypotheses about the incident, as well as about many other strange incidents involving animals. However, there are no clear and unequivocal logical answers. Do animals also have extrasensory abilities, like people?

Telepathy between humans and animals is a phenomenon that is known to many people for whom a cat or a dog is one of their best friends. I have already become accustomed to seeing my adopted street cat waiting for me on the path leading to my house every time I get back from somewhere, even after I have been away for a few days. He sits there as if he was just waiting for me to arrive, and accompanies me into the house. My Boxer bitch, Kaya, loves to wander around the yard, and sometimes finds ways to get out and stroll around in the street. Sometimes, some unexplained feeling causes me to leave my computer and go outside to see where she is. In most cases, she is not within my field of vision, and I sigh, knowing that tomorrow I'll have to look for the new hole she found so that she could go out for a walk in the street. In four out of six cases, a few minutes after I get back to the computer, Kaya comes into the house and looks at me as if I had called her.

Another special phenomenon that I discovered while observing her profoundly is as follows: About five or ten minutes before one of my closest friends comes to visit me (a friend who always plays with her for a long time, and sometimes seems to be visiting her rather than me...), Kaya begins to wag her tail, go to the door, yowl, watch me and the door alternately, and show signs of impatience, as if to inform me of his arrival. It makes no difference whether he arrives on foot or by car, or whether his visit is prearranged or unexpected. She is so consistent in her advance knowledge that when I see her beginning her series of tail-wags and yowls of joy, I know that in five or ten minutes, my friend will appear on the doorstep... Initially, I thought that perhaps she heard his car pulling up, even though my house is situated far away from the road, and it is necessary to go along a path past several other houses in order to reach it. However, when I told my mother the story, she was not in the least surprised. My parents' dog, who met my father "by chance" as he was walking down the road and "adopted" him, always knows when my father is coming home, even though he does not have a fixed time for getting home from work – he sometimes comes home late at night and sometimes in the afternoon. My parents live on the seventh floor of a condominium on a busy street. About 10 minutes before the downstairs buzzer sounds, heralding my father's arrival, the old dog, who generally lies inert on the mat for most of the day, sits erect next to the door, howling with joy at the top of her voice. She always provides accurate "information" – everyone in the building knows when my father is arriving according to the dog's behavior.

Many dog-lovers that are in the habit of observing the fascinating behavior of the animals who live with them and pay attention to these phenomena that repeat themselves in a regular pattern, are not surprised at such stories. In fact, this phenomenon is not at all rare. However, the question arises as to how the dog or cat knows when his friend is approaching – sometimes a relatively long time before the person actually gets to the house.

## Seismic sensitivity (sensitivity to earthquakes)

There are many stories about animals who behave strangely a day or two before an earthquake. This pattern repeats itself so regularly that earthquake researchers have begun to examine this phenomenon scientifically and in depth in order to utilize it for predicting earthquakes. In Japan, where earthquakes are relatively common, scientists are now studying the behavior of dogs, rabbits and cats after it was discovered that these animals begin to behave strangely before the occurrence of an earthquake. Before the famous Krakatoa earthquake in 1883, an enormous number of animals fled from the region. In the city of Copigo in Chile, too, in 1922, a similar event was reported, in which the street cats and the domestic cats fled outside the city a short time prior to the huge earthquake that destroyed most of the city!

In contemporary Japan, people who live in regions that are prone to earthquakes keep goldfish, since they begin to behave in an agitated and abnormal manner shortly before an earthquake.

Before the big earthquake in Japan, it was reported that the dogs began to behave abnormally about an hour before it occurred. In California, too, before the mild earthquake in 1974, the abnormal and agitated behavior of two horses who were normally quiet and calm was reported a short time before the earthquake. Dr. Jack Aberdoon from the Institute for Geological Research in the United States, found that the horses were located exactly above the epicenter of the earthquake.

Before the big earthquake in Santa Cruz, California, too, in October 1989, the strange behavior of cats was reported hours before it happened.

These stories are reliable reports that were studied and found to symbolize the repeated behavior patterns of animals before earthquakes. However, are they connected to extrasensory perception? Not necessarily. It depends on how we define extrasensory perception. It is possible that to us, as human beings, a premonition regarding earthquakes would attest to a highly developed extrasensory ability, but for animals, it may simply stem from a far deeper sensitivity to geological changes that occur in the world than that of human beings.

However, the plethora of phenomena that are incomprehensible to us, as human beings, in the animal world, evokes a great deal of wonder.

From observations and studies that have been performed, it has been discovered that squirrels tend to hoard much more food before a long, difficult winter. Moles dig deep burrows before a severe winter, but shallow ones when they expect an easier winter. Are these examples of instincts or proof of sensory and advanced perception abilities? Human beings tend to define all unusual abilities among animals as instincts. Examples of these are the massive migrations of certain birds and fish. How does the salmon manage to leave the river in which it leaves and swim in the ocean and then return to the same river many years later in order to procreate? Scientists have learned that the salmon, like the birds, is guided by the sun. This guidance enables the salmon to reach a distance from his birthplace. Afterwards, his sense of smell enables him to return to the river or pond of his birth unerringly. Are those instincts or extrasensory ability? Scientists have not yet succeeded in providing an unequivocal answer.

Bird migration seems to involve an extrasensory element, because the birds set out on their migratory journey only in suitable weather conditions – when they "know" that these conditions will prevail all the way. This is because even when these conditions prevail, the birds stretch their physical abilities to the limit, and a severe storm will down many of them.

For years, farmers observed the behavior of their animals, and in more ancient times, they tended to attribute magical powers to them because of their ability to "know" things. Bees, for instance, are very sensitive to the earth's magnetic field. In various places, it was customary to use bees for forecasting thunderstorms. Before the storms, bees become agitated and disturbed, and return to their hives in large swarms. Other animals are very sensitive to changes and variations in weather and temperature. Until the days when scientists succeeded in explaining some of the phenomena, many animals were considered to possess mystical properties. But the fact that it is possible to explain many of these phenomena is not proof that animals are devoid of special powers and are only driven by instincts. Actually, there are many incidents and situations that science has not yet managed to explain.

In the eighth volume of the minutes of the Association for the Study of Supernatural Phenomena, there is a report about two dogs that saw a ghost. One of them hurried toward it, wagging its tail and jumping excitedly, thinking it was a person. When it realized its mistake, and that the being in front of it was not human, it fled in terror with its tail between its legs. There are many documents containing reports about animals that were frightened by ghosts. Sir William Bart, a renowned researcher of supernatural phenomena who lived in the 1920s, documented the stories of two sisters who were riding their horses, when suddenly they saw a ghost crossing the path along which they were traveling. Their horses halted. Initially, the horses trembled with fright, and then they went wild. Bart himself documented many cases of this type. Since Bart's documentation and forecasts, many studies have been conducted on extrasensory phenomena and abilities in animals. One of the most famous of these is the study on "the wise stallion" that occurred at the beginning of the 20th century.

The stallion, which earned the attributive "wise," was a horse of average breed that revealed astonishing and unexplained abilities. He was able to perform addition and subtraction, spell words, and do other such amazing tricks. The stallion would tap out his answers with his foot.

Prof. Stampf from the University of Berlin studied the behavior of the wise stallion and made an astounding discovery – the horse could answer questions only when the asker himself knew the answers and when he was present! Stampf discovered that the stallion could read the asker's body language. Although this is an impressive ability, it is not considered to be supernatural. As a result of that study, skeptical researchers and scientists to this day recall the "wise stallion effect" when they get hold of results of studies on the supernatural abilities of animals. However, scientific explanations have still not been found for many of the phenomena.

Joseph Rhine, the famous investigator of supernatural phenomena, conducted research with his wife, Louisa, under the auspices of Duke University on animals that returned home from enormous distances. They investigated more than 50 unexplained but extremely reliable cases of animals that had returned home from distances of over 50 kilometers, and found that the homing instinct could only be explained as an extrasensory phenomenon. In most of the cases, the animals were conveyed from one place to another in a vehicle, which meant that they could not rely on their memory or on the sense of smell in order to find their way home. One of the most famous cases is that of a Collie whose owners lost it while on vacation in Indiana. The dog returned to its home in Oregon a year later. He covered over 3,500 kilometers on his journey!

*Performances demonstrating the supernatural powers of animals.*

## ∞ THE SIXTH SENSE ∞

Animals have many senses that are far more developed than ours. Dogs' sense of smell is much more acute, and they can hear sounds that are out of our range of hearing. Cats can see well in the dark. They live in the same world, but hear, smell, and see things that we cannot. They can also communicate differently than us. Animals communicate verbally in the same way as people do, but they also use body language a great deal, and can communicate among themselves, with other kinds of animals, and with human beings. In addition, many of them are gifted with telepathic ability. Many people have noticed that when they think loving thoughts about their dog, even when the dog is sound asleep, it wags its tail or reacts in some other way. After profound observation, I noticed the same property in my dog. When I look at her, even from behind, while she is lying in such a way that she cannot see my face or body language, and I feel feelings of deep love for her, she turns her head and looks at me with the same loving look, and wags her tail. One of the things I noticed is that when I am suddenly concerned about her whereabouts, or remember her spontaneously and passionately wish that she would come to me, she always shows up. On the other hand, when I tried to conduct "trumped up" experiments by using the computer to call her name, she generally came into the house from the yard, but would not come to me. Many dog-lovers say that the moment they think about taking their dog for a walk, or feel like leaving the house, the dog reacts by standing at the door ready to go out, before they have even made the slightest indication of their intention. The phenomenon of the dog that knows about its imminent bath is extremely widespread. Of course, when you take the towel or special shampoo out of the closet, the dog knows how to recognize the signs and begins to react with joy – or by running away (depending on how it feels about a bath). However, many people describe strange but common cases in which the dog knows about the intention to give it a bath even before any preparations for it have been made, but rather at the very moment the person decides to do it. Many dog trainers claim that it is impossible to deceive the dog by saying one thing and thinking another. A dog will often obey a command that was given in the person's thoughts instead of a command that was given vocally. Guide dogs are particularly outstanding in this area.

One of the most famous cases of telepathy in dogs was investigated by the Russian scientest Vladimir Bachtarov, who was bewitched by a performing dog at a circus. During the performance it seemed as if the dog reacted to its trainer's thoughts. Bachtarov asked the trainer's permission to carry out a study on the dog's abilities. He discovered that the dog was able to react to his thoughts, too, as well as to those of his research colleagues. The telepathic communication with the dog was amazingly easy and fast. Bachtarov discovered that the dog obeyed orders even when he himself was concealed behind a screen in order to preclude the possibility that the dog would read his body language, and sent him telepathic orders from there.

Cats also have clear telepathic abilities, but they tend to be somewhat stubborn and do not always react to telepathic orders. Having said that, many cat-lovers reveal that it is sufficient for them just to think about their cat, and it will show up in a minute or two.

Just as animals can pick up our thoughts, so we can pick up theirs. Many people say that they found a lost cat when the cat itself "called" them. I myself experienced a peculiar occurrence of this type at the beginning of my acquaintance with my feline friend, Chi. Chi was found in a street by a girl who studied at the holistic school where I was studying. When she found him, he was suffering from a serious neck injury after a gang of children had abused him. He was about three months old. Since she already had a dog, and the two did not get along, she pinned a notice on the notice-board at the school. Up until then, I had not had many encounters with cats. In my limited experience of them, they seemed to me to be somewhat mystical, elusive figures, and I did not think that I could adopt a creature like that. However, for some reason, I felt a fierce need to respond to this notice. During the first few days after Chi came to my home, I reached the conclusion that I was apparently "a dog person," since I found it very difficult to like him. He, on the other hand, loved me from the first moment, and felt at home. A few months passed until I got used to him and could give him the love he needed. He would wander freely around the neighborhood, and would come home to eat and be petted whenever he felt like it. Therefore, when he didn't come home for long periods of time, I wasn't worried.

One day, when the cat was not at home, a strange feeling enveloped me. Suddenly, I began to worry about him. I tried to calm myself – he'd probably be home later to eat, he always wandered around like that, and so on. But I could not calm down. Although I was busy, the tiresome feeling forced me to leave everything and go outside. I walked along the path between the buildings of the neighborhood without really knowing where I was going. When I got close to the road, I stopped, and suddenly began to call him. Above me, from a distance, I heard a whiny cry, and when I raised my head, I saw Chi on the roof of the three-story building next to me. He was looking at me from up there and crying. I asked the owners of the apartment if I could climb onto their roof and take the cat down, and when I came out onto the roof, he jumped on me and cuddled up close to me, yowling and crying. Evidently he was frightened that he could not get down from the roof. The amazing thing was that the entire time I had been walking in the road, no thought had come into my mind. I just walked, without really thinking where I was going. Without that strong feeling that gripped me, I would probably have thought to look for him only a day or two after his disappearance, since it wasn't very unusual for him to disappear. Deep inside me, there is no doubt that Chi was calling me and directing me to the building on whose roof he was stranded. Stories like these, in which lost animals call their friends to find them, are not unusual. Generally speaking, the messages of animals in distress are so strong that they can even rouse people from their sleep.

Just as animals can communicate with us, so we can communicate with them. Certain people use their supernatural powers (many of them claim that those powers are completely natural, but most people simply aren't aware of them and don't use them) to communicate with animals. Dr. Monica Diedrich, who works in the United States and in South America, is one of the most famous of them. Dr. Diedrich has succeeded in treating a large number of animals suffering from unexplained problems – peculiar behaviors, fears and phobias, aggressiveness, and physical problems whose origins even specialist veterinary surgeons could not understand – simply by communicating with the animal itself. She does this by asking the animal about its problem and condition telepathically, and picking up visions, scenes, and feelings from the animal. Dr. Diedrich explains how she operates: "Communication with animals is the ability to pick up pictures by means of the third eye, pictures that are transmitted by the animal. In a state of deep concentration, with eyes closed, I pick up kind of 'clips' and pictures of a few seconds' duration in my mind's eye. The pictures and clips are similar to a preview to a movie and go on for two to three seconds, and then they repeat themselves over and over again. There is always a message of movement in the pictures. At other times, I see before me perfect color pictures. In two cases, the pictures were accompanied by a feeling I felt in my body, which is the animal's feeling, so that if he is sad, happy, worried, or hurting, I can explain this to its owners in a way that they will understand its condition. Frequently, when the animal begins to feel at ease, it initiates a kind of faster and more precise communication. At this point, words, even whole sentences, are added to the messages I receive, and are then added to the telepathic feeling, the physical feeling and the pictures. I join everything I have picked up together, and then explain in simple terms to the animal's 'guardian.' At this point, I can translate a fluent conversation between the animal and the human." Moreover, Dr. Diedrich can communicate with animals that have departed this world and tell the person what their purpose and deeds in this world were.

## What exactly is communication with animals?

"The animal does not open its mouth and release a flow of words," say people who communicate with animals. "However, animals do indeed communicate in an astounding, non-verbal way. They communicate by transmitting pictures, emotions and feelings. Often, the information comes in the form of words, sometimes in a feeling in the communicator's body, or in pictures or symbols that the animal transmits via telepathy." Communicators claim that the telepathic experience with animals occurs in a language that is universal to the entire animal kingdom.

"Telepathy between human beings and animals is not very different than telepathy between two people," says Raphaela Pope, a famous communicator with animals. Pope believes that people are in fact born with telepathic ability, but tend to repress or forget it when they learn to speak. Telepathic communicators with animals believe that animals are conscious beings with aims, choices, and world-views of their own. Many animal-lovers who live with them on a daily basis agree with them.

One of the most incisive proofs of the validity of this hypothesis is Coco, the talking gorilla. Coco can use more than 600 signs from blind and deaf language in order to communicate. She can communicate quickly and easily, describe her feelings, and build whole sentences using sign language. One of the clearest proofs of the fact that she does not only repeat the signs she has learned, but also understands their meaning, occurred when a brush was pointed out to Coco, and she used a movement describing a comb. The investigators interpret this "error" as true understanding of the nature of the instrument that was shown to her – combing and brushing, which indicates ability to understand the meaning of the words. By means of sign language and the use of a special Macintosh computer, Coco can easily, and even "chattily," describe her wishes and feelings regarding various situations.

Back to telepathy with animals. Just as the concept of telepathy between human beings was not understood or appreciated for many years, while today it seems so self-evident to many people, including many investigators and scientists, so too the ability to communicate telepathically with animals has not been accepted by many people, and has not yet been accorded official endorsement by many scientists. If this were as clear to us as the possibility of telepathy between people is clear to us today, would people still relate to animals with the same lack of respect, exploitation, and attitude of superiority?

The telepathic ability of animals places them on the same level of awareness as human beings. Indeed, their shape is different, as are their ways of communicating, but from telepathic communications, it is certainly possible to understand that they too have certain aims in this world, and they too have insights, feelings, and knowledge of their own. It is possible that just as today, many people in the Western world feel remorse for their conduct toward peoples they once called "savages," such as Africans and Indians, in less than a century from now, the world will feel contrition for its present attitude toward animals. It is only a lack of insight, obtuseness, and an unjustified feeling of superiority that cause man to "allow" himself to abuse animals and exploit them for his own purposes. Many people think that this is one of the reasons why not enough studies examining telepathic communication in animals are being conducted.

Bachtarov, who examined the astonishing telepathic communication with the circus dog in his research, tried for several years to get other scientists to continue with this type of study. However, for somewhat mysterious reasons, no one acceded to his requests, even though his studies were accepted as reliable. Most likely, many large companies and well-heeled people would lose the source of their exploitative income when more and more studies on the subject proved the existence of such abilities in animals and the implications thereof. These people, who make a fortune from exploiting animals, will find themselves in the same state of stupefaction as the slave-owners were when laws were promulgated to liberate the slaves.

In order to facilitate reading, I must mention that most people who communicate with animals, and like them, many sensitive people, do not call dog-lovers or guardians "dog-owners." They prefer to call the person who has bound his life to the animal "friend," "guardian," or simply, "his person." Frequently, they call the person by the name the dog himself calls him, and this can be "Mom" or "Dad" or "Friend" or "Brother." When parapsychologist David Ashdown told me that my dog calls me "Beloved Sister," I was not in the least surprised, because I had often picked up this pet name from her eyes.

People who communicate with animals do not rely solely on animals' ability to communicate, but can also communicate with them at will. Raphaela Pope describes an encounter she had with a German Shepherd bitch called Helga: "Helga's person, Joan, told me that Helga's left ear was badly torn. She wanted to know how Helga had been injured. When I tuned in to Helga, she showed me a picture of digging at the wooden fence that surrounds her enclosure. Helga tried to push her head under the fence, and was cut by a piece of barbed wire. Afterwards, Joan asked Helga to show her exactly where the barbed wire was. Helga led her to the spot, and Joan found old, rusted barbed wire twisted around the base of the fence!"

Penelope Smith, who is considered to be the most famous communicator with animals, and one of the first, wrote two books in which there are numerous anecdotes of this type.

Actually, almost anyone can communicate with animals. People who communicate with animals offer some useful tips. Leora Simpson, who communicates with animals, relates: "I discovered that one of the secrets of effective communication with nature is to be clean and clear inside yourself from the emotional and mental point of view, and to let some emotion flow into the communication with the animal. Allow yourself to see, listen with your heart, speak with emotion, and trust the link you have created with the animal."

Raphaela Pope recommends: "Imagine the thing that you are trying to cause them to do, or the thing that you are trying to say to them. Send them your emotions and feelings, too. If your intention is for your message to reach them, it will reach them. Try not to overwhelm your animal with the expectation of hearing its message, or what it is trying to transmit to you, but rather sit quietly, relax, and loosen up, and let the animal's thoughts and emotions reach you. The basic steps of telepathic communication with animals are creating a state of tranquillity, quiet, and acceptance, in order to receive the telepathic transmission, to transmit a message of your own, and to receive a response."

Many of the people who are reading these words feel that they are not telling them anything new – many animal-lovers have already tried out these forms of communication with animals, simply without calling them "telepathic communication with animals." In contrast, people for whom this topic is new often ask: "How will I know that this is really a true, authentic experience, and that I am picking up the animal's thoughts and not my own? How can I be sure that this is really the animal's answer? It seems as if I'm inventing it!"

If you are in a quiet, calm state, without investing a lot of thought or a great deal of emotion, and not trying "forcefully" to cause a transmission to go or come through, the information that comes to you is from the animal. Since it is coming to you via your feelings and thoughts, or via your visual perception, this can be felt as if it is yours. However, when you receive an unexpected answer of the kind that you yourself are not inclined to create in your imagination, you will know that it is a message from the animal.

One of the strongest proofs of the success of communication with an animal is its practical success. This happens when you receive a message from the animal concerning its health, for instance. After receiving the message, you implement the required change in its nutrition or in anything else that will help it feel better, according to the information you received from the animal itself, and you discover that the particular "piece of advice" was in fact beneficial to the animal.

Danielle D., a well-known communicator with various forms of life in nature, tells of an unusual event that served as a trigger that led her to a profound understanding of communication with nature.

"A long time ago, I looked after a litter of six-week-old kittens that had lost their mother two weeks previously. Without a mother to help them, the training of the little kittens was unbearably difficult and became a serious problem. I became frustrated with the whole thing. A friend suggested that I take them to a barn that was in desperate need of a few mouse hunters, but I wasn't too enthusiastic about the idea... until one scorching summer afternoon, when I came home after a long series of meetings, exhausted and slightly irritable. Next to the door of my bedroom, I was greeted by three balls of fur that were happy and excited to see that 'Mommy' had come home, and a stench that could make even the strongest stomach turn over... There were little 'gifts' all over my beautiful bedspread, on the floor, in the closet, everywhere – everywhere, that is, except in the cardboard box I had put out for them. The box was still sparkling clean. All this terrible mess had been made in the eight hours I had not been at home. 'Enough!' I yelled, 'Maybe you're barn cats, after all! That's it, guys, if any of you wants to stay around here, you're going to have to learn to control your bowel movements right now, otherwise you'll find yourselves outside. I'll take you to the barn!' A few seconds after I had shouted those words, little Joey (who ultimately remained with us) was in the cardboard box, and a few seconds later, all the kittens were raising hell in the cardboard box in order to demonstrate their new 'awareness' – and there were no more little 'accidents' in the house!"

Danielle suggests several methods for communicating with animals:

**Thought** – Notice the words and thoughts that come into your mind when you link up to your friend, the animal.

**Emotion** – Notice the pictures and emotions that arise in you.

**Heart** – Pay attention to the strong and amazing messages of love that your friend the animal transmits to you, and notice the understanding and knowledge that are evoked in you when you link up to the animal's feelings flowing to you.

**Body** – Pay attention to how your animal behaves when the two of you are communicating. Slight trembling and eye movements show that you have succeeded in making contact. Notice the feelings or messages that seem to arrive from your own body.

**Confidence** – Learn to trust the feelings that arise in you, the feelings of your body, the emotions, the pictures, and the thoughts. Although all those feelings arise in you yourself, since the animal does not speak in words, there are good reasons for the fact that you are receiving these particular transmissions, or that certain pictures arise in your imagination. It is possible that the message you receive will be, "Quick, open the door, I have to go out and do my business," or "The water in my dish is not clean, please change it." Very common messages are, "I love you, I'm so happy that I have a friend like you. I want to be with you everywhere, always!" (a common canine message). However, you can also receive amazing messages in which the animal tells you about himself, his past, or about his previous life, as well as about the relationship the two of you had in a previous life!

I received an incredible feeling of communication with animals at one of the festivals I attended recently. It was a music festival, one of many that have been taking place over recent years, and I was very sorry and rather angry to hear that animals were forbidden. (What kind of "ecological" and "natural" festival was this if man's best friend was discriminated against and wasn't allowed in?) After the first day, my friend and I noticed that there were many dogs there, and they were enjoying themselves and having a great time. We immediately decided to go back and pick up Kaya (since she had succeeded in creating very strong ties with all my friends, and everyone felt her absence). Of course, we managed to get her in very easily. She arrived at the festival in the afternoon. Since the festival was taking place over a very large area, and our camp was deep among the trees, I decided to take her for a walk on a leash so that she could become acquainted with the place. In the evening, we had to leave the camp to go to the performance. I debated for a long time. I knew that Kaya could go wild, barking and jumping when she saw people dancing and heard loud music – since that is her way of attracting attention and participating in the festivities. The problem is that many people who see a giant Boxer barking and jumping do not understand it, and tend to become slightly hysterical… I also knew that I wanted to dance, and I was afraid that if I approached the stage, she would get lost in the crowd and wouldn't know how to get back. With a heavy heart, I thought I would tie her to one of the trees next to the tent. However, when I began to explain to her (in words, but with deep emotion) why I wanted to tie her up, I received a clear message in words: "I want to go with you. Don't worry. Trust me. I know the way, and I understand how you want me to behave. Take me with you, and you'll see that there is no reason to worry. Trust me, you don't need to take me on a leash." The message was so clear that I didn't listen to my friends, who know how she behaves generally and begged me to leave her in the camp. I took her with me, without a leash.

When we reached the performance, in the dark, I was slightly apprehensive. Thousands of people were dancing and letting their hair down, singing and jumping, in a manner that really begged for a minor vocal disturbance from Kaya. But to my surprise, she looked completely relaxed. I danced with my friend, and the whole time, Kaya sat quietly next to us, watching the people. I could feel that the music was too loud for her sensitive ears. As a result of the commotion, and without noticing, my friend and I moved further toward the stage, and after a few songs, I suddenly remembered Kaya. I looked around – we were already deep in the dancing crowd, and there was no chance of my catching a glimpse of her. I felt anxious and began to run around. To my horror, I didn't even remember the direction from which we had reached the center of the crowd! Suddenly, I could feel a clear message that pulled me in a certain direction. The message was so strong and clear that I went in that direction without hesitation, jostled by the crowds of dancing people. Within a few minutes, I got out of the crush and continued quickly forward. While I was walking and looking down to see Kaya, I nearly bumped into one of my friends who had chosen to stand at the side and listen to the performance from a distance. Next to him sat a quiet and smiling Kaya, who lifted her head and looked at me, as if to say: "You see that you can rely on me? You worry too much. Everything's OK. I'm managing by myself."

During those four days we were together in nature, Kaya taught me over and over again that I could trust her, and that she knew how to look after herself very well. Of course, every time I got lost and couldn't find the camp, all I had to do was transmit to her, in thought and full of emotion: "Kaya, we're not just having a walk, I'm trying to find the camp and not succeeding, and it's making me nervous. Help me," and she immediately stopped wandering around and sniffing, ignored the dogs that came to sniff her, and led me quickly to the camp.

At that same festival, something happened that to this day I don't know how to explain. On the same afternoon of Kaya's arrival at the festival, I was walking with her on a leash so that she could familiarize herself with the place.

We were walking with a friend of mine in the stall area, when he stopped to chat with an old friend. I stood with Kaya at a slight distance so as not to disturb what seemed to me an intimate conversation, when suddenly Kaya began to pull me toward the hot-dog stand. I could feel that she was hungry, and in my feeling, although it wasn't so "logical," I felt that she wanted to eat hot-dogs. Since I perceive her as a good friend, and not as a "dog" that belongs to me, I did the same thing I would have done if any other friend had asked me to buy her a hot-dog – I stood on line and waited my turn to buy her a hot-dog. However, after a few seconds, she began to pull me, which was unusual for her. I followed her, and she led me to a large area behind the stand, where people were sitting on cushions, opposite low tables, eating hot-dogs. She didn't stop. She pulled me further and further into the place. When she stopped, I also did, and some people sitting there began to talk to me about the beautiful dog. Suddenly I looked down at her. Kaya was sitting on one of the cushions, at a low table. On the table lay half a bun, completely devoid of any ketchup, mustard, or relish, and on it was a hot-dog. The two girls who were sitting on the other side of the table shouted enthusiastically: "Look, look how she's taking the hot-dog out of the bun!" With some trepidation, I asked them, "Does that belong to anyone? Is it yours?" but they answered that they had no idea who it belonged to. In fact, they hadn't noticed the hot-dog there at all. Kaya ate the hot-dog, and was ready for action again. To this day, I don't know how she knew exactly where to go without looking around, stopping at another table or looking at the people who were eating. She simply "knew" exactly where the perfect meal was waiting for her!

# Automatic writing

Automatic writing is occurs when some kind of entity from another dimension transmits messages via a writing instrument – pen/pencil and paper, typewriter, computer keyboard, and even via various artistic techniques (to be discussed later on). The nature of automatic writing is the communication of the will of some entity by means of the written word. Sometimes, the message may arrive in a foreign language that is unfamiliar to the person who is holding the pen or typing on the keyboard. In this case, the person serves as a "conveyor" of the messages. Frequently, the conveyor does not recognize the handwriting on the paper as his own. Sometimes, the words appear without spaces between them or without punctuation. Sometimes pictures, drawings, symbols or sketches appear as part of the message.

Some of the people who have experience with automatic writing know who sent the messages to them. Sometimes, the transmitter of the message informs the receiver of the message of his name and background. Others, in contrast, do not know who transmitted the message to them, or receive messages from various interchangeable entities. Generally speaking, when the energies are felt to be comfortable and pleasant, the entity reveals its name or gives various hints within a short time. When the energies are felt to be uncomfortable, when the information is not positive, or the entity transmitting the messages is felt to be non-positive, the person must stop writing.

Certain mediums can hold a pen, relax their body and calm down their train of thought until "something else" begins to write, using the hand holding the pen. In most cases, some kind of spirit or entity takes control of that hand and actually performs the writing. Sometimes, the subconscious or even the conscious of the medium himself is the producer of the writing. This is automatic writing. Entire books have been written in this way. A Brazilian writer produced 70 books that were written by 70 different authors in this way!

Inspirational writing is also a form of automatic writing, but it is performed in a slightly different way. The medium writes in a regular and normal manner, but discovers that the information has been transmitted to his brain by some kind of entity. The famous Australian medium, Val Higson, has several friends who are not human beings, but rather spirits, and they dictate poems and articles to her. She sits at her computer, requests the help of the spirits, and her fingers immediately begin to move at an incredible speed over the keyboard. In the same way, unusual church sermons are dictated to Val Higson.

Ruth Bennett, who serves as a priest in the Windsor church, is sometimes granted entire sermons that are dictated to her by spirits. She discovered the marvelous ability one Sunday, when she was standing in her living-room and ironing. It was an ordinary day, and she was very absorbed in her task – to the point that she was almost "meditating" while ironing. (It is interesting to point out that prolonged automatic actions, such as ironing, sweeping relatively large surfaces and so on may send the person into an unintentional meditative state!) Suddenly, Ruth Bennett felt a tremendous need to grab a pen and write something down. What, she had no idea, and she did not even think about it, but simply rushed to take a pen from the table and quickly wrote down a strange message that had been sent to her. After reading what she had written, it transpired that it was a perfect church sermon! Every Sunday in the Windsor church, a certain medium would go up to the pulpit and deliver a special sermon to the congregation. She took the sermon with her, and, very surprisingly, it turned out that on that particular afternoon, the church's regular medium had not arrived! From then on, Ruth Bennett was sent many messages and sermons on an almost permanent basis. This is an example of inspirational writing. It is different than automatic writing in that the entity is not the one that "holds" the pen that is in the medium's hand, but rather sends the messages to his brain, and he writes them down. Many writers attest to the fact that they wrote entire books in this way. The renowned Charles Dickens and the children's writer who is known to many of us, Enid Blyton (whose "Famous Five" series is very popular in many countries) related that some of their writings were transmitted to them in this way.

They said that they did not invent the story by themselves, but rather certain images appeared in front of their eyes and "forced" them to write their story, or acted in front of them, as if in a play or movie. They simply wrote down what was acted out to them or told them. Enid Blyton wrote hundreds of books in this way.

Inspirational creation can also produce additional works, such as sculptures, paintings, and so on. Artist Matthew Manning, who works in pen and ink, produces his works in this way. His pictures begin in one corner of the paper and grow and fill up most of the surface. He describes the process as if the picture itself grows on the paper like a kind of plant. Musicians are sometimes also granted musical works in this way. Mozart once received an entire symphony in one second, and after that spent many days writing it. The British medium, Rosemary Brown, is granted visits by dead composers who come to her and dictate new musical works. Music critics who investigated the works she produced claim that they are indeed high-level musical works that are characteristic of those composers!

# Extrasensory powers in the service of the superpowers:

## The Soviet Union and the United States in a race to develop extrasensory weapons

While Dr. Rhine was beginning his research in the West, and the first signs of serious scientific interest in extrasensory phenomena were starting to appear, Soviet scientists were already relating to this topic very seriously. However, their interest in the study of extrasensory phenomena was far from purely scientific and philosophical. They were more interested in the possibilities for practical application inherent in this new science than its benefit for humanity.

Behind the Iron Curtain, under conditions of great secrecy, the Soviet scientists worked on war solutions and intelligence means based on extrasensory phenomena. As far as we know in the West today, formal experiments began in the early 1920s, but they may have begun before that. There is no doubt that the conception of the ideas and the initial grounding of the studies had begun several years previously. The Soviet scientists focused their studies on a number of levels:

- the extrasensory effect of telepathy, psychometry and hypnosis on human beings, with the aim of preparing "human" weapons – people who would serve as spies and assassins under the influence of hypnosis and telepathy;
- military espionage by means of clairvoyance and "reading the minds" of people in key positions in enemy countries;
- telekinesis (the effect of the power of thought on objects), whose objective was to neutralize/activate explosives at a distance by means of the power of thought;
- tools charged with psychotronic energy (we do not know much about the aim and success of these studies);

and several more research areas about which there is not yet sufficiently clear information. For decades, information about these experiments was completely classified. However, while Western scientists themselves only had a vague idea about what was happening in the Soviet Union, it seems that the US government and its intelligence agencies possessed substantial information about the directions of the Soviet research. Just as the Unites States did not hesitate to try to catch up with the Soviet Union in the nuclear arms race and in space research, so the Americans did not agree to take second place in this field, either. Of course, these experiments, some of which trampled the known moral limits underfoot, were and still are top secret.

But it was the first revelations about the Soviet activities in the field of the extrasensory that promoted public interest in extrasensory phenomena. While research such as that of Prof. Rhine interested very few people – mainly people who were "into it" and people with a scientific or philosophical interest – the thought of the extrasensory threat on the part of the Soviet Union caused the general public to open their eyes and begin to consider extrasensory phenomena as a matter that went beyond philosophical or "unscientific" dabbling. Although the Soviet involvement in extrasensory phenomena was far from innocent, it must be admitted that as a result of the serious studies and research, the scientific basis of some of the extrasensory phenomena was understood, and stable and proven scientific theories, as well as technical means for converting and using these energies, were propounded as a result of the studies.

Many journalists and researchers attempted to investigate and discover information about the experiments that were being conducted behind the Iron Curtain. However, the credit for the discovery and publication of some of these studies for the general public goes to two investigators who published the first book on the topic, based on tested and reliable information.

In June 1968, the Canadian, Sheila O., and the American, Lynne S., were invited to an international conference on ESP in Moscow. The person who issued the invitation was Edward Nomov, then 36 years old, one of the chief researchers of Soviet supernatural science. A few years beforehand, such open and public interest in matters like these would have cost Nomov a long sojourn in Siberia. However, in the mid-1960s, with the advent of *perestroika*, the gates opened up to interest in Soviet research in this field. Three years prior to the invitation, Sheila and Lynne had corresponded with Soviet scientists and researchers and exchanged information with them on these topics. They went to the conference, which, because of political disruptions, disbanded early. Sheila and Lynne were forced to flee to Prague before the end of the conference that had been disrupted. That aside, however, during the political respite that enabled the two women to take an in-depth look at the Soviet research and discoveries, they produced a book that opened the eyes of the world to the amazing breakthroughs that had occurred in extrasensory research thanks to the studies that were being conducted in the Soviet countries. The book, *Psychic Discoveries Behind the Iron Curtain*, was published in 1971, became a bestseller in New Age circles, and is considered a classic today. Although the book was snapped up by the people who were interested in the topic, the lack of media interest in its publication in those days (and I'll mention again that it is a book that is based on tested and serious findings) evoked a great deal of puzzlement.

Up until that time, most of the information about extrasensory phenomena in the West stemmed from Dr. Rhine's studies and experiments at Duke University during the 1950s. While some of his findings were positive and dramatic, their effect on the general public was dulled by the dry research language and the obtuse statistical terminology. But the publication of *Psychic Discoveries* had a dramatic effect. The description of the experiments that were conducted on the topic that until that time had mainly been the province of fantasy and science fiction, shocked the world. The understanding that the phenomena that could easily be attributed to the world of fairy tales served the Soviet government in such a concrete way caused feelings of terror mixed with enthusiasm and curiosity. The authors of the book declared that these discoveries could lead to a Utopia on the one hand, if they were used properly, or to the annihilation of the human race, on the other.

Although the book and its topics, like other books that had uncovered information behind the Iron Curtain, were sensational, the press, like most of the public, did not agree to deal with them for 25 years. Like the events that were linked to the discovery of UFOs, in this case too, there were people who claimed that these were simply attempts to conceal information. Relating to these books, Uri Geller (who wrote an introduction to the third book in the series) said that the CIA itself had a parapsychological program that included a person by the name of Pat Price, who could see through walls. This revelation about research conducted by someone called Turner in 1971 did not create the tiniest ripple in the press!

Although the revelations concerning the Soviet experiments were not widely publicized, they nevertheless created a revolution that gradually seeped into consciousness of the general public. The same book also exposed the experiments and discoveries of Kirlian and his wife Valentina, discoveries that placed the concepts of "aura" and "delicate bodies" in the province of science and removed them from the esoteric and mystical realms. This is one of the most powerful links connecting the mystical world and the occult world to the reality of everyday life and science that can be measured and proved. One of the results of the couple's discoveries sparked a completely new understanding of the ancient Chinese art of acupuncture. A Russian surgeon, Dr. Mikhail Geikin, succeeded in showing that the colored auras themselves that emanate from the body and can be seen clearly in Kirlian photographs derive from the 700 acupuncture points.

Before the publication of *Psychic Discoveries*, several books about the unique and strange dimensions of the Great Pyramid at Giza were published. However, thanks to Sheila and Lynne, who went to Prague after the international conference in Moscow, the world was granted new and dazzling revelations concerning the power of the pyramid. In Prague, the two women were invited to meet Karl Drabel, a Czech radio and television engineer who had discovered that small pyramids whose dimensions were identical to those of the Great Pyramid could sharpen razor blades! Apparently, a pyramidal form constructed according to the appropriate dimensions concentrated cosmic energy when it was placed exactly on the north-south axis, energy that could operate on the crystalline shape of high-quality steel.

All the Soviet researchers who were interviewed when the Iron Curtain fell expressed the hope that those discoveries would only serve good purposes. In reality, the researchers cooperated with intelligence authorities and proposed methods of espionage and counter-espionage such as the world had not known before. Some of their discoveries can be used to create weapons of mass destruction.

However, it was not only the Soviets who conducted many experiments on this topic, but also the CIA. At the same time as the Soviets were conducting their experiments, various governments, first and foremost the United States government, did everything in their power to follow the Soviet research and keep track of their results, at the same time trying to conduct similar experiments. During the Cold War, the two powers were involved in a wild contest to perfect and invent extrasensory weapons, but, as happened with the space program, it is possible that today the two powers are working jointly.

With the publication of the book, the world was informed of the Soviet developments concerning the control of behavior and consciousness by means of telepathy. In experiments that began in 1924, the Soviet scientists succeeded in getting the subjects into a hypnotic trance and to rouse them from it telepathically at a distance of thousands of kilometers. From the moment the contact was made, the subject's behavior was manipulated by long-distance suggestion, similar to face-to-face hypnotic suggestions. The subjects were able to converse and operate "normally" while they were in the hypnotic trance. The CIA, unable to ignore the new discoveries, picked up the gauntlet, and began an intensive investigation of the possibility of using similar extrasensory weapons.

In Prague, the two researchers met Robert Paulita, the inventor of the psychotronic generators that render 20th-century weapons as obsolete as the bow and arrow. In a documentary movie, Paulita is shown with his psychotronic generators, small and strange-looking metallic objects. In the movie, Paulita explains that the secret of the generators lies in their shape. The generators amass human energy, and it is then possible to concentrate this energy for various actions. Paulita and his daughter Jana charged the generators by staring at them in a special pattern. After the generators had been charged, they were turned by propellers, and drew non-metallic objects to them, accelerated the growth of seeds, and purified polluted water. This human energy had been given many names already in ancient times – prana, chi, life energy, animal magnetism, etheric power, orgon, bioplasmatic energy, and psychotronic energy. The two women visited Paulita's home, examined the generators and watched Paulita's own demonstrations at first hand. Paulita's daughter volunteered to be the guinea pig for solving the greatest mystery of all: What happens when the generator is aimed at a human being? As a result of the experiment, Jana felt extremely dizzy and lost her sense of orientation in space. When the generators are aimed at insects, they can kill them instantly.

General Kalogin, one of the heads of the KGB, began to supply information at the beginning of 1990. He claimed that instructions to concentrate numerous means and resources on extrasensory warfare had been given at the beginning of the 1970s, and that some 500 million rubles had been invested in these studies. As a result of the studies, the Soviets developed sophisticated psychotronic generators (based on Paulita's archetype). Dr. Nikolai Koklov, who worked for the CIA, discovered over 20 laboratories, guarded by tremendous military might, that were working on psychotronic instruments for military use in the 1970s. It is possible that some of the operations were being conducted jointly with the USA.

One of the most fascinating experiments performed in the Soviet Union was an experiment with telekinesis (the effect of the power of thought on objects), which is known as "Nola Michaelova's experiment." Nola Michaelova, after whom the experiment was named, was a famous medium who also participated in some of the experiments. The aim of the experiment was to check the possibility of using cerebral energy for affecting inanimate objects. It is possible that the experiment or experiments that followed were not limited to investigating the effect of human cerebral energy on objects, but also dealt with the effect of animals' brainwaves on objects. However, the information on this topic is not clear enough. In order to perform the experiment, about 400 subjects with telekinetic abilities, most of them women, were assembled in one of the research institutes near Moscow. All of the subjects went through the identical experimental procedure for examining their ability to move lightweight objects over a surface, to lift light objects into the air without any physical contact, and as a final test, to keep a pair of scissors in the air and open and close them by means of the power of thought. Despite the complexity of the tests, about 30 subjects managed to pass the final test, which was immortalized in photographs and in a 16-mm color movie. The subjects that passed the final test were immediately awarded the rank of officer in the Soviet army and moved on to the next stage of the experiment – the more practical stage. Here, they had to try to affect objects such as compass needles, navigational instruments and parts used in aiming guided bombs. As a result of the experiments, the researchers reached the conclusion that there was a possibility that human beings could use the power of thought to affect various objects – even from a distance of up to 2,000 kilometers.

*The scissors are in the air without any hand contact!*

The idea of using the power of thought to affect the enemy's navigational instruments and parts that influence the operation of enemy bombs was not alien to the people conducting the experiment. It is interesting to point out that a plane crash that occurred at the same time in the Soviet Union, after the pilot reported unusual changes in the operation of the navigational instruments, was attributed to an experiment in telekinesis that went out of control.

In addition to finding people with powerful thought energy, the research on telekinesis (also called psychokinesis) also focused on finding ways to fortify the intensity of brainwaves and creating a powerful thought wave that would exert a will-controlled and steadying influence on objects. During the course of the experiments, various machines for fortifying brainwaves by means of psychokinetic exercises were devised. One of them, which reached the West, consisted of a small carousel to which a row of colored lights was connected. There was only one electrical contact with the lights on the carousel, and the role of the subject was to cause the carousel to revolve using the power of thought and turn on the lights according to the examiner's demand.

Another topic that was accorded a great deal of attention by the Soviet researchers was applied telepathic research. One of the studies that earned a great deal of acclaim because of its potential for military use was the experiment in transmitting messages by means of the telepathic Morse system. As we know, Morse is based on the transmission of flashes of light or of flashes of electricity marked by dot/dash. It is possible to use different combinations of dots and dashes to create all the letters of the alphabet.

The scientists conducted the experiment in parallel in two institutes, one in Moscow and one in Leningrad, 600 kilometers apart. However, as opposed to the usual Morse transmission, the Morse message chosen by the researchers was not transmitted by means of electricity or any kind of electronic instrument, but rather by the power of thought. Several groups participated in the experiment, and after in-depth work, they succeeded in transmitting relatively long messages by using hot/cold imagery. The best results were achieved when the transmitter of the message focused on a feeling of a burn, or of burning fire, to symbolize a dash, and on a mental thought/feeling of a block of ice in order to transmit to the receiver the symbol of a dot. Two types of reception were common among the receivers of the messages. The first, intuitive reception, a kind of guess or knowledge of the sign, telepathic reception that was expressed in the mental (thought) layer, had a success rate of about 90%! In other words, in nine out of ten cases, the receiver was able to guess and identify the transmitted words telepathically. The second type was considered to be even more accurate. By means of a physical examination of the changes that can be measured in blood pressure and pulse, it was possible to identify when "cold" thoughts (dots) were transmitted and when "hot" thoughts (dashes) were transmitted. It was therefore possible to identify the entire words that were transmitted to the receiver, who was connected to an instrument that measured blood pressure and pulse. American scientists also performed this experiment, and succeeded in transmitting telepathic Morse messages between New York and Miami. As the American research progressed, a small portable instrument was invented for recording the changes in blood pressure in accordance with the reception of the telepathically transmitted messages. The instrument recorded the message in Morse signs – dot/dash – that were subsequently used to compose the entire verbal message.

The Soviet researchers worked tirelessly. They managed to pluck people (mainly women) who were gifted with developed extrasensory abilities from isolated places all over the Soviet Union, sometimes against their will.

One of the most interesting cases that reached the West in great detail was the telepathic experiment that was conducted with a subject called Natasha. Natasha was gifted with involuntary telepathic powers. She had a certain degree of control over them that the researchers tried to intensify, but in principle, she could "read thoughts" without any effort.

The astonishing experiment took place at "The Russian Military Institute for the Applied Research of the Sixth Sense for Military Purposes." This institute was located in the environs of Moscow, and information about it first arrived with the defection of Alexei Nerovsky to West Germany. The threatening appearance of this institute, which consisted of a row of gray buildings surrounded by a high barbed-wire fence guarded day and night by sentries and vicious dogs, was reminiscent of a mental asylum or a prison for particularly dangerous criminals.

Inside one of the buildings of the institute, in a small room, impermeable to all external noise and devoid of decoration, sat a fair-haired, blue-eyed girl. In front of her was a wide table on which a large relief map was spread. Around the map there were little plastic models of tanks, planes, ships and soldiers. Besides the girl, the chair upon which she sat, the table, the relief map, and a video camera that recorded every single one of the girl's movements, there was nothing else in the room: just telepathic Natasha. The girl's movements were transmitted to two large TV screens in the adjacent room. Opposite the screens, tense and fascinated, stood the top echelons of command in the Red Army. They were waiting for the signal that would indicate the beginning of the experiment.

At the same time, in another room at the far end of the camp, a group of high-ranking officers sat around a table on which there was a relief map that was identical to the one that was opposite the girl. This room, too, was devoid of any instrument, except a video camera that transmitted what was happening in their room to one of the two screens in the room occupied by the top brass.

When the signal was given, the officers began to place the plastic tanks, planes, and soldiers that were lying beside them on the relief map, as if imitating strategic moves.

The top brass opposite the screens held their breath. On one screen, they clearly saw the movements made on the map in the officers' room. A few seconds after the officers began to move the plastic figures over the map, Natasha, concentrating, began to place the plastic figures on the map in front of her, moving them in perfect coordination with the movements of the officers. Seconds after the officers had decided on a particular strategic move among themselves, Natasha made exactly the same move on the map in front of her!

A murmur of excited amazement swept through the control room. "How does she guess the moves?" asked one of the generals aloud. "She doesn't guess," answered the scientist who was in charge of the experiment. He had spent many hours of work and research with Natasha, and had succeeded in deciphering parts of her amazing way of operating. "She doesn't guess the moves. Before performing the action, the officers in the war room think of the moves they'll make. Natasha succeeds in picking up their thoughts or perhaps their intentions. Natasha is a living example of involuntary telepathy. She accurately picks up the thoughts of the person or people at whom she is directing her mind..."

The general was silent for a moment, as if considering. "Can she read the thoughts of any person?" he asked the scientist. The answer he received might have calmed him down a bit. The "use" of people with extrasensory powers could have a boomerang effect, and the thought of a person who could read anyone's thoughts so accurately posed something of a threat.

"No," answered the scientist carefully. "Natasha must know the person; she needs certain information about him. She can pick up his thoughts even without knowing him personally, but she must know as many details as possible. Prior to the experiment, Natasha read the files of the officers in the war room. The better she knows them, the more clearly and accurately she'll pick up their thoughts. As you can see, her level of accuracy is above and beyond..."

"...above and beyond anything we've seen up till now," one of the generals in the room completed the sentence, staring at the screen. A murmur of agreement went through the room. The scientist smiled. As he already knew, Natasha was not the only girl who could do this.

"We are still at the edge of the camp. Tell me, up to what range can this... Natasha activate her ability?" asked the general, without moving his eyes from the screen.

"So far we have succeeded in achieving satisfactory results in a range of three kilometers... but we are now working with a girl of Tatar origin. If the continuation is as fruitful as the beginning, she will be able to pick up thoughts – waves of telepathy – from double the distance..."

Even the most obdurate of the Soviet officers found it difficult to hide the excitement that gripped them. The tremendous benefit inherent in the girl's ability made them dizzy. It is easy to understand them – the thought of a spy who could sit at a distance of several kilometers from the control center of the enemy and read the thoughts of the enemy officers even before they performed any action would excite and ignite any army person.

The American top brass did not remain indifferent when the first news of the institute and the research being conducted there came in. The concrete threat inherent in this type of ability roused them to act immediately. As soon as they received the initial information about what was going on at the institute (in order to get this information, the Americans used the "old-fashioned" methods of espionage – defectors and double agents), the heads of the American army gave one of the research institutes in South Carolina the task of finding a substance that would prevent the passage of "telepathy waves." They demanded that a substance that would help render war rooms impermeable to "tracking with telepathy waves" be found urgently. Within a short time, they diverted most of their efforts to another channel, which I will talk about in detail – making their brains "impermeable," or "deleting information" from the heads of people who possessed information that must remain secret. To this end, the American scientists did not disqualify any substance or method, from hypnosis to heavy drugs, hallucinogens, and drugs that undermined the long-term memory.

Of course, the Americans did not focus only on "preventing" access to the brains of people who possessed secret knowledge, but also on the "counter-attack" of the brains of key people on the enemy side. Dr. Rhine's studies of telepathy, which stemmed from pure scientific curiosity, became the substance of war in their hands. In a characteristic experiment in the study of telepathy, the American scientists sat a girl in a room that was impermeable to and insulated against every sound. Her eyes were covered with a cotton cover with a black band on top of it, and her ears were blocked with earplugs that blocked out sound. The objective was to insulate her against any sensory stimulus from the outside world for the duration of the experiment so that she could use only extrasensory powers.

In another room, at a distance of hundreds of meters from the girl, sat the girl's partner who had lived with her for about two years. The boy sat in an impermeable room, his mouth gagged. Out of a library of some 300 movies, one movie was chosen randomly. It was an ad for a tourism company. A few minutes after the broadcast of the movie commenced in the room where the boy was sitting, the girl began to speak quickly. Every word she said was recorded. For six minutes, the girl spewed out words very fast. It seemed that she was nervous. She said, "White, high and white, cold! I want a coat, thick – oh, something is moving fast – strange shoes – she's fallen! High! The people below are so small!" She continued talking excitedly for a few more minutes and suddenly fell silent – a few minutes after the end of the broadcast of the movie her partner had watched. While the girl's boyfriend had been watching the ad for ski resorts in Switzerland, she described the scenes and her feelings. The girl used words to describe the feelings, sights and sounds that were evoked in her as a result of the telepathic reception. After a half-hour rest, during which they both remained in their impermeable rooms, another short movie was screened to the boy, the transmitter. About a minute after the beginning of the transmission, the girl began to speak. This time, she sounded calmer, and her voice was steadier. She said: "...Oh, it's useful! It suits our living-room... I feel like cooking... I want one like that for the bedroom!... Did I bring my credit card? I'm not sure..." The movie that was shown to her boyfriend was an ad for a large household appliance store.

In this experiment, the researchers relied on the relationship between the transmitter and the receiver, a situation in which the two telepathic communicators knew each other well. Similar to the Soviet experiment with the girl Natasha, the American researchers also discovered that transmission and reception between people who knew each other in some way was likely to be clearer and more powerful. In this case, it transpired that the transmission of feelings and emotions, and the transmission of the general feeling telepathically, produced good results and afforded the receiver a general picture of the scenes being viewed by the transmitter. There are obvious physical markers for the telepathic effect, as was already discovered in the experiment with telepathic Morse. When the girl's boyfriend was shown a movie that showed two people dining in a fancy restaurant, eagerly eating the mouth-watering dishes on the table in front of them, the girl's salivary glands began to work energetically.

Another interesting experiment that was conducted in the United States involved the participation of a married couple. The experiment was conducted in a similar fashion to the previous one, in which the two members of the couple sat in rooms far away from each other, totally insulated from the outside world, but in this experiment, the woman was the transmitter. Here, most of the focus was on the physical effect caused by the telepathic transmission. The transmitting woman was shown 16 short movies, one after the other. Eleven of them showed children playing, and five showed erotic clips. Each time the transmitting woman watched one of the erotic movies, her husband, the receiver, had an erection.

However, these "innocent" experiments were just a preparation for more in-depth – or, should we say, more dangerous experiments. The efforts expended by the Soviet Union in developing means of extrasensory warfare and espionage raised the threshold of anxiety among the people in the American administration, and within a short time, the CIA began to perform experiments in the extrasensory realm, whose hideous repercussions can still be felt today.

This is what the EDOM (Electronic Dissolution of Memory) program was like. The objective of the CIA in this experimental program was to attack the long-term memory and turn the person into a zombie devoid of memory by means of blocking the neurotransmitter acetylcholine and electronic interference in the bioplasmatic (etheric) body. As we shall see, this technique served (and may still serve!) to neutralize former agents. This possibility was developed from the MK-ULTRA program that was conducted in the 1960s, in which bizarre experiments were performed on volunteers, prisoners, and the mentally ill. The experiments in the MK-

ULTRA program included the introduction of hard hallucinogenic drugs into the food of the mentally ill and the prisoners, various brainwashing techniques, mental and telepathic pressure, hypnosis and various actions to undermine and damage the memory. This brutal program was halted by Congress in 1976. However, once the immoral mechanism of using extrasensory and hypnotic techniques was activated, it was difficult to stop it – a situation that led to one of the most distorted developments in memory control. This technique drew its inspiration from the severe mental disturbance that is known as multiple personality, which is considered to be a special form of schizophrenia (split personality).

The CIA investigators succeeded in artificially planting multiple entities in a single body, each one with its own personal memory bank. Similar to the situation that occurs in the psychiatric disorder, here, too, the many entities do not have information about one another or access to one another's memory banks. Gil Jenson, a CIA psychiatrist from Oakland, California, claims that he created a personality by the name of Arlen Grant in the body of the famous supermodel, Candy Jones, in the 1950s and 60s. To this end, he claims that he used hypnosis and memory-altering drugs. The personality that was created, Arlen Grant, was trained as a superspy and was the recipient of a perfect memory and highly classified information, which the model Candy Jones knew nothing about. Every time Jones was invited to celebrity events and trips throughout the world, Grant – the secondary personality – was invited telepathically by means of a series of electronic sounds and received instructions to perform her espionage missions. The nuclear personality (the model, Candy Jones) could not retrieve information from the secondary data bank (which belonged to the spy Arlen Grant, who lived in her body), even under severe pressure and torture, thus creating a perfect spy. Today, this program is called "radio-hypnotic intra-cerebral control," and seems to be based on Soviet discoveries that were linked to bio-magnetic manipulations of the bioplasmatic (etheric) body.

These worrisome developments bring back memories of the lost continent of Atlantis. According to legend (which is being investigated in depth nowadays, because of findings that emerged from Edgar Casey's channeling), the existing information that we possess concerning the use of extrasensory abilities is just the tip of the iceberg of the information that the people of Atlantis had at their disposal. The use of extrasensory means and telepathy as an everyday means of communication, just as we use the telephone today, was a way of life for the people of Atlantis. However, the lust for power, strength, conquest – the unbalanced ego that constitutes an obstacle in the path of healthy spiritual development – caused the people of Atlantis to use their extrasensory powers to create destructive weapons. Apparently, it was the use of such weapons that caused Atlantis to sink into the depths of the ocean and disappear.

Pernicious use of extrasensory abilities is like fouling one's own nest. It means that the source of these abilities, the source of the cosmic energy that activates the network of communication and extrasensory knowledge, is totally ignored. When this power is used for evil, it will ultimately be turned against the user like an energetic boomerang.

# Astral travel

Try to remember whether this experience is familiar to you. You come home after an exhausting day's work, spend a few hours in front of the TV, and feel drowsiness enveloping you. You turn off the TV, shuffle tiredly toward the bedroom, and expect to fall asleep in a few minutes. However, suddenly and mysteriously, you find your body paralyzed. Noises echo in your ears, flashes of bright light pass through your closed eyes. And then you feel as if you are beginning to float. A moment later, you open your eyes, and find yourself floating above your body. You are really floating in the air – and you can look down at your body and gaze at it, and you can look at everything in your room and see what is happening there. You do not feel judgmental or worried – it seems as if your brain has been completely liberated from the limits of the body and the subjective mind, and you feel a sense of expanded awareness, and a kind of feeling of freedom and lightness. And as you begin to understand and wonder about the nature of the situation you find yourself in, you experience a blackout of a fraction of a second, and then you "wake up," and find yourself inside your body, lying in your bed.

If this experience sounds familiar to you, you have experienced astral travel. This experience is not so rare, and many people have it, even if they do not know that it should be defined as an "out-of-body experience."

In astral travel, the astral body leaves the physical body. The astral body is one of the seven energetic bodies that exist around the physical body.

Certain people can go off on astral travels naturally. Others are afraid of leaving the physical body and fight against it, so they do not succeeded in going on astral travel.

In astral travel, we remain linked to our body and to this dimension by means of a silver cord (like the umbilical cord) that joins the astral body to the physical body, but we cannot always see it. During the course of astral travel, the person may reach different places, different dimensions of awareness. He may visit some place in the present – and be there while things occur (mainly places where there are people who are dear to him or places where he has a special interest in the events that are occurring there), or some place in the past or the future, which exists in other dimensions. Many people describe seeing temples or unfamiliar holy places during their astral travel. Sometimes, when the astral travel commences, a white horse or a black panther appears, symbolizing the beginning of the journey.

Stories about various kinds of spiritual journeys that we are supposed to consider as astral travel can be found in many ancient writings. In most cases, the attitude toward these cases resembled the attitude toward folk legends. However, one of the cases that changed the somewhat derisive perception of astral travel was the publication of the experience of the British scientist, Oliver Fox.

One afternoon in 1913, in a quiet London suburb, Oliver Fox was dozing in his room. He had not yet sunk into his afternoon nap when he began to feel his spirit leaving his body and going through his bedroom without opening the door, going out and evaporating, weightless and transparent, through the heavy metal door at the entrance to his house.

Fox found himself in the street. He passed along the street where he lived, and was swept, or perhaps pulled, to a small and pleasant park that he had never visited. He saw several children playing in the park and some people having a picnic, but continued moving onward until he reached a quiet residential area. The front door of one of the houses was open. Fox went inside, wondering if anyone in the house would sense his presence. Since there was no one on the ground floor, he moved up the carpeted flight of stairs to the second floor of the house. There he entered a room that looked like a bedroom. A young, good-looking woman sat on a low chair opposite a dressing-table mirror, combing her hair. She did not seem to sense his presence. He advanced toward her and stood behind her. The image of the young woman appeared in the mirror, combing her long hair – but Fox's reflection did not appear in the mirror! At that moment, he realized that he could see but was unseen. He wondered: Can the woman discern my presence? She does not see me, but can she sense me? He placed his hand on the woman's bare shoulder and could feel the softness of her skin beneath his fingers. Suddenly a violent shock-wave passed through the woman's body and there was terror in her eyes. At that moment, Fox felt his body swept far away from the room, and he woke up lying in his bed.

As in the case of telepathy, the out-of-body experience attracted scientists and researchers to examine the topic in depth. In his book, *Leaving the Body*, Scott Rogo, from Kennedy University in California, presents many studies dealing with the out-of-body experience. One of the first studies on this matter was conducted at the beginning of the 1950s by Dr. Hornell Hart, a sociologist from Duke University in North Carolina. Dr. Hart asked 155 students about the out-of-body experience, and discovered that 27% of them had had at least one out-of-body experience in their lives. During the 1960s, Celia Green conducted an identical study in England. She randomly chose 115 students from the University of Southampton. Nineteen percent of them admitted that they had had an out-of-body experience. When Green conducted a similar study with 380 students from Oxford University, 34% of the responders began to talk about their out-of-body experiences! Studies that have been performed in recent years provided similar findings. After many studies of this kind, performed either with university students or with different groups throughout the world, Scott Rogo makes the well-founded assumption that one out of every five people has had at least one out-of-body experience in his life. This is a relatively enormous number for an extrasensory experience, and it shows the out-of-body experience to be a fairly common experience. The experience can occur under various circumstances and in a broad range of situations.

In old occult writings, the experience was described as mystical and unique, and sometimes even as dangerous. In contrast, in studies that were conducted in recent years, it transpired that the experience is so widespread that it might be one of the qualities that exist in all human beings, and it is possible to learn or acquire the art of voluntarily activating the experience. In inquiries and debriefings that were conducted among people of different age-groups and personality structures, it was found that most of them described the experience as "pleasant and liberating," and many of them were prepared to undergo it again. Many people who had this experience in a natural way did not dabble in the occult or belong to any kind of New Age trend.

A researcher who investigated the matter in depth together with a relatively large group of well-known researchers from several universities in the United States, succeeded in finding several general characteristics of the out-of-body experience, based on the inquiries and debriefings of a large number of people who had undergone the experience. Seventy-nine percent of the responders who had had this experience had been in a calm emotional state and their bodies were relaxed when they had the experience spontaneously. The remaining 21% had a spontaneous experience while giving birth, as a result of the anesthetic, or as a result of fierce stabs of pain during an illness or a serious injury. Moreover, he found that people who practiced meditation displayed a great tendency to have spontaneous out-of-body experiences. The fact that 79% of the people who had had the experiences were not in any state of crisis, pain or distress may attest to the fact that the out-of-body experience is a normal human experience and not one that is caused by a severe crisis or a life-threatening situation, as was thought previously. Most of the responders said that they had heard a thundering in their ears, like waves of noise, before the beginning of the experience; they felt themselves "leaving their body" and saw their body remaining in the place it had been prior to the experience. Many passed through walls and ceilings during the extrasensory experience.

But the fact that astonished the researchers more than anything was the innocence of the responders regarding the experience. About one-third of the people who had experienced an out-of-body experience in no way expected such an experience, and many of them did not even know that such a thing existed. No less surprising is the fact that most of the people who underwent the experience enjoyed it! Eighty-five percent of the responders in a study that was performed in Kansas defined the experience as "pleasant," of them about half defined it as "extremely enjoyable." Likewise, it seems that the experience affected the world-view of many of the responders, as well as their views regarding life and death. About two-thirds of the responders said that the experience helped rid them of their fear of death and caused them to believe in life after death. Forty-three percent of the responders defined the experience as "the most awesome thing that has happened to me in my life." Most of them were keen to have more out-of-body experiences. Almost all the responders were certain that they had not been dreaming when they had undergone the experience.

The results of the Kansas study, which was performed by a group of psychiatrists, presented the three researchers with the following question: "Must the person who has the out-of-body experience possess special personality traits? Must he be 'different' in something than the rest of humanity?" Many researchers were interested in this question.

A questionnaire that was sent to the homes of the subjects who had undergone the experience helped the researchers answer the question. The researchers were looking for answers to questions such as: "Are people who undergo out-of-body experiences gifted with a more than normally active imagination?" "Are they more hysterical or neurotic than other people?" "Do they have a greater than normal ability to adapt?" After the questionnaires were handed in, it was simple to answer these questions.

After checking the answers, the researchers reached the conclusion that people who had undergone out-of-body experiences were in no way different than people who had not!

These psychological findings are of great importance, since many psychiatrists tended to attribute the numerous stories of out-of-body experiences to various psychotic syndromes. After an in-depth study by the group of psychiatrists in Kansas and other researchers, it was concluded that the psychiatric syndromes to which various psychiatrists attempted to ascribe the experience were completely different, and the out-of-body experiences did not attest to any psychological or physical problem in the slightest.

Most astral travel experiences occur spontaneously, that is, sometimes even with people who are not at all aware of the possibility of leaving the body. In contrast, many experts claim that it is an ability that can be acquired, and there are even people who can go out on astral travel any time they so wish. The parapsychologist, Charles T., conducted one of his studies on the topic with a woman who could go out on astral travel "on demand." In the laboratory of T.'s parapsychology institute, the woman was hooked up to an ECG monitor in order to record her brain-waves, so that it would be possible to examine the states of brain-waves that enabled her to leave her body. After being hooked up to the machine, she was asked to perform a complicated exercise: if she actually could leave her body, as she claimed, she would have to identify the title of the book that was lying on a high shelf, near the ceiling. The woman succeeded in going out on astral travel by means of her will power, and identified the required title, even though her body did not move at all.

In the 1980s, I wanted to perform a similar experiment, without the use of an ECG monitor, on a person by the name of Robert Johnson, who claimed that he could go out on astral travel any time he wanted. I asked him to lie down on a mattress while I sat on a chair about 10 meters from him. When he had reclined and was beginning to prepare himself to relax his body, I wrote down five words in a notebook I was holding (in such a way that he could not see what I was writing) and I added three small drawings below them. I held the notebook in both hands, open, close to me. A few minutes after I finished writing and lifted up the notebook, I felt a strange sensation, a kind of discomfort behind my back. The person before me lay motionless and seemed to be asleep.

About 10 minutes later, Johnson sat up on the mattress. His eyes were turned toward me, but it looked as if he were staring at a picture in his memory. Within five seconds, he rapidly pronounced the five words. After a short pause, he described the three drawings and added that there was a spelling mistake in one of the words – I had written the letter E instead of the letter A. His accuracy was perfect.

One of the common reasons for the belief that astral travel occurs in states of distress or in situations in which the physical body cannot tolerate what is going on around it, stemmed from Ed Morrell's book, *The 25th Man*. As stated previously, in current studies, it has been found that only a relatively small percentage of out-of-body experiences originate from some kind of physical suffering or state of distress. Ed Morrell was an inmate of an Arizona prison about 60 years ago. During his four-year prison term, Morrell experienced extreme abuse at the hands of the wardens who conspired against him – physical violence and lengthy periods in cramped, dark solitary confinement. However, fortunately for Morrell, his soul found a way to get away from the physical tortures. Every time he spent a long time in solitary, Morrell would have an out-of-body experience, and his astral body would visit faraway and much more pleasant places. Morrell had good control of the direction and destinations of his visits during his out-of-body experiences. He could get to any place his soul desired and he met many people. After his release, he went to meet them and discovered that they really did exist in those places. Among other things, Morrell also met his future wife on his astral travels. In Morrell's case, when his terrible experiences in prison ended after he had been released and had begun to live a normal life, free of pain and pressure, his unique out-of-body experiences also ended.

In many cases of leaving the body, the person who is experiencing the astral travel relates to the astral body that leaves the physical body as a double. In such cases, the person himself is in a state of clear consciousness, which even enables him to channel with the "astral double" and receive messages and information from him. The famous French writer, Guy de Maupassant, related that occasionally, while he was writing one of his stories, his etheric double would "bother" him. This situation occurred relatively frequently with Maupassant, and he said that his double even dictated some of his most successful stories.

Certain stories about astral projections describe the presence of the etheric "double" in the company of friends and loved ones while the person himself was in another place. The Swedish playwright, Strindberg, deeply missed his family after he had moved to Paris following his divorce from his second wife. During those moments of profound yearning, his body floated to Sweden, where he lingered next to his mother-in-law, who was playing the piano, for a few minutes. Several days after the experience, Strindberg received a letter from his mother-in-law in which she wrote that she had seen his double that evening.

The English poet, Shelley, also experienced a projection of his astral body to a place where he longed to be. In an out-of-body journey, Shelley saw his etheric double in the company of Lord Byron and other friends while he himself was someplace else.

The American, Sylvan Muldoon, author of the book *Spotlight on the Astral Body* (published in 1921), described the following event in the journal, *The Occult Review* in 1931:

Mrs. B., an American, experienced astral journeys and could relate in detail what happened to her during these journeys. Most of the astral travel was involuntary, spontaneous, and generally occurred before dawn. Before actually leaving her body, Mrs. B. usually experienced a sensation of the physical dulling of the senses. The sensations that preceded the out-of-body experience included swift flashes of headache alternating with moments of a feeling of lightness. Her general feeling was that she had been caught in a powerful sweeping current. During the course of the out-of-body projection itself, Mrs. B. could not direct or navigate her astral body, but was conveyed involuntarily in a kind of sailing or floating manner. Uncharacteristically, her out-of-body experiences were accompanied by sensations of discomfort and pressure, distress, a feeling of suffocation, and sore throats. The unpleasant sensation would become stronger until it caused Mrs. B. to return to her body within a short time.

One of Mrs. B's journeys was unusual as compared to her other experiences. During the journey, she found herself in the parlor of a fancy house, luxurious and somewhat strange. From the living-room, her astral body floated up a staircase that was unique in its tremendous size, and from there, her astral body passed through an expansive hall into a room in which an elderly woman was lying. Mrs. B's astral body approached the old lady's bed with a kind of inexplicable hesitation – since she knew that during astral travel she was invisible. Suddenly, the old lady woke up, and it seemed that she could see Mrs. B! She looked into Mrs. B's face as if she was seeing a ghost. Mrs. B. describes her feeling at that moment: "I felt very embarrassed to be in that house, like a thief or a burglar, without an invitation. I moved backward with inexplicable fear, toward the winding spiral staircase, and instead of going down in a circular manner, I moved straight back. All at once, I felt myself falling down with a sharp sinking feeling in my stomach. Suddenly, a long whistle deafened me, and I found myself sitting in my bed, inside my physical body, breathless."

If it were possible to try to dismiss Mrs. B's experience as a dream or a fantasy, the events that occurred two years after this incident contradict that assumption. Mrs. B's cousin went to live in the town of Concord, about 60 kilometers from where Mrs. B. lived in New Hampshire. Her cousin had just purchased the house from the estate of an old lady whom Muldoon calls Mrs. M., who had died shortly before Mrs. B. went to visit her cousin. Mrs. B. had never seen her cousin's new house before. When she stood at the entrance to the house, a strange feeling came over her. A servant opened the door and led her to the parlor. The strange feeling became stronger in Mrs. B. and disturbed her. Her glance swept over the large space, which was somewhat familiar, and she had a powerful feeling that she had been there before. Only when her cousin came down the huge, winding staircase to greet her did Mrs. B. realize that this was the house she had visited during her astral journey. Afterwards, it transpired that the old lady who had seen Mrs. B. on her astral journey was none other than Mrs. M., whose house had been purchased by Mrs. B's cousin after her death.

The British researcher of extrasensory phenomena, Carrington, relates to Muldoon's stories with great faith and considers them to be a fascinating documentation that sheds light on the astonishing phenomenon. Muldoon, who, because of his many journeys and his documentation of them had been nicknamed "the astral traveler" in the United States, says that he could leave his physical body voluntarily and go out on journeys in his immediate surroundings and remain fully aware of what he was doing.

Muldoon's childhood had been spent in a house in which extrasensory phenomena were related to seriously. His mother was very interested in spiritualism, and when he was 12, she took him and his brother to a spiritualist camp in Iowa during the summer vacation. During their first night at the camp, Muldoon woke up with a feeling that he was somewhere else. He could not move his body, nor could he see or hear anything. It seemed as if his senses were not working. He only felt as if his body was floating, hovering up and down in the air rapidly, involuntarily, without his being able to control it. Suddenly he felt a blow on his head, and his body began to float in the air again, in zig-zag movements. While he was floating, his senses gradually began to function. The first sense to "return" to him was the sense of hearing, and after that his sense of sight also began to function once more. When he could see again, Muldoon identified his surroundings, and understood that he was floating near the ceiling of the house where he was staying the night with his mother and brother. He looked down and saw his physical body lying in the bed. He was anxious, because he was sure that he had died and that was why he could see his body below him, while he was ascending and floating near the ceiling. Instinctively, he hurried to wake his mother. He went to the second room and when he tried to open the door, it turned out that he was already on the other side! He had simply gone right through it. He went to his mother and touched her in order to rouse her, but she did not feel him at all. No one in the house sensed the frightened boy who was trying to wake them up with all his might. He felt that all his senses were functioning, except the sense of touch. He touched the sleeping people, tried to shake them – but they did not feel anything. The young Muldoon was shocked by the experience. He heard the wall clock chime twice – it was two o'clock in the morning. About 15 minutes after the chiming of the clock, Muldoon felt that he was being swept and drawn to his body in the bed, floating vertically in the air and rejoining his physical body. As he rejoined it, Muldoon woke up in his bed, covered in cold sweat and frightened.

The experience Muldoon had at age 21 evokes additional questions, similar to the story of Mrs. B. Do people who experience astral travel aim in some inexplicable way to meet particular people who can see them / identify with their state / experience similar states of consciousness? What creates the contact between people who have this experience spontaneously? Does the fact that a person who is familiar with the out-of-body experience has the ability to accept and understand make the astral visit of another person in his life possible? Does the ability for openness and extrasensory reception (that sometimes stems from a particular physical and mental state – such as the case of old Mrs. M.) help in the encounter between the astral traveler and the person who can feel his presence or see him? And like the amazing case of Ed Morrell, who met his future wife during astral travel – is there such a thing as a "guiding hand" or an unconscious ability of the "upper I" to guide the astral traveler to a place where there is someone he has to meet?

This special case occurred in the summer of 1924, when Muldoon lived alone in a small town near Wisconsin. One warm evening, Muldoon was eating a late dinner alone in the cabin where he lived. He was feeling low, and he decided to go out for a short stroll before going to sleep. The weather was pleasant and relatively warm, and the full moon illuminated the path. Muldoon walked slowly along the paths near his house, hoping that the pleasant weather and the moonlight would cheer him up. After walking for a while without the slightest improvement in his mood, he returned home gloomily. He locked the door and went back to bed. Just as he was beginning to doze off, he felt his body float up into the air and pass through doors and walls. In a few moments he was outside. He began to be swept and pulled uncontrollably, but not in such a threatening way as during his first experience. Within a short time he found himself in the living-room of a strange and unfamiliar house. He looked around. There were four people in the room, but one of them – a pretty girl of about 17 – attracted his attention. He stood opposite her and looked at her, momentarily hypnotized by the movements of her fingers that were embroidering white lace for a sleek black velvet dress. After a few minutes, he resumed floating in the room and examined the furniture and objects carefully. After that, he left the house and returned to his room.

*Illustrations from Muldoon and Carrington's book – Spotlight on the Astral Body.*

He etched the trip in his memory, and went on with his life as usual, trying to invest all of his energy in his college studies. Two weeks after the incident, when he was walking home from college, a familiar movement not far away attracted his attention. He approached, and saw the same girl he had encountered during his journey going into the house of one of his neighbors. The door closed behind her, and he decided to wait for her to come out. When she came out of the neighbor's house, Muldoon was waiting for her at the fence. She passed by him, and he hurried after her. Since he knew that she did not live in the area, he asked her without hesitation where she lived. The girl was astonished at the audacity of young stranger's question. In those days, it was plain rude to go up to a girl you didn't know and ask her such a personal question. Muldoon tried to calm her down – and actually did so when he began to describe her house very accurately. He recalled the heavy furniture in the living-room, the way it was arranged, the few ornaments and even the odd pictures hanging on the wall. Surprisingly, the girl's astonishment waned and she was silent for a few moments, looking at him with such interest that Muldoon succumbed to the temptation of telling her how he knew all these details. To his surprise, the girl did not express any skepticism about his special experience, and told him that she herself had had similar astral journeys! They became close friends, and could share their special experiences freely and openly.

Muldoon's out-of-body experiences occurred fairly frequently throughout his life. The wonderful experience of meeting people astrally without them seeing him near them and afterwards actually meeting up with those same people also recurred throughout his life. He began to take a greater and greater interest in astral travel, and began to investigate the phenomenon. One of his hypotheses regarding the origin of the phenomenon was that the underlying reason for out-of-body experiences was a serious physical illness or an emotional shock that changed the person's physical balance, and the astral body was a kind of cosmic energy that emanated from the body and continued to move and travel to different places.

One of the famous "astral travelers" is Robert Monroe, who transformed the out-of-body experiences into an art, researched it in depth, invented a popular method for doing it, and even established an institute for brain research and astral experiences in Virginia. Because of his great importance in this field, I will briefly present his biography.

Robert Allen Monroe was born in Lexington, Kentucky, to a mother who was a physician and a father who was a university professor. He began his studies at elementary school at age four, and completed his academic studies at the University of Ohio, where he studied paramedical engineering, arts and sciences. Upon graduating in 1937, he began to work as a writer and producer in radio stations in Cleveland and Cincinatti.

In 1939, Monroe moved to New York, where he wrote and produced his first program for the "Rocky Gordon" radio networks. After he had worked as a producer and the manager of a radiophonic advertising agency for a time, he established a company called RAM, which produced radio programs up until 1956. At that time, Monroe's company was producing some of the most successful contemporary radio programs. Monroe's reputation spread far and wide and he became a kind of celebrity, and in parallel began to publish personal columns in the press. Monroe, who was blessed with multiple talents, did not make do with producing radio programs and writing in the newspaper. He began to compose music for the radio, the cinema, and for TV programs.

With the expansion of Monroe's company into other states in the US, the name of his company was changed to "Monroe Industries" in 1956, and the company began to engage in the development and installation of cable television.

Monroe's interest in human consciousness began in 1956, when he initiated a small research project for developing programs for the New York branch of his company. The aim of the research was to check out the possibility of learning while sleeping. In 1958, key data were found – an almost unknown state of consciousness, differentiated from and different than the physical body. The group of researchers coined the name "Out-of-Body Experience" (OBE) as the scientific definition for astral travel.

Today, this concept is used by scientists and researchers who are interested in exploring astral travel. In the years following, Monroe and his group of researchers began to work on means and methods to invoke and control this ability, at the same time conducting studies on additional states of consciousness in their research laboratories. All of Monroe's researchers, and Monroe himself, were considered to be unique experts in creating effective sound patterns as part of their work in radio and TV research, and of Monroe's personal and professional affinity to the sound processed in electronic instruments. They used these abilities as a basis for their research. Their efforts ultimately produced clear and significant results scientifically, sparking international interest. Scientists, physicians, psychologists, physicists, psychiatrists, research engineers and even non-professional people began to take an interest in the results of the studies of Monroe and his group. Monroe took out three patents in his name dealing the reception and entry into various states of consciousness, and they become known throughout the world. After Monroe's magic touch, the idea of astral travel turned from an abstract mystical idea to a fascinating and viable scientific topic. In 1973, the "Monroe Institute" was established by the original nucleus of the group of researchers and began to hold study seminars meant both for the general public and for professional people in various fields whose interest was the ability to control human states of consciousness. The seminars were held in several places inside the United States as well as outside of the country. Nowadays, the research and studies are held mainly at the Monroe Institute in Virginia, which, besides auditoriums and seminar rooms, also contains research labs and recording studios. The research activities of the Monroe Institute created a new popular-scientific facet in the attitude toward astral travel – toward the out-of-body experience and toward understanding different states of consciousness, and toward the control and use of the abilities of the human brain. In 1971, Monroe's book, Journeys Outside of the Body, was published.

The course of Monroe's life and the chronology of his professional success are very interesting in relation to his abilities to embark on astral travel. If we look at his life, it seems that his entire professional path, from the beginning, led him to developing and making the general public aware of the various states of consciousness. His *modus operandi* is the dream of every creator and scientist. On the one hand, it consisted of in-depth research, with a holistic ability to see the different functions that could help in the development of the research, as well as creative and unique thinking that combined art, medicine, science and awareness into a single whole. On the other, it demonstrated the ability not only to make his research topic popular with, understood by and interesting to the general public, but also to stimulate the curiosity of the scientific community. Monroe's success-filled life and self-realization inspire the question: Did some kind of guiding hand guide young Monroe's steps? Did the creative and far-reaching information that formed in his brain gain the continuous and directing support of the universe?

Monroe's becoming a successful TV producer and one of the first people to support cable TV (which afforded him tremendous financial resources for the continuation of his scientific-creative-spiritual activities) is not mere coincidence. Thirty years before the invention of television, when he was still a child, Monroe predicted the television era and its undoubted influence on human awareness.

Monroe's astral journeys did not begin at one magical moment. They were gradual and filled with distinct unpleasantness. In an attempt to pinpoint the moment when Monroe experienced the beginning of his expanded consciousness, we can mention the day in his youth when he lay on his bed and began to feel agonizing cramps and convulsions in his entire body. Lying in pain on his bed, Monroe let his arm slip down and hang loosely next to the bed.

Suddenly, he felt his fingers passing through the carpet. He pushed his arm, and his whole arm went through the floor without any resistance from the solid matter! Many years later, Monroe said that he had no doubt that he was completely awake at the time. As he grew up, the attacks of pain and cramps became stronger and stronger. In one incident, when he was already a young married man, the pain was so intense and out of control that he fell on the floor. As he fell, he felt that he was going through the floor, and the sensation of intense pain changed into a feeling of light floating, like a balloon drifting in the air.

Suddenly, the feeling of lightness changed into astonishment and rage – he saw his wife lying in their double bed with a man. He scrutinized the man who was sleeping peacefully in the bed – and identified himself. At that moment, he tried to return to his physical body, and succeeded in doing so easily. He woke up in his bed next to his wife, who was fast asleep.

In contrast to Muldoon and Ed Morrell, Monroe did not visit only known places on earth in the present, but also other dimensions, which he called "realities" – reality A, reality B, and reality C.

The first reality is the reality of the world in which we live in the present.

The second reality is the world of thought, the mental world, which Monroe considered to be the natural environment of the astral body. In the second reality, Monroe saw what people are inclined to define as "heaven and hell," and there he met the spirits of people who no longer lived in the first reality.

The third reality Monroe visited was the reality of a world similar to ours, but its technological level and several of its properties were different from those that we know. In that reality, Monroe met people who looked like people who were in the first reality (our world, as it is here and now), visited cities and saw roads and buildings that were similar to those that exist in the reality that is familiar to us. However, the customs of the people in this reality were different, and it was based on a technology that was different than ours. For instance, in that realty, the use of gasoline did not exist, and it even looked as if the development of science in that reality was less advanced, or different than what we know. But Monroe would go out to visit this reality, adopting his other, astral body, which was a "physical body" in the dimensions of that reality, and live a different life than the life experienced in the reality that is known to us.

Today, the idea of different "realities," different dimensions, is no longer only the province of science fiction, but a possibility that is being seriously studied by several research bodies in the world of physics and science.

# Projection outside the body

This story happened in Canada in 1996, and I myself was involved in it as a result of my curiosity about matters concerning the sixth sense. At the request of the parties involved in this event, I have changed their names.

In 1996, I was living with three girl friends in a large house on a collective settlement in the center of the country. At the time, my friend Yael and I were studying complementary medicine, Yonit was studying political science, and Michal was studying social work. Some time before this, Yonit had broken up with a boyfriend with whom she had had a painful and unhealthy relationship that had engendered in her negative feelings about the male sex in general.

We had many arguments in the living-room regarding Yonit's attitude toward men. We tried to explain to her that even if she had known two or three exploitative guys, not all men are like that. Yael and I decided to "educate" Yonit with the aim of changing her belief, which derived from the bad relationship between her parents, and stated that all men are hurtful and dangerous creatures. We explained to her that this belief is what caused her to attract exactly that kind of man. Yonit was skeptical about the various theories we presented to her, but agreed to perform a daily series of awareness exercises that would help her get rid of the inhibiting belief patterns to which she adhered. But this was not enough for Yael and me. We kept our eyes and ears open, and looked for a "match" for Yonit that would reveal the nicer sides of the male character to her.

During one of the breaks, one of the girls in our class began to tell us about her brother. He was Yonit's age, and, from his sister's description, was a sensitive, charming and special guy. When his sister mentioned that he did not have a girlfriend at the time, Yael and I immediately knew what to do. The sister was impressed by Yonit's stories, but mentioned one problem. Yonit was not inclined to believe in spiritual matters, while Ilan, her brother, engaged in extrasensory activity on a daily basis. However, Yael and I saw the positive side of the whole thing – perhaps through Ilan, Yonit would open up and free herself of her persistent skepticism.

That same evening, we came home satisfied, with Ilan's telephone number in hand. After a barrage of persuasion from her three friends, Yonit finally gave in and agreed to call him. She sat in the kitchen, and we could hear her conducting a calm conversation from the living-room. Finding it difficult to overcome our curiosity, we sat in front of the TV, which was on at a low volume, one ear directed at the kitchen. Two hours later, we began to signal her that, with all the sympathy and love in the world, there were other people who were waiting to use the phone.

When she replaced the handset, we pounced on her with questions such as, "What does he sound like? What did he say?" But the only information she was prepared to give us was that she had just spoken to one of the most charming men in the world. There was no need for further interrogation, however. The smile on her face said everything.

The next morning, Yonit was up before anyone else (an unusual event). She was excited, even slightly hysterical. In a flood of words, as if she had been waiting for us to wake up, she told us what had happened to her during the night:

"I went to bed smiling and excited because of the conversation with Ilan. While I was doing the awareness exercises you gave me, I recalled incidents from my parents' home, which depressed me a bit. In order to feel better, I went over details of the conversation I had with that sweet guy in my mind, and I fell asleep smiling.

"At around three in the morning, I woke up with a strange feeling. I felt as if someone was in the room. I pulled the blanket over myself, trying to understand the nature of the strange feeling. I felt someone approaching me and sitting next to me on the bed. The feeling was very weird, but at the same time it wasn't scary. When I overcame the natural fear of the feeling itself, you could even say that it was a pleasant feeling. I lay awake in bed for some time until suddenly, as if someone shut off music that had been playing continuously, the strange feeling stopped. I sank into a deep sleep again, and woke up early feeling great. I don't know what it was, but – don't laugh – I think it was Ilan."

Yonit herself was no less surprised at what she was saying than we were. We didn't know what to say. She was unable to explain where the feeling came from or the knowledge that it was Ilan, and did not understand how it was possible. Finally, she added that it might only be her imagination, because she so wanted to meet him after their very special conversation. She tried to find rational explanations for the strange feelings, but none of them sounded credible.

Yael and I did not know what to say. During the first break, we went over to Ilan's sister. Since we knew her to be a special person with experience in the extrasensory realm, we decided to tell her about the incident without mentioning that Yonit thought that it was Ilan who had visited her. She listened attentively. Suddenly she asked, "Tell me something – did Yonit call Ilan yesterday?" We nodded. She looked at us seriously and told us casually, "Then it's possible that Ilan came to visit her during the night."

When we got home that evening, Yonit was on the phone again. I could no longer restrain myself, however. Was it Ilan? I asked her, even though I knew. She nodded, and I grabbed the receiver from her hand. "Hi Ilan, I'm a friend of Yonit and your sister. Did Yonit tell you what she felt last night?" Yonit put her ear next to mine, and the other girls rushed to pick up the handset of the other phone so as not to miss a word. "No, not yet," said Ilan apologetically, as if he knew exactly what I was talking about. "Ilan, I have to ask you a slightly weird question," I said. "Is it possible that you 'visited' Yonit last night?" Ilan hesitated slightly, and then shyly answered "Yes." "She wasn't feeling so good… so I wanted to cheer her up a bit…," he added, as if apologizing. I watched Yonit. There was a slightly skeptical expression on her face, not devoid of shock, but also flattered at his sincere concern. "How does he know how I was feeling?" she whispered.

From the other phone, Yael's excited voice interrupted the conversation. "If you really visited her last night, how does her room look? Can you describe it to us?" "Yes," answered Ilan calmly. None of us expected such an accurate description of Yonit's room. Yonit, completely surprised, stared at me in wonder. "I didn't tell him anything about your room, I swear!" I whispered to her. Ilan described where the bed was, where the desk was, and even mentioned that it was untidy. He knew where her disk-holder and her stereo were, and described in detail the special clothing shelves that Yonit had constructed by herself – shelves that rested on red bricks, the jug containing peacock feathers and the large mirror on the wall. Finally, he asked whether Yonit had made the two large ceramic sculptures standing in the corners of the room herself. "How did you do that?" I asked him emotionally. "It's... a long story..." he replied. "I'll try to explain it to you when I come and visit."

We let Yonit carry on chatting to him. After the conversation, Yael asked her over and over again whether she had described her room to him in their first conversation, until Yonit got annoyed and burst out, "You all listened to my entire conversation, so what do you want from me? I don't understand it any more than you do!" Having said that, she was surprised that the strange occurrence had not put her off the guy or caused her to be afraid of him, and that the natural affection she felt for him had not changed.

Yonit and Ilan became involved in a deep and protracted relationship that helped Yonit get rid of all the inhibiting beliefs she had entertained about men. For the first time in her life, she had met a guy who supported her completely and did not hurt her in any way. We also liked him a lot, and appreciated him for the support he gave her and for the way in which he helped her open up to things that she had not even been prepared to listen to before. I interrogated him at length about levitation techniques, teleportation and astral journeys, which he had known intuitively from a young age, and I gained valuable knowledge.

# Life after death

The question of life after death is a question that has preoccupied people on the philosophical, spiritual, and personal level for thousands of years. Religious leaders worked hard to convince their followers of life after death, and even used vivid colors to depict the reality of other worlds (heaven and hell) that exist after the person's body has been buried in the ground. However, even before the emergence of the great religions, man believed that his spirit did not disappear along with his physical body. Various findings revealed that even prehistoric man was in the habit of burying the dead with objects that had been useful to them in this world, so that they could use them in the next world, too. This stemmed from a belief that the next world would be similar to this one.

The attempt to answer this question has gone hand in hand with constant attempts to receive any kind of information from the world beyond the "world of the living" – some clue, information, message. If "life" exists in the world beyond, what's stopping us from making contact with it?

According to many beliefs, the inhabitants of the next world do not tackle existential questions as we do in this world. For this reason, many people considered communication with the spirits of the dead to be a useful channel for receiving answers and solutions to questions, and tried to predict the future with their assistance. This was the case with Saul and the soothsayer, for instance. The latter, as she is described in the Bible, was the same as a present-day medium, who uses various means to try to make contact with the spirits of the dead and to receive answers regarding the future from them. At the very least, the medium tries to prove his extrasensory abilities by using his mediumistic abilities. For this reason, a stigma has been attached to this profession, since many of the famous mediums used tricks and deceit in order to create an illusion of communication with the dead, and exact substantial sums of money from innocent people who wanted to communicate with loved ones that were no longer in the land of the living.

In this chapter, we will review some of the means employed by mediums, such as seances and Ouija boards. We will present some stories describing the activities of mediums with genuine powers, and, in contrast, several stories about famous mediums who mainly employed trickery in order to satisfy their lust for fame and fortune.

# Mediumistic abilities:

Most of the mediumistic abilities can be divided into two main categories: mental and physical.

## Mental mediumistic abilities:

**Trance** – The medium's ability to detach himself from his body, thereby enabling another entity to enter and speak through him. This state can be induced both in the dark and in the light.

**Clairsentience** – The ability to sense the presence of entities and spirits, and the ability to sense the nature of the messages or information being transmitted. Sometimes this ability is entwined with clairvoyance. The ability to sense the presence of spirits and entities and their messages (often by feeling the entity itself) is among the foremost mediumistic abilities to be discovered or developed.

**Clairaudience** – The ability to hear messages from entities and spirits clearly, always differentiating between personal thought and the external message.

**Clairagostine** – The ability to sense entities and spirits via the sense of taste. Some people also include the ability to "smell" the presence of entities via the sense of smell in this category. The medium smells a certain odor that indicates the presence of some kind of entity in his vicinity, and sometimes even helps him characterize it or pick up the message it brings.

## Physical mediumistic abilities:

**Direct voice** – By using the ectoplasm (the radiation that emanates from his body) of the medium and sometimes of the participants in the seance, spirits and entities can create ethereal vocal sounds by means of which they can speak. Some mediums use a kind of long megaphone in order to amplify the sound so that the seance participants can hear it. In this situation, there is no need for the seance participants to have an audio ability. Frequently, the megaphone rises up and wanders around among the people in the room and above them without any physical help from the medium, who is in a deep trance.

**Transfiguration** – During the trance, the spirit or the entity uses astral matter and the ectoplasm that emanates from the medium to cause the figure of the medium to resemble that of the entity that is speaking from within him.

**Scotographs** – A photographic film is placed on the solar plexus chakra of the medium and draws ectoplasm from the medium. After the session, the film is developed and pictures of entities appear.

**Writing of messages by spirits** – During the medium's trance, the spirits can use the ectoplasm from him, astral matter, or small quantities of ink that are extracted from pens that are lying on the table in front of the medium, in order to draw pictures and write messages on sheets of white paper.

**Pictures on silk** – The entities used the ectoplasm of the medium and of the seance participants to create pictures of themselves and of their dear ones on pieces of pure silk.

**Etherilization** – This form is rare and considered to be extremely dangerous. For that reason, very few mediums use it. The entities draw ectoplasm from the medium and the seance participants in order to construct a life-size picture of the entity itself, from which the entity can speak.

**Portraits in drips** – The entities use ectoplasm, ethereal matter and drops of color from the surroundings in order to create a picture (generally of themselves) on a clean canvas. Frequently, the resulting picture on the canvas changes its shape some time after that.

**Extrasensory art** – Via various shapes and methods, spirits and entities transmit to the medium what should be painted or drawn. Often, the entities enter the painting itself and change in it in order to leave a certain message or image.

**Automatic writing** (see the chapter on this) – In mental mediumistic abilities, the entities transmit to the medium what should be written. In physical mediumistic abilities, the entities activate the medium's hand in order to produce a written message.

**Writing on a slate** – By using a piece of chalk and ectoplasm, the entities write messages on slates.

**Volleying** – The entities break objects down into astral matter, move them into the seance room, and, by using the ectoplasm of the medium and the seance participants, reassemble the objects and transfer them to the seance participants.

Mediumistic activity, in its various forms, has been known for thousands of years. However, it became popular at the beginning of the 19th century. Several spiritualist movements emerged during those years, and many mediums became famous and even gave performances for the general public. The seance became a "party game" in the high society of Europe and the United States, and ways of communicating with dead spirits were perfected, as well as people's desire for conclusive proof of the authenticity of the messages that were being received by the medium. Scientific means of checking the correctness of the transmissions did not exist, nor did means of checking the biochemical changes in the body of the medium. Although the medium had to prove the truth of his transmissions, the flourishing of spiritualism was a convenient field of action for various phonies, who amassed fame and fortune from their ability, which was sometimes nothing more than sophisticated ways of pulling the wool over people's eyes.

The more popular the seance became, the more the number of phonies who roamed the United States, England and France introducing themselves as spiritual mediums increased. These phonies gave the profession a bad name. They wandered around these countries, seeking to establish contact with rich people, widows, or mentally unstable people who were easy to manipulate. By gathering information, they learned about the relationship between those people and their dead loved ones, about the lifestyle of the dead relatives, and even about the property that was in the possession of the living relatives. When they held a spiritualistic seance, they used the information they had gotten hold of to prove their credibility, and after they had gained the unequivocal trust of the asker, who was sometimes a person who was having a hard time rebuilding his life after the death of his dear one, they used their powers to extract money and property from the people who trusted them.

One of the famous cases, which greatly accelerated the waning of the "medium fashion" at the beginning of the 20th century, was the letter of Eileen Bradford. Eileen Bradford was a well-known medium at the time. She worked in cahoots with her husband, a retired police officer. With an extreme lack of caution, she wrote a letter to her friend, which led to her losing her status as a famous medium. In this letter, she wrote, among other things:

"...When I know something about the bedroom habits, eating habits, or other personal habits of the dead person, everything is in my hands... I warned T. not to let any man kiss the mole on her belly, which her husband loved so much. She burst out crying and fell into my hands like a ripe fruit..."

As a result of this incident, in which the dead husband of a rich widow "spoke through Eileen's mouth," the deed of ownership of a large estate in New York City "fell into her hands like a ripe fruit." The Bradfords tried to transfer it into their name. Eileen's friend, who was upset at what she had read in the letter, decided that she could not let her get away with such an ugly scam, and she passed the letter to the family attorney, who exposed the scam in a widely publicized court-case.

The activities of the family that succeeded in entering the annals of modern spiritualism as one of the founders of the modern spiritualist movement and as the main players in making the whole matter popular have also come under suspicion.

## The Fox sisters – pioneers of modern spiritualism

The Fox sisters – Margaret, Leah and Kate – were the daughters of a religious farmer and a housewife, who moved to a small house in the state of New York in 1847.

A few months after they had moved to their home in New York, strange sounds and mysterious knocks began to be heard in the house, especially at night, frightening the young girls. The situation became so serious that the father wanted to sell the "bewitched" house and move to another house. But soon things changed dramatically, and what had seemed to be a "curse" turned out to be a blessing for the Fox family.

*The Fox sisters.*

One night, upon hearing the knocking sounds, Kate Fox began to react to them, as if she were trying to persuade the mysterious knocker to play a children's game with her. She shouted, "Do what I'm doing!" and clapped three times. From the depths of the house, three knocks sounded, in the identical rhythm. Kate's two sisters also joined in the "game." They clapped and called to the ghost to repeat the number and rhythm of their knocks. The mother of the family, calming down a little from her fears, also joined in the bizarre game, except that she steered in a different direction: She began to ask the ghost questions and asked it to answer her with one knock for "yes" and two knocks for "no." Very soon, a dialog developed in the dark room in which the mother asked questions aloud, and the ghost answered by knocking.

It did not take long for the strange occurrences at the Fox house to become widely known, involving, as they did, communication between the living and the dead, and the Fox house became a shrine for aficionados of mystery, religious leaders and researchers. The father claimed that he had found a corpse in the basement of the house, and that the knocks were a means of communication with the ghost of the dead person.

The Fox sisters became adept at communicating with the ghost. It seemed that they had an answer for every question they were asked, an answer that came in the form of mysterious knocking sounds. Word of the Fox house spread outside the United States, and people from various European countries came to see the mysterious happenings. Questions for the "ghosts of the Fox house" even arrived from royal courts in Europe. The press competed for every shred of information from the house, the sisters were interviewed, and their pictures appeared on the front pages of the newspapers. With the massive publicity the Fox sisters were getting, the spiritualist movement began to amass power, and spread quickly throughout the United States and Europe. People began to hold seances in their homes, and people who claimed that they were mediums – until that time they had been related to skeptically at best and contemptuously at worst – found themselves inundated with work and their pockets bulging with money.

That particular case of a haunted house with noises and knocking sounds and three young, "brave" girls who fearlessly communicated with the spirits of the dead, led the entire world to believe that communication with the dead was possible, and provided a means for receiving answers to various questions.

However, at the beginning of the 20th century, diaries and letters of the Fox sisters were published, in which they described how they had been directed by their parents to answer questions. The wheel of fortune turned once more, and the Fox sisters were shown to be mediumistic phonies. Was the Fox sisters' communication really all a scam? Or was there perhaps a shred of truth at the basis of the communication, which the parents decided to milk for all it was worth in order to amass fame and fortune? No definite answer has been found to this day.

The first spiritualist conference was held in Rochester in Britain in 1848. In spite of long years of parapsychological research (which did not fulfill scientific criteria), the active parapsychologists had still not reached one definitive conclusion about the form of life after death. Most spiritualists believe that the spirits of the dead are found in various spiritual spheres, and that every person, with the help of innate abilities or acquired skills, can reach these spheres, and thus obtain information from the spirits of the dead or communicate with them. The prevailing belief among active parapsychologists states that some of the souls of the dead come back to life in a different form and another consciousness – without remembering their previous life (similar to reincarnation), while some of the souls remain in spiritual spheres of some kind.

When modern spiritualism became popular, spiritualist churches emerged in the Europe and America. The objective of these churches and the people who gathered in them was to communicate with long-dead relatives or friends. According to their belief, the spirits of the dead could guide the believers during their everyday lives, advise them and answer their questions, on the assumption that life in the world "beyond life" contained much more information than life in this dimension. The groups in the spiritualist churches communicated with their dear ones via a medium, who would go into a state of trance, as a result of which he would begin to communicate with the spirits of the dead.

One of the tools used by the medium is the seance. Seances have become popular over the last 200 years, even though there have been many warnings about them. Most of the serious healers and parapsychologists advise against holding seances, since there is no proof that the so-called answers that come up during the seance are actually correct. Moreover, cases of mental derangement or of "disturbing the spirits" as a result of seances are not uncommon. Some of the professional mediums begin the seance by imparting basic information about the spirit with whom they are about to communicate. In a seance that is being held in order to communicate with a spirit that is familiar to the person who has requested the seance, the medium begins by imparting information that is known only to the asker and to the spirit he is raising. Quite a few cases have occurred in which the medium gave extremely personal details in the presence of a group of people, causing a great deal of embarrassment to the asker. Although the details provided by the medium are sometimes validated by the asker of the question, who knows them himself, there is no way to determine if it is actually the spirit that is giving the details. The medium may be gifted with telepathic ability and can therefore use this gift to obtain the information from the asker, who is sitting opposite him. This is one of the reasons why people in the extrasensory professions are overwhelmingly skeptical about seances.

Some of the mediums use various means to help the spirit communicate. One of the best-known means is the Ouija board. Recently, the popularity of this device has increased. It is a board marked with the letters of the alphabet and the words "Yes" and "No," and quite a lot of people use it. The popularity of the Ouija board stems, possibly, from the desire of people nowadays to receive some kind of "proof" of the communication with spirits. As opposed to channeling, which requires mental powers, intuition, and familiarity with the world beyond the senses, as well as the ability to believe in the intuitive messages that are received, many Ouija board users are not skilled in extrasensory channeling and are liable to harm themselves. The use of the Ouija board is often doomed to failure in two major ways. The first is that these people are mostly unsuccessful at making any contact with the spirit world, and no information or message arrives. The second is less pleasant: the people who are waiting for some kind of proof from the spirit world receive "too much proof" when they do not succeed in controlling whatever is visiting the seance and their Ouija board.

The following is a typical story about the use of a Ouija board:

"My friends and I began to see some kind of movement on the board. Neither of us was touching it. Then a sweet little boy appeared in front of us. We spoke to him for a time. He said that he had died years ago in this area, and was happy that he could talk to us. When we decided to clear the table and put the board aside in order to end the seance, he began to look very angry and cursed us. When I told him to leave, books began to fly at me from the shelves. The Ouija board flew up into the air and hit one of my friends on the head. We got rid of the Ouija board, but from then on we had lots of problems."

One of my friends, who has innate extrasensory powers, told about a series of seances he had held in his youth with one of the members of his family. In this case, the effect of the series of seances was serious. The spirit that communicated with the two managed to convince them that one of them was the Messiah. We are talking about two very rational people, who to this day are unable to explain how the spirit succeeded in convincing them. The situation reached the point where they began to save up money for a trip to Australia, where the spirit had commanded "the Messiah and his companion" to go. Fortunately for them, the intervention of their parents, who had noticed that the two youngsters had begun to act extremely strangely, put an end to the seances. A long time after that, the two still suffered from the effects of the spirit, until one day, inexplicably, the harassment ceased, and with it the strange belief in the Messiah and the trip to Australia. They cannot explain how they could have believed in such things. Their feeling at the time was as if they "weren't themselves," thinking and acting in a way that in no way resembled their normal way of thinking and behaving.

The messages received from spirits at seances are not reliable. Even if the spirit introduces itself as Elvis, Napoleon or Cleopatra, it does not mean that it really is Elvis, Napoleon or Cleopatra. Like human beings, spirits can also lie. Frequently, when ignorant and inexperienced people open the Ouija board, they get a low-level spirit, which may be an entity that "sucks" energy. Sometimes, these entities create an energetic link with the inexperienced communicator by appearing to be nice – they may say that they are the person or friend with whom the communicator wished to speak, or appear as a little child. When they succeed in creating the energetic link, their behavior may become unstable.

By the time the person realizes that he has been deceived by the spirit, and that it is not positive, the spirit already has a firm grip on his energies, and tries to extract as much energy from him as it can. The more the spirit succeeds in frightening the person, the more energy it extracts. The person's fear serves to deliver energy into the spirit's hands. Several parapsychologists who worked with people who had been harmed by seances say that often a state occurs when the avenging spirit introduces itself as "Satan" himself. Of course, it is not Satan, and is nothing like Satan, but is generally speaking a low-level energetic entity that would do anything to get hold of more and more energy, and the easiest way for it to do so is by means of intimidation. In view of everything that has been said here, anyone who is not absolutely certain that he can get rid of a non-positive, tiresome, harassing entity must not mess with the Ouija board. In contrast, the few people who do know how to deal with non-positive entities are not in the least inclined to use a Ouija board and generally relate to it with undisguised contempt.

Although the mediumistic profession is controversial, there are quite a few cases of genuine communication with entities from the world beyond. When the famous parapsychologist, Myers, died in 1901, scores of mediums all over the world began to receive messages from him via automatic writing, messages written in Latin and Greek, and messages in a complicated language and handwriting that were characteristic of Myers when he was alive.

Another unexplained and fascinating case is that of the American medium, Rosemary Brown, who in 1924 began to compose complex music in the unique styles of the great composers – Beethoven, Bach, Liszt, Rachmaninoff, Brahms, Debussy and Chopin. This occurrence was particularly surprising since Rosemary Brown's knowledge of music was minimal. Brown claimed that the spirits of the great composers communicated with her and dictated their works to her in order to prove to the world that they still existed. During the "dictation," Brown wrote down the complicated notes at an incredible speed. She claimed that the music that was dictated to her had already been composed by the composer, and he was simply dictating it to her. He was not composing it while dictating, and that explained the tremendous speed. This phenomenon particularly astounded experienced musicians who were present during this type of dictation, since even an experienced composer is unable to write entire pages of complex works so quickly, even from memory. Brown named one of the most beautiful and complex works that reached her "Beethoven's Tenth Symphony." It was meant for a large orchestra and was very similar to his Ninth Symphony.

Generally speaking, Brown understood only intuitively what she was writing, and could not play the melody. Most of the composers communicated with Brown in English. Liszt spoke French or German when he got excited, while Chopin sometimes spoke Polish. In those cases, since Brown did not know those languages, she wrote phonetically, by ear only, and used the services of a translator in order to understand the words. The Rosemary Brown phenomenon sparked interest among many musicians, some of whom agreed that there was a great similarity between the works of the medium and the original works of the great composers.

Another famous medium was Mrs. Paladino. She lived in Naples in the 19th century, and many researchers were impressed by her abilities. During one of the seances she held in 1891, the spirits went inexplicably "wild." Prof. Cesar Lombroso, a famous Italian criminologist who was known for his skeptical attitude toward spiritualism, three other professors and five physicians attended the seance. During the seance, one of the participants, Prof. Poo, a professor of pathological anatomy at the University of Torino, tried to test the medium's powers by placing a photographic plate on the table around which the seance was taking place. Mrs. Paladino herself sat behind a screen. The moment the professor laid down the photographic plate, a hand appeared from behind the screen and tried to snatch the plate away. Prof. Poo grabbed hold of the mysterious hand, but it eluded his grasp and struck him. It seemed as if the spirits were angry at the blatant intervention in the seance and at the expression of doubt in their existence as reflected by the photographic plate. They began to attack the table, which rose into the air above the heads of the stunned spectators. When one of them tried to seize the table, it floated over the screen, where it began to break apart noisily. The table flipped over, and one of its legs was torn off. It continued shattering into splinters behind the screen, apparently by itself. The nine astonished spectators watched the scene wide-eyed and shocked. When one of them wanted to shake the spirit's hand, the spirit instructed him via the medium to come closer to the screen, and then the fragments of wood flew at him and struck him.

Mrs. Paladino was examined by many scientists in research laboratories in the United States and in London. They were impressed by her abilities but unable to explain or understand them. One of the scientists said: "No one has managed to explain the medium's supernatural powers. Mrs. Paladino remains one of the greatest paradoxes in history."

A broad spectrum of supernatural phenomena can occur at seances. The most common of these (which false mediums can also produce by means of various tricks) are the table rising into the air, objects moving, knocking sounds, blows, and so on. The appearance of a cloud in the room is also not unusual. One of the more unique phenomena that accompanies a seance occurred during a set of experimental seances held by Dr. Crawford, a mechanical engineering lecturer at the University of Belfast, with the medium Kathleen Gulliger. During the course of the seances, all the participants lost weight! After the first seance during which this odd phenomenon occurred, the participants and the medium herself began to weigh themselves before and after each seance. Once, when the medium weighed herself after the seance, she had lost over 20 kilograms! No explanation was found for this strange and rare phenomenon.

Sometimes, the spirit appears at a seance in a concrete, two-dimensional form, which can be photographed. The first photograph of ghosts was taken by William Mabler in Boston, in 1862. Mabler, who was attending a seance, aimed his camera at the chair on which, according to the medium, the ghost was sitting. When Mabler developed the film, he discovered to his astonishment the image of a young girl sitting on the chair. The girl's face and upper torso were quite clear, while her waist and lower body were covered in the picture by a kind of mist. Mabler excitedly identified the image in the picture – it was his niece who had died at age 22.

## An unwitting medium – or a strange case of reincarnation?

Connie Islin, who has been examining different aspects of the extrasensory world and supernatural phenomena for many years, relates the following case, which she calls "the Paulina fantasy."

The incredible case began with a telephone call to Islin from the principal of a special boarding-school for dyslexic children in the province of Burgundy, France. The principal, who had read several of Islin's articles dealing with extrasensory phenomena, was calling her to request her help. In her school, there was a 16-year-old girl of German origin by the name of Paulina S. The principal said that Paulina was a very quiet girl who did not cause any unusual problems. Recently, however, she had begun to spend a lot of time – during lessons, too – scribbling and sketching strange drawings, numbers, letters, and words. There was nothing exceptional about that, of course, except that the sketches and symbols that appeared in Paulina's drawings were unusual, and the principal had identified some of the words as Latin – a language that Paulina did not know. There was a mystical element in the drawings that disturbed the principal. She asked Islin to come and spend a few days at the school in order to fathom the nature of the phenomenon.

When Islin reached the environs of the school, she was not sorry that she had agreed to the request. The school was located in a breathtakingly beautiful area, on a hill in the middle of a virgin forest, and the school building itself was an ancient castle that may have served one of the nobles of the region in the past. Around the school building was an impressive stone wall, and, in spite of the renovations that had modernized the building, it had maintained its ancient exterior. As the gatekeeper was taking Islin to the main building, she caught sight of an interesting etching above the entrance gate – a circlet of grapes containing a large cross.

A total of about 60 people resided in the castle precinct – 30 pupils, 10 teachers, and various service-providers. Everything was in readiness for her arrival, and she rested for a few hours in the pleasant room she had been allocated. Then she went to meet the principal and look at the pages about which the latter had spoken so agitatedly in their telephone call. She opened the black folder the principal placed before her and was stunned. Although the scribbles that appeared on the sheets of paper looked childish, Islin immediately identified the Latin inscriptions she recognized from previous research. In front of her eyes appeared a kind of ancient Latin shorthand, which the convent clerks were in the habit of using for taking notes. On some of the pages, there were dates written in Roman numerals, indicating the year 1691. On one of the pages, she identified the watermark that was imprinted on sheets of paper during the Middle Ages. She carefully examined the pages before her. The pressure of the nib on the paper and the style of writing attested to the fact that this was not contemporary writing. It did not take her long to realize what was bothering the principal. On many of the pages, there were crude drawings of naked women and next to them sketches of candles, dogs, men and flogging whips. Islin could hardly conceal her astonishment at the drawings.

When she looked up from the pages crowded with drawings and sketches, she asked the principal: "Who used this castle before it became a boarding-school?" The principal did not have the faintest idea, but Islin knew that it would not be difficult to find some kind of information about the castle's history. She gathered the papers, returned them to the black folder, and asked to meet Paulina for a brief conversation. She spoke to the girl for about 15 minutes, but did not reveal her objective. Paulina gave the impression of being an ordinary girl, quiet, devoid of any unusual characteristic for a girl of her age. After the meeting with Paulina, Islin made a quick tour of the castle, lingering especially in Paulina's classrooms and bedroom.

Islin debated at length about how to define the phenomenon. Was it a unique case of reincarnation? Or was Paulina serving as an unwitting medium for the spirit of – someone – linked to this castle? Islin's senses told her that there was a close connection between the place Paulina was in – the castle – and the strange drawings. She was faced with two courses of action that she would have to take simultaneously (1) finding all possible information about the castle itself, and (2) investigating the subject of the phenomenon – the young girl, Paulina.

Islin got down to gathering all the information she could lay her hands on about the ancient castle. She used her many contacts, and within a fortnight, had managed to get hold of a great deal of information about the castle. She invited two French researchers from Paris to go through the drawings, and they stated without hesitation that they were "original drawings" – the drawings of a clerk at a Catholic convent – whose name even appeared on Paulina's drawings: Bartholomeus Benini. Bartholomeus served as a kind of "inspector" for the bishop, and his job was to "put out fires" in convents where events occurred in contravention of the strict rule of the church. Islin checked Bartholomeus' name, which appeared in Paulina's drawings, in the church records and found the information she was looking for. In the church records was inscribed: "...March 1691, Brother ... (B.B.) was sent to the convent ... All his expenses will be covered... He has two donkeys for his use..." Later on in the records, it was mentioned that Brother Bartholomeus Benini stayed in the convent for eight months.

The castle that serves as a boarding-school nowadays once served as a convent called "The Convent of the Holy Virgin." From the land registry documents, Islin learned that the convent had been built in about 1240, and served as a castle and as the center of the large forest estate. In 1450, there was a huge fire that badly damaged the castle, and about 60 years later, the castle and the estate were rebuilt by the Catholic church in its present form. Until 1860, the castle was used by the church, and then it passed into the hands of the local authority, from which the management of the school leased the estate. In the few documents concerning the castle that Islin found, there was no mention of any unusual event – no stories of witchcraft, evil spirits or other religious scandals, which are not so rare in the context of ancient castles and monasteries. On the contrary, the castle was amazingly free of stories of this kind. Islin wanted to examine the convent records in order to find out additional details about what went on in it, but discovered that these documents had been lost in the great fire of 1450.

She managed to lay her hands on a number of documents written by Bartholomeus Benini – not from the convent – and compared them to Paulina's records. Bartholomeus' original handwriting was astonishingly similar to Paulina's handwriting in her peculiar records. It must be mentioned that the girl's handwriting in the records was very different than her normal handwriting. The scribbles were in fact made in the Latin shorthand style, and the records matched the agricultural crops and the activity in that region in the 17$^{th}$ century. Of course, Paulina herself had no way of knowing about these things – in-depth research and good connections had been necessary in order to check out such details. Islin discovered that the strange drawings of women that appeared in Paulina's sketches were secret drawings from "The Books of Sin and Obscenity" – drawings that had been made following the confessions of the girls who lived in the convent, and sometimes, in worse cases, as a result of the exposure of the cases and catching the girls red-handed. More than any other figure in Paulina's drawings, the girl stood out, and the sketch of the candle or some other object next to the figure indicated her confession about the use of a particular object for purposes of masturbation and so on. In one case, Islin even managed to identify the name of the girl that appeared above one of the sketches – she was the daughter of one of the families of the local aristocracy – and even obtained a photograph of her gravestone in the family burial plot. But the dates are what mostly astounded Islin. On almost every page on which Paulina had "scribbled" her strange sketches, there were dates written in Roman numerals. The sequence of the dates astonished Islin. With the assistance of a calendar, she managed to track Bartholomeus' daily routine almost day by day. During all of her years as a researcher of extrasensory and supernatural phenomena, she had never encountered such an amazing phenomenon!

She had to check out another topic in depth before she could attempt to define the phenomenon she was facing. She had to check out Paulina's memory. As Islin writes, the power of the memory can sometimes be so great that looking at a book or a certain document, even in the first years of childhood, can bring about a state of photographic memory, in which the person can write down, detail by detail, entire pages from the book or document. But the possibility that Paulina had seen records from the convent was almost nil. First of all, most of the convent records had been lost in the fire. Second, the records known by the name "The Books of Sin and Obscenity" had been kept in locked safes, and even nowadays it is virtually impossible to look at them.

With the help of Prof. François Dijon, Islin tried to find out whether it were at all possible that Paulina saw something in the convent itself. For a month they scoured the convent, but without any success. At the same time, Paulina was still sketching these types of drawings every day, with sequential dates.

Islin decided to continue her research, and moved into the castle. She began to track Paulina on a daily basis. Paulina did not display any unusual behavior patterns or any other signs of extrasensory perception. Other than her daily sketches, everything was perfectly normal. Islin requested the principal's assistance in creating "laboratory conditions" for examining Paulina, and received her full support. She discovered that Paulina drew her sketches at the same time every day – between 11 and 12 in the morning. She decided to keep Paulina occupied at that time in order to see what would happen. With the principal's permission, that time became a special physical education or handicrafts lesson for Paulina, under the scrutiny of Islin. The girl demanded to go to the bathroom, took her notebooks with her, and spent a long time there. When Islin followed her to the bathroom, she found her sitting next to the sinks, vigorously sketching her mysterious drawings. Islin tried to present her with Latin words, but there was nothing about Paulina, verbally or in her facial expression or body language, that attested to the fact that she had any idea of the meaning of the Latin words. Paulina herself did not know what she was writing down or what it meant. She had no idea!

Islin believed that the castle lay at the root of Paulina's drawings. From her experience, she knew that in many cases of reincarnation, evil spirits, ghosts, or other involuntary mediumistic forms, there is a close connection between the place in which these things took place or in which the figure lived in the past and the present manifestation. For that reason, she tried to distance Paulina from the castle. Initially, Islin took her for walks in the forest. Paulina continued to make her sketches at the same fixed time, even when she was at some distance from the castle. But when Islin traveled a distance of 25 kilometers from the castle with her, Paulina stopped drawing, but displayed obvious impatience and agitation. Paulina herself was unable to define what was bothering her so much. Islin even tried to keep Paulina in the dark at the time when she made her drawings. She was not surprised to discover that Paulina continued to sketch the same drawings in the dark. She drew and wrote mechanically, without even looking at the paper in front of her.

At the same time, Islin continued her historical research and obtained a record of the history of the convent in 1691. She knew that now she was in the last third of Bartholomeus' sojourn at the convent, and was sure that there was a close tie between him and the messages Paulina received. According to the records, Islin anticipated the sketches that Paulina would draw, and was correct in at least two cases. Paulina drew sketches of a battle that took place in the forest next to the convent, after which the monks collected the armor and all the weapons and buried the dead. She also recorded in the "Book of the Sins and Obscenity" the expulsion of the girl from the convent after she had committed the "sin of the cross" (masturbation with a cross containing the figure of Jesus). There were solid historical witnesses to both of these incidents.

Islin planned her next research move. She found out where Bartholomeus Benini had gone to after finishing his tour of duty at the Convent of the Holy Virgin, and did everything necessary to go there with Paulina. She was sure that Paulina would continue her communication with the spirit/brainwave of Bartholomeus in the new place as well. And indeed, as she expected, exactly at the time when Bartholomeus completed his tour of duty in the convent, Paulina stopped drawing completely! It was obvious that the messages had ceased once Bartholomeus had been transferred from the convent. Islin wanted to continue the fascinating research with Paulina, but the girl's parents intervened, and refused to let her take the girl with her to continue the research.

Following the Paulina affair, Islin propounded her hypothesis concerning the brainwaves that exist in the universe. She surmised that it is possible that people produce pictures, feelings and thoughts consciously or unconsciously on brainwaves that we do not yet know how to identify. The resulting brainwaves are sent out into the immediate surroundings, like the radiation that is emanated to the aura (whose existence was proved by Kirlian in his research and photographs). Every brainwave has a certain frequency, unique to the person who is emitting or to the event – thought, emotional, and so on – that is being transmitted. Islin thinks that every brainwave can be picked up, if the person on the receiving end is a "key" that is exactly suitable to the emitted brainwave. This reception can be immediate, during the transmission itself, or delayed, when the receiver is in a place where the brainwaves were emitted – which might have been the case with Paulina. This theory provides an original explanation for the functioning of certain mediums. Islin continued to develop her theory, from the perception that space around us is full of an almost infinite quantity of brainwaves, which carry pictures, words and sensations from ancient times until today. In order to link up to those "channels" and receive the messages, a certain "key" is needed.

Three months after concluding the investigation of the case of Paulina, Islin had the opportunity of researching her theory and perhaps even proving it. When she was in London, she received information about a young Serbian girl, who, it seemed, not only held one "key" to the "lock" of a certain brainwave, but even a "master key" to every lock.

## The Irina Teshenova affair

Irina Teshenova was a 19-year-old medium from Serbia. Her mediumistic talents were prodigious, and her ability to pick up extrasensory communication was exceptional. When she was 11, Prof. Anatoly Washrensky discovered her, and performed laboratory experiments with her for about two years. Mediumistic reception abilities are not that rare. But Irina's uniqueness lay in the fact that she could adapt herself to every "extrasensory transmission." Moreover, in contrast to most of the mediums who tend to pick up messages consistently in a certain way (as we saw in the categories of mediumistic abilities), Irina could pick up pictures, sensations, words, signs and letters with equal success. It seemed that Irina had the ability to "get onto the energetic wavelength," like a person who looks for a radio station, but Irina picked up dozens of stations at the same time, and managed to scan the spectrum of frequencies that reached her into her brain, isolating one frequency from among them and picking it up precisely.

Islin describes Irina as a "simple-looking girl, overweight, unprepossessing." She came from an uneducated family, and her parents raised pigs. She only spoke Serbian, and knew a few words of Russian. Islin was forced to hire the services of an interpreter in order to communicate with her. There was no chemistry between them, but the resulting distance was advantageous to Islin's research work. Islin was aware of the fact that Irina and her family received financial grants because of Irina's abilities, so she chose an unusual research environment that would totally prevent Irina or her parents from knowing what was going on there. In this way, she ensured that no information reached Irina before the start of the research.

Islin had gotten hold of an in-depth study about Wharton House, a manor house in Kent, which appeared on the list of "Houses in which ghosts have appeared." She had made contact with a young researcher, Alan Preston, who had written a whole book describing and documenting the history of the house. The book had not yet been printed (at the time of Islin's research) and had not yet been sent to a publisher, so that the only copy of it was in Islin's hands, and no information from it had been leaked. In order to avoid a situation in which Irina would pick up thought messages from Islin herself, Irina only read the even-numbered chapter in the book. In this way, she could know for certain whether Irina could pick up messages from the interior of the house itself. In order to prevent any possibility of information reaching Irina in other ways, Islin sent Alan Preston to Los Angeles on vacation at her own expense, and rented the house, which was empty.

Islin had all the tools for valid scientific research – a laboratory (Wharton House), a research object (Irina), and a basis for comparative research (the history of Wharton House). The hypothesis that Islin set out to check was that in the haunted house there were telepathic brainwaves that carried messages that Irina the medium could pick up and decipher. She took care to prevent any possibility of error, falsification, or coincidence.

On their way to Wharton House, Islin explained her research method to Irina by means of the interpreter. As a first step, she had chosen eight defined weeks in the 18th century. She knew exactly what had happened during four of them, but as for the four other weeks, she had no idea (the information was in the odd-numbered chapters she had not read).

Irina listened to the interpreter indifferently, chewing gum noisily. When the translator had finished, she straightened her shoulders and began to speak fluently. Islin waited impatiently for the translation. "She says there's no problem," said the interpreter, "but she'd like to eat something on the way… and she needs to find a place to urinate…"

Irina's big advantage as a research object was her ability to "compress time." As opposed to Paulina, who lived Bartholomeus' events in real time, day after day, which required a lengthy period of research, Irina could race backward and forward between the events, very fast or very slow, according to what Islin wanted.

As soon as they arrived at Wharton House, Irina began to wander around the large house and its courtyards. She requested an extension of three days to "feel" the house. On the fourth day, she informed Islin that she was ready to begin.

The first stage that Islin had to go through was determining some kind of point in time from which she could continue. Islin got the tape recorder ready, and checked that the video camera for recording the event was working properly. Irina sat in a large armchair in a gloomy room, her eyes half-closed. On the small table in front of her, Islin placed a writing pad and pens. A few moments later, Irina began to enter a mediumistic trance. Islin followed Irina's facial features in astonishment as they changed, softened, and looked less coarse and more pleasing. In a few minutes, Irina began to utter various sentences, words, and parts of words, in languages that she did not know at all! Islin tried to follow what she was saying. She did not manage to identify any clue that would place Irina's mutterings at any particular time, until suddenly, Irina began to speak French, and Islin watched her fascinated, beginning to understand the course of events and connect them to what she knew about Wharton House.

Irina spoke French in a deep, slightly hoarse, guttural voice, like the voice of an elderly man. Islin could understand every word: "...We encountered quite a strong wind... the ship was pushed onto the rocks, and some of the barrels rolled off the deck... You should have seen the ladies! They shut themselves up in the little cabin and vomited their guts out..." And then, abruptly, Irina's voice changed, and sounded like that of a young girl, speaking French in a sharp, petulant voice: "Father, you promised me that you wouldn't talk about that!"

Islin knew what was going on, and identified the voices in the incident. This was her first marker. One of the members of the household had brought a French bride for his son in 1837! In records from those times, the bride's dowry was well documented, and included, among other things, a large cargo of barrels of wine. Islin also knew what had happened during that week. She signaled to the interpreter, and he began to speak to the girl in Serbian, repeating the same sentence several times. Islin had asked him to tell her to try to speak more slowly. Irina's voice became calmer. She uttered short sentences, alternately in French and English, changing voices in accordance with the person who was speaking. She displayed life in the house, day by day, to Islin, playing the roles of all the participants, but her facial features did not change.

Islin glanced at her watch. Irina had been in a trance for almost two hours, which was a very long time for mediumistic communication, and Islin knew that she had to stop soon, because such protracted mediumistic communication is really dangerous. But just as she was about to ask the interpreter to instruct Irina to stop, a voice calling for help emerged from Irina's mouth. Islin froze. "No… no… please!" And then the voice of a man speaking English erupted from Irina's throat: "Shut your mouth, you French bitch!" Irina's mutterings became faster and more disjointed and unclear. Disjointed syllables emerged from her mouth, and she slowly began to calm down. "You got what you wanted, what," said a harsh male voice in English, from her mouth. And then suddenly, Irina screamed in a sharp feminine voice, followed immediately by a male scream. She began to release a rapid stream of words in French: "…He was stronger than me…Oh… What have I done? Now he won't want to marry me… How can I look him in the face now?"

Connie Islin was astounded. She knew that before the wedding, one of the brothers of the English lord of the manor died in a peculiar hunting accident, when he went out one night to hunt a wolf (that is what was written in the historical records of the house). Now she was hearing the real story from Irina's mouth – how the young bride, her father and her maid took the body outside, pulled the string of his bow and released it after leaning his body on it, how they made the event look like a hunting accident, and how they hid the signs of blood.

This was information that nobody had known about. Irina had no way of inventing the story or of picking it up from Islin's thoughts, because the latter herself had not known the truth behind the "hunting accident."

Islin asked the interpreter to halt the girl's flow of speech. As if nothing had happened in the room, as if she did not understand anything of what she had said before, Irina straightened up, stretched her arms, and became the same simple Serbian girl once again. The first words she uttered were, "I'm hungry. Can we go eat now?"

Islin was dizzy. She was sure that she had gotten hold of a gold-mine, and that the rest of the research would be as successful as the beginning had been. But she was in for disappointment. Irina did indeed continue to get onto wavelengths and brainwaves, but what issued from her mouth was a strange mixture of sentences, words, and bits of words in various languages, and Islin did not succeed in finding any common denominator among them. The things that were said during the following times when Irina served as a medium seemed to be unrelated to the history of the house.

The question that was still valid for Islin was: What caused a sentence or a certain picture to become a brainwave that is preserved and can be picked up by a person with mediumistic properties? She asked herself why Paulina had picked up Bartholomeus' inscriptions in a precise and organized way, but did not pick up anything about his life or his personal impressions about what he wrote. Not a shred of his personal life reached Paulina.

The hypothesis that something traumatic, something extremely powerful and upsetting, like rape and murder, remained in the memory and turned into brainwaves that could be picked up, could not be verified after the encounter with Irina, since she picked up everyday and completely insignificant and meaningless conversations to the same extent. After several encounters in which Irina delivered confused and insignificant information, Islin had almost given up – until one day, toward the final date of the tests, when another surprising event occurred.

As on the other days, Irina sat in the heavy brown armchair in the slightly gloomy room. This time, however, instead of sitting quietly as she usually did, Irina began to squirm around restlessly in the chair. For the first time since Islin had brought her to Wharton House, Irina reached toward the table and took a pen. Several seconds later, she discarded it and looked for a pencil, which she also discarded immediately. Islin wondered what she wanted. Finally, irritated and impatient, Irina asked the interpreter for a paintbrush and an inkstand. It was the first time that Irina had wanted to write or paint. Islin found a fine paintbrush and an inkstand for her. Irina grabbed them, bent the paper, dipped the brush in the ink, and wiped the excess ink off with her lips. With the fast and confident movements that Islin knew from studies in which she saw communication by means of automatic writing, she began to draw. Irina began to make strange signs on the paper, signs that looked like pictures – it was Chinese writing!

She filled an entire sheet with these signs, and then rested and became herself once more. Several days after the incident, Islin, with the help of experts, succeeded in deciphering what was written on the paper. It was a Chinese poem, written in perfect and precise writing. Irina, an uneducated girl from Serbia, who had never had any contact with the Chinese language, had written a well-known Chinese poem on the paper with complete accuracy in every stroke! There is no doubt that the brainwave Irina picked up was that of a person who was an expert in Chinese language and literature, who wrote with the skill of a Chinese author, skill that had been learned over many years.

Islin returned to the book about the history of Wharton House in order to try and solve the mystery. In one of the chapters she had not read, written in 1884 (not the year that Islin had chosen as a test point), a Chinese scholar had stayed in the house. He had been brought over by one of the members of the family who had returned from the Far East and possessed a large and valuable collection of Chinese porcelain.

Most regrettably, the last incident was just about the end of the road with Irina. Islin propounded the hypothesis, which derived from many years of research, that a medium or a receiver may not improve with time, but the opposite. The medium is exposed not only to transmissions from the past that he tries to pick up and decipher, but also recent transmissions, no less powerful, and sometimes even more so – transmissions of people who expect an answer from him, a revelation, a communication. It is possible that this pressure greatly erodes the medium's sensitivity. In many cases she investigated, Islin discovered that the first transmissions that were picked up by the medium were the clearest and most accurate.

## Communicating with spirits without a medium

There are forms of communicating with and receiving information from spirits without a medium – without a "professional" medium, that is, since other means, even various mechanical ones, can also serve as non-human "mediums" for picking up messages from spirits and entities. One of the best-known methods is by using a tape-recorder, and one of the most renowned cases of communication with spirits by means of a tape-recorder is that of the Swedish movie producer, Friedrich Jorkenson.

One day in 1959, Jorkenson was sitting in his home, preparing to listen avidly to a recording of birdsong he had recorded in one of the forests he had visited. He pressed the button and activated the tape, and suddenly, instead of the chirping of birds, there was the voice of his deceased mother calling to him, "My little Friedel, can you hear me?" When Jorkenson got over his astonishment at hearing his mother's voice speaking to him from the tape (it took him a few days), he began to take an interest in and study the topic of recording the voices of the dead with a tape-recorder. From then on, Jorkenson recorded hundreds of voices of dead people on his audio tapes. In general, the spirits uttered a few words. Because of his interest in the topic, Jorkenson met Dr. Konstantin Raudiv, a psychologist of Latvian origin, who was spending the year in Sweden and was interested in parapsychological research. They began to make outdoor recordings together. By 1968, Raudiv had recorded over 70,000 voices of dead people, among them the voices of Sir Winston Churchill, Tolstoy, Stalin, Hitler and Nietzsche. The most common messages on the tapes were things like, "The dead are alive, Konstantin, please believe that." In one of the last recordings they made, one of Raudiv's assistants, who edited the recording, heard: "We want Kostie." Raymond Cast, a researcher of the voices of the dead, heard recorded voices on a tape-recorder, saying: "This man, Raudiv, is close to the grave." Three months later, Raudiv died.

## False mediums

Cases of false mediums were so numerous and so common in the 19th century and at the beginning of the 20th century, that the French researcher of supernatural phenomena, Camille Flammarion, declared that "All the professional mediums are frauds." The cases of deception by mediums are so numerous that I will present only the most infamous of them here.

### The seance of the medium Florence Cook

The English medium, Florence Cook, was considered to be one of the greatest mediums in England at the end of the 19th century. Not even the exposure of her deceptions diminished her popularity.

One winter evening in January 1880, a group of people from London's high society sat in Cook's seance room. Holding seances was fashionable at the time, and the medium Florence Cook easily found her way to the heart of England's high society. The seance room was in total darkness, except for the light of a single candle that cast bewitching shadows on the wall. The group crowded around the table upon which the candle flickered was not a doubting group. They believed, and wanted to believe, that the vision that was about to be revealed to them would be genuine. Indeed, what was revealed to them was extraordinary. Florence Cook concentrated for a time, when suddenly she began to speak about a young girl who had identified herself by the name of Mary. The people were fascinated, and a light tremor passed over their flesh when they heard the weak, almost "dead" voice of the young girl. Their astonishment increased when Mary's spirit suddenly began to take on skin and bone, and she assumed a flesh and blood image. She appeared in front of the astounded spectators dressed in a white gown, and began to dance in front of them, singing a bewitched and enchanting song. However, one person among the spectators was too skeptical to believe in the scene. He got up suddenly and grasped the "singing girl's" arm. The figure began to wrestle with him. The seance ceased abruptly, and one of the spectators turned the light toward the figure of the girl. It was none other than Florence Cook herself, dancing around the room dressed in a white nightgown...

The deception was revealed and exposed. And Florence Cook? She held another seance for a new group of naive people the next night.

The British researcher, Dr. Harvard Harrington, reached the conclusion that many mediums are tempted to use sleight of hand when their supernatural powers become weak, or when they want to impress their audience and cope successfully with the competition in the "medium market." Even famous mediums, who were gifted with supernatural powers that had been confirmed by laboratory tests and serious studies, were caught more than once in acts of deception and various magic tricks. Even Mrs. Paladino, the famed and esteemed Italian medium, was caught knocking on the table during a seance, and once even lifted the table with her knees.

The number of tricks, feats of wizardry and deceptions performed by professional mediums was so great that a substantial number of books exposing these tricks was published, and various people turned the exposure of the mediums' deceptions into a lucrative profession that led to considerable renown. One of these people was David Abbott, one of the first researchers to set himself the goal of publishing a book of mediums' tricks. In 1907, he published his book, *Backstage with the Mediums,* which was very successful. In his book, Abbott described 100 ways to perform technical tricks used by mediums of the time during their seances. Of course, the technical methods have improved immeasurably since those days, and the book is not as relevant today. After watching many seances, Abbott reached the conclusion that a substantial portion of mediums' work was nothing but trickery and deception. He compared mediums' work to a popular theatrical performance or a magic show in which the mediums created an illusion of communication with the dead by means of considerable sophistication and inventive ability.

In his book, Abbott described one of the seances he attended. The seance took place in a theater and the medium was a woman. After a mystical and highly impressive opening in which the woman presented her successes, her credentials, and her stories about communications with famous spirits from the past, the medium asked the audience to write down their questions on a piece of paper, to sign their names, and to keep the paper with them. The people in the audience wrote down their questions. During the entire time, the medium did not budge from the stage where she was sitting, and did not get up. After the people had finished writing down their questions, the medium concentrated, and, with the help of "the spirit who delivers messages to her," began, with what looked like an extremely high degree of concentration, to repeat aloud people's questions, quoting them word for word! After quoting every question, she answered it, and once more, the information came from the spirit "that communicated with her." The effect of this sight on the audience was tremendous. People nodded enthusiastically – "Yes, yes, that's right! That's exactly what I wrote, it's exactly the question I asked, she repeated it word for word!" These were the whispers that were heard among the audience. The medium was given thunderous applause.

However, one person in the audience was not prepared to have the wool pulled over his eyes. That was Abbott. By means of a good ability to read body language and facial expressions, it took him only a few minutes of sitting in the audience to identify several people who seemed "overly enthusiastic," their eyes sparkling as if they were playing a clever deception game. Even when the medium's assistant went through the audience, a thick notebook in hand, asking people to write down their questions on a page of the notebook, tearing out the page on which they had written the question and giving it to them, Abbott saw that there was something suspicious about the notebook. Moreover, he noticed that some of the people who had looked suspicious to him were more interested in what the unsuspecting person next to them was writing – if he used his own piece of paper and pen – than in writing a question of their own in the notebook. When the medium's assistant reached them, he could see a spark of recognition in their eyes.

Abbott put two and two together, and checked out his hypothesis after the performance. It was correct. With the help of "collaborators" who were planted in the audience, and of the assistant holding the pen and notebook, a fantastic deception was possible. Since most of the people came to the show without pen and paper, the assistant passed among them with notebook and pen. The pages of the notebook were atypical – they were wax pages. Every time one of the people wrote his question in the notebook and the assistant tore out the page and gave it to him, the marks of his writing remained clearly on the page beneath it and the assistant folded the pages back, as is normally done with a notebook, and this is how copies of the questions remained in his hand. Abbot did not take his eyes off of the notebook, which lay casually on the medium's table, this being the only place the remaining papers could be put on the stage. With a brief glance, the medium could look at the writing that appeared on the pages that were lying on the table, and discover the name of the writer and his question. There were people who took paper out of their bags and wrote their question on ordinary paper that belonged to them (some of them needed a pen, and Abbott noticed that it was always the same people who jumped up to offer a pen to whomever needed one, at the same time watching the question being written, as if they were waiting for their pen to be returned to them). The medium's assistants, both the ones who went through the audience with paper and pens and the ones that actually sat in the audience, hurried to glance at the questions, write them down, and pass them on to the medium at the first opportunity. The actions of the gang of assistants were perfectly coordinated.

Abbott stared at the audience in disbelief. Was it possible that no one saw the deception? He watched the excited and enthusiastic people.

"Perhaps they don't want to see the deception," he answered himself. His answer turned out to be accurate, since even after the exposure of the medium's deception, the stream of people who came to see her did not stop, and her income was not affected in the least.

The performances of that medium occurred in the first years of the 20th century. With time, the mediums' means of deception improved. The most well-known and renowned medium in Britain, William Roy, a person whose name was adorned with embellishments such as "Seer of the occult" and "Communicator with the world beyond" and other such superlatives, used far more sophisticated means to pull the wool over the eyes of his spectators. Roy, who was considered to be one of the greatest mediums ever, was the only person responsible for his downfall, and that was because of his greed for money. In 1955, Roy himself exposed his deceptions in a special interview granted by one of the newspapers in return for a huge sum of money. He received what he had always coveted, and all the means justified the fulfillment of this lust for money and fame. After his exposure, the British spiritualist association's newsletter, *The Two Worlds*, defined him as "the greatest fraud of all time."

In the interview, Roy exposed his sophisticated deception routine bit by bit. This is what he told the interviewer: "When the spectators reach the seance venue, my assistants ask them to leave their coats and bags in the entrance hall. I sit in the seance room at the end of a long corridor – this creates the impression that I cannot hear anything that is happening in the entrance hall – preparing for the tremendous mental burden of communicating with the spirit. I am hooked up to a small microphone, which picks up everything that the hidden microphones in the entrance hall pick up. The assistants ask for the names of the people who are entering in order to check which of the people who booked tickets for the performance have arrived and which have not. They don't write anything down, so as to avoid arousing suspicion and to ensure that the effect of my knowledge is more powerful. I pick up everything through my little microphone. One of the assistants leads the people through the corridor to the seance room. In most cases, the people are momentarily stunned by the darkness and the mysterious atmosphere I have created in the seance room. At the same time, one of my assistants goes over to the bags and starts to go through them. He is looking for every shred of information that he can find: bills, letters, telephone books, cards, and so on, and sometimes finds very personal objects in the coats and bags that give away something about the owner's character. After that, the people who 'provided' my assistant with the most unique information will be the 'stars' of the seance and will receiver far more attention during the seance. My assistant is hooked up to the microphone, and he slowly reads the information he found, and sometimes adds a personal impression. All of my assistants are very skillful. I myself can discover a great deal about the person just from looking at the expression on his face. Sometimes the assistants give me information from things that happen in the entrance hall, which can attest to certain aspects of the nature and behavior of the people. It's very simple..."

In the seance performance Roy gave, he would tell the people that the spirit who assisted him was Tunka, the spirit of a wise and mystical Indian.

After he had finished handing his secrets over to the journalist (he seemed very amused at the whole situation, and looked as if he had enjoyed exposing his deceptions and the way he "tricked people"), he boastfully added, "You see, even after this confession, which will create tremendous waves in the media, I can still fill many seance rooms and get people to believe me." Roy really boasted about his ability to deceive people. Thirteen years after that interview, which caused the entire spiritualist community to ostracize him, Roy appeared again, in 1968, as the medium "Silver," and convinced the audience that he was communicating with beings that lived on the planet Venus. This time, Roy used even more sophisticated tricks, benefiting from the rapidly developing technology.

According to spiritualist belief, during the communication with spirits, a phenomenon of etherylization is possible. This is a state in which the spirit draws ectoplasm from the medium and the seance participants in order to materialize. As we said before, this form is considered to be dangerous and rare, and mediums who succeed in "causing" the spirit with whom they are communicating to appear as a two- or three-dimensional image create an entity that can talk. Not many mediums use this method – and those who can do it earn a great deal of esteem.

For this reason, the phenomenon of etherylization has engendered a broad range of fraudulent methods and techniques. The ability to photograph in the dark by means of a good-quality flash put an end to the phenomenon of deception that many mediums used when creating the illusion of etherylization. In a number of cases, the "ethereal cloud" that emanated from the medium's mouth – a phenomenon that left the astounded spectators breathless – turned out to be a piece of transparent white fabric, or even white paper that the medium pulled out of his mouth and manipulated, until gradually it took the form of a human being who, in the darkness of the room, at some distance from the spectators, and with the help of quite a lot of dexterity, could look like a pale human figure, a "ghost."

No less interesting are those mediums who are not aware of their own deceptions. This is a fascinating phenomenon in and of itself that has still not been explained sufficiently clearly. The researcher of supernatural phenomena, the American, Prof. James Hyslop, studied a case of this type of medium. While holding the seance, the drums and bells that accompanied the medium's "communication" would play by themselves. The seance was held in total darkness. Hyslop asked the medium if he could photograph her while she was holding the seance, using a special camera that was adapted to heavy darkness. The medium agreed willingly and confidently. She herself was interested in the photograph and expressed a desire to see what went on in a seance from the side, and not as a person who served as "the link between the spirit world and this world." She was more surprised by the actual fakery when the photographs were developed. In the pictures, it was clear that the medium herself was the one who was playing the instruments with her own hands. The strangest thing of all was that she herself was not in the least aware of the fact that it was she who was playing the instruments!

# Haunted houses

There are many situations that look as if a house or a person is haunted by entities that are not of this world. It is important to differentiate between these situations and evil spirits, poltergeist activity, disturbances that stem from the use of a Ouija board and seances, and thought products. All these are liable to look like haunting by spirits, but are not.

The most widespread phenomenon is the one in which people feel that their house is "haunted." In such cases, the surroundings, namely the house, estate, or piece of land, assume the characteristics of the most energetically powerful event that occurred there. According to the theory, if a war of any kind, a battle, a murder or a brutal rape occurred on the tract of land upon which your house is built, you can, in theory, expect the deed to recur over and over again, like in a movie. This situation does not constitute a danger for people in the vicinity since the spirits themselves are not there, but "traces" of the event continue to exist in the place. Sometimes, the energetic pattern of the emotions of the participants in a battle or in a murder – usually the energetic pattern of the victim himself – continues to exist in the place.

Take, for example, the story that occurred in the environs of the Black Forest, which was the scene of the rape and murder of a young girl. When I was in the place, I could see the emotional pattern of the girl – the same emotional part of her aura that continued to exist in the place, as well as the course of the rape and strangulation as if I were watching a movie, without anything bad happening to me.

The only "dangerous" thing about these cases is the fear of the new inhabitants themselves, which is liable to create thought products of terror and fear that exist as separate entities in the house, even though they are the fruit of the thoughts of the inhabitants themselves. A parapsychologist who lives in the United States told me about a case in which he was called to a house in which the family saw a girl running down the passage every night, stopping at one of the doors, and whispering something to herself.

When the parapsychologist visited the house, he did not find any signs of a spirit in the place, but only the tiresome presence of her emotions connected to the event, which he succeeded in viewing exactly like a movie.

The sensation of entering a home or business, which is accompanied by a feeling of powerful discomfort without any visible reason for it, is familiar to many people. You may have experienced this feeling once or twice in your life. It is created when we "get onto" a frequency of energetic tracks leading to an event that occurred in the past. Sometimes, this event occurred only days or a few hours before you entered, and may not be as dramatic as a war or a murder, but rather an event in which a very powerful energetic pattern was sent into a room – a serious row, powerful anger, clear and strong sorrow. The tracks of these events continue to exist sometimes for several hours or days, in accordance with their intensity and with the intensity of the emotions that were evoked in it. Many people do not feel emotional-energetic tracks. In contrast, people who are very sensitive energetically are liable to "get onto" the frequency easily and feel great discomfort as a result.

As we said before, in most cases, there are no spirits present in the place – just emotional tracks. Sometimes, the event may or may not be physical, but rather an ongoing state of non-positive emotions of a certain kind. For example, if hostile or angry emotions existed in a certain place for a long time, even after the people who transmitted the hostile messages have moved out, it will still be possible to feel the energetic tracks of their emotions. In most of the cases, the energetic prints fade and pass with time. If the feeling is severe and disturbing (especially if you are a person with high energetic sensitivity), it is recommended that the place undergo energetic purification. This problem is mainly common in workplaces where there is a chain of workers with negative behavior or emotions who come to the workplace one after the other. Although the workers do not know one another, one of two things, or both, is liable to occur: there could be energy of anger, dispute, hostility and so on in the place, and the workers are liable to "link up" to this energy and act accordingly. The second thing is connected more to the managers of the place. If they, too, adapt themselves to the negative energetic pattern that exists in the place, they will attract workers who "respond" to the negative energy pattern of the workplace, a pattern that is "activated" by the managers who give it energetic power with non-positive energy. Fear and worries are also included in these emotions.

It is important to mention that if you feel great discomfort in a particular place, it need not be because it is "haunted." There could be many different reasons for this. Sometimes, energies that are not known to us – not necessarily non-positive ones – can cause us discomfort in a particular place, until we get used to it and adapt to it.

A situation of "haunted places" that is no less common is the visits of spirits. These are cases in which a spirit returns to a certain place in order to communicate. Although this can be a bit frightening, because of the fear of the unknown, in most cases these visits and communications are completely safe. In such cases, you must remember, first of all, that these spirits are not likely to be alien spirits, but rather the spirit of a person who died and was connected to you in some way – a relative or a friend. If you are engaged in channeling, you will have the opportunity to try to listen to the spirit's message, or to enable it to show you something it went through. Like a person who goes to a psychologist and bares his soul to him, a similar type of behavior exists with spirits. In order to liberate themselves of a certain event, they sometimes want to "talk" about it to a person who is strong energetically and knows how to listen. Another thing you must remember is that spirits do not have the real physical capability of harming you, and the only thing that can harm you is your own fear. For that reason, it is preferable not to be afraid in this type of situation, but rather to remain as calm as possible. If the fear is too strong, you may want to use one of the "defense" techniques. You can even ask the entity what it wants, and you can also ask it to move on and leave. Often, the entity leaves after it has been requested confidently and assertively to do so. If you feel any kind of guilt because of a feeling that this is the spirit of a familiar and loved person, but you do not want the uncomfortable feeling to continue, you can declare something like: "Please understand, I don't understand this situation; if you are …., I love you, but you have to go." If, in some cases (although it is rare), there is some kind of violence linked to the spirit that has appeared, you will have to seek the help of a parapsychologist or professional channeler who can communicate with the entity and make it go away and not come back.

The third most common case that can look like "supernatural haunting" could be the result of some kind of religious or occult objects that are in your home. In most cases, there is nothing to worry about when there is a sacred item in the house. Sometimes, however, various artificial elements crystallize in order to protect a sacred item of some kind. This is the perception behind "the curse of the Pharaohs," a powerful example of which we saw in the chapter dealing with Tutankhamen's curse. If you do not have a profound understanding of the sacred items and their use, it is preferable not to keep them at home. Old furniture and clothes, too, as well as old toys, can contain "energetic tracks." You can purify them with incense or with some other purification method, but if you continue to feel discomfort in their vicinity, it is preferable to simply get rid of them, because the energetic tracks they contain may not suit you. Objects that were purchased in stores that deal in black magic, even if they are not dangerous in themselves, can absorb the energy that emanates from the rest of the objects in the store, as well as from the people who touched them and worked with them. These people may have non-positive energies or energies that do not suit you. New objects generally do not carry energetic tracks, but if you feel any kind of energetic discomfort when in contact with them, you can purify them using one of the methods for purifying the aura. It is advisable to find out the background of old furniture, toys and clothes that you found or received. They may have a spurious genealogy. When purchasing old objects, it is always advisable to purify them with incense before bringing them into your home, and necklaces and strings of stones and crystals must always be purified before placing them on the body. A precious stone or crystal that has not been purified must not be worn or held, since the energetic absorption power of crystals is tremendous.

After describing the more common forms of haunting, we get to the real haunting of spirits that are "trapped" in the concrete dimension.

These spirits, and sometimes "parts of spirits," that is, a certain layer of the entity that was whole when it lived in the concrete world and was very "confused" at the time of death, undergo some kind of trauma or shock, or simply want to remain here in the concrete dimension. For whatever reason, that spirit, or part mind or part soul, was unable to "reach the light," return to the source, or be reincarnated. Those beings are "trapped" between the dimensions, or between the worlds, until they understand and learn how to release the pattern that is trapping them between the dimensions, or until they receive help and assistance for the transition. Genuine "hauntings" are extremely rare, since the nature of the soul is to long for the light and for linking up with the source. To remain tied to the concrete dimension after death is actually going against the rules of the universe. Spirits that are tied to the concrete dimension are liable to take energy through fear or by drawing life energy from energetically weak people, people who succumb to fear and live in it, or sick and physically weak people, as well as newborns. They may also learn how to draw energy from machines and appliances. Various parapsychologists claim that the longer the spirit remains tied to the earth, the more it learns numerous or powerful methods and ways of maneuvering energy for its benefit. In such cases, spirits that are tied to the concrete dimension and refuse to leave it are liable to be very dangerous.

As we said before, such cases are rare. A parapsychologist from the United States tells of an encounter with a spirit that was bound to the earth and learned to draw energy from a machine. It caused her such a powerful electric shock that she could not use her right hand for hours. Not all spirits that are bound to the earth are "evil." Most of them are simply confused, often because of the way they died. A spirit may become bound to the earth in a situation of fleeing from a murderer, for instance. The spirit is so busy trying to escape that it does not notice that it has died. This can create a situation in the haunted house in which the new inhabitants see a person fleeing in fear from a knife-wielding murderer every night, because the border between the worlds becomes thinner at night. Moreover, the magnetism of the entities spreads out and decreases during the day, and is recharged at night. These situations, as we said, are rare, but may occur. When a disturbing event of this type occurs, it is important to check the history of the house and of its environs.

If you are not skilled in communicating with spirits and you are not very strong energetically, physically and emotionally in parallel, you will have to contact a parapsychologist or channeler who is experienced in expelling and halting disturbances of this kind. If there are any young infants or sick people among the family members, action must be taken to get rid of the disturbance speedily.

# Evil spirits

There are many legends about evil spirits, and every single one of them is terrifying. The thought of the spirit of a dead person entering a living body is frightening, of course. For this reason, it is important to point out that this is an extremely rare occurrence that exists more in legends than in reality, even though it does exist. The ordinary, healthy person walking innocently down the street has no reason to fear evil spirits. These things don't just happen, and there is no point losing sleep over it or eating oneself up worrying about it.

In order to create the circumstances in which some kind of entity is liable to come and take possession of a living body, the person has to reach such a profound level of depression and despair that his lack of spiritual vitality causes him to surrender his life force to a certain entity that can then take possession of him. Vital, happy and calm people have no reason in the world to fear things like that, since the basic energy of happiness serves as a very powerful shield against all unnatural extrasensory disturbance. This point is important especially for people who engage extensively in channeling. They must remember always "to be happy," so as not to attract extrasensory disturbances that exploit sadness and depression in order to obtain energies.

As we said previously, in order for some kind of entity to take possession of the body of a living person, that person must feel great helplessness and an extreme lack of self-worth. Signs of despair and surrendering life force are a lack of physical and mental strength, self-doubt, a lack of emotional stability, illness, alcohol and drug abuse, harming oneself, self-hatred, and so on. Of course, conditions like this rarely incur evil spirits, since the latter are themselves rare. However, in any event, such conditions tend to endanger the person from the spiritual point of view. Ninety-nine percent of people suffering from such syndromes will never suffer from evil spirits, but in most cases, a person who does suffer from an evil spirit will show those signs and emotional and thought patterns of that kind before possession by evil spirits becomes possible. After the entity takes possession of the body of the person and begins to manipulate his consciousness, these signs become extremely severe. In most cases, the entity is "sucking energy" from a low energy level. The entity exploits the person's feeling of a lack of self-worth. On certain levels, the person is in such extreme thrall to his despair and to his pessimistic perception of life that he cannot fight against the entity that has entered his body at all. At other times, the person is completely unaware of what is happening until the mental manipulation begins to occur.

Another way in which a person is liable to attract an evil spirit is by inviting an entity that he cannot control into his body. This situation occurs when an unskilled person, who has not learned enough about the energetic arts in which he is dabbling, begins to channel and tries to "play" at being a medium, or engages in black magic. People who practice black magic and voodoo tend to be harmed in such matters because of their view that arousing the entity will endow them with the power they long for, instead of learning how to use the power they have, invoke it and increase it, in order to change their lives for the better. Probably, when a person opts for dark paths in order to fulfill his wishes and desires, the universe also responds to the dark way he has chosen. In such cases, since the spiritual process of the person has not reached a sufficient level of perfection, and his mind and soul are not purified and distilled, the person cannot see what kind of entity he has aroused. Instead of channeling with a positive and supportive entity, which will serve as a spiritual guide, he arouses an entity from a low energetic level that is seeking ways of sucking energy, and then that amateur does not know how to get the entity to leave. Of course, according to the energetic laws of the universe, the entity is supposed to leave and is not supposed to take possession of an individual's body. But the amateur who engages in things that are beyond his comprehension tends to become frightened and anxious, cannot think clearly, and sometimes does not have the tools to deal with the situation he has gotten into, either. Feelings of anxiety, fear, and lack of self-worth develop, and enable the entity to have a tighter grip on the person.

Various parapsychologists think that wizards who engage in black magic have the ability to arouse and catalyze such situations by exhausting the person and creating a situation in which the person surrenders the power of his belief and his spiritual strength to them. For these or other reasons, it should be known that practicing black magic, as well as visiting wizards who practice black magic, is not advisable, to put it mildly. Every action that can be performed by means of black magic can be performed by means of white magic, healing, and work on spiritual self-awareness. In contrast to black magic, however, these ways of coping lead to growth, prosperity and development, and do not demand a heavy and dangerous price from the person who practices them. After the wizard who engages in black magic succeeds in getting the person to surrender his strength to him (surrendering the strength occurs as a result of the faith the individual has in the wizard), the wizard is liable to send some kind of entity to haunt the individual. Having said that, the success rate is generally low.

In places in the world where the use of voodoo and black magic is widespread, it is first of all important not to make contact with or visit a person who practices black magic, and second, to pay attention to your surroundings and to the people whom you befriend. It is not advisable, to say the least, to live in the vicinity of a person who practices black magic. This situation does not constitute a real danger of an evil spirit, but if a tourist who is living near a wizard of this type becomes ill, or suffers from depression and despair, the energetic waste that is emitted from the wizard's actions is liable to make his situation even worse, and he may find himself harassed by various entities that are emitted by the spells or invited into the surroundings by the wizard.

Another point that is important to mention in such cases is that in most of the places in which black magic is widespread, the local people tend not to talk about such matters at all. For this reason, you should keep your ears and eyes open, since even local friends will mostly not give you any information about it (because of the belief that even speaking about such things is dangerous). You must be careful and pay attention when making contact with people, rely on your inner intuition, and fortify yourself energetically by means of defenses, prayer, or linking up to the power of the universe and to the known guides of the soul.

Wizards who practice black magic are liable to possess the ability to link up to the physical body of others in an attempt to "cheat" death or in order to control somebody. The Western occult tradition relates to this like it related to an evil spirit. Some of the New Age movements have created a somewhat romantic aura around this topic. When various people claimed that there are entities that create a kind of "contract" with the individual in whose body they reside, they often claim that these are beings from another world, "aliens" that have come here in order to illuminate human beings' awareness. In most cases, there is no basis to these claims, since positive and enlightened entities will find other ways to channel with human beings (via voluntary channeling of the channeler with the entities from another world, for instance), and the idea of the control of a person's soul or body is fundamentally non-positive.

It is important to deal with cases of evil spirits (and again, I will mention that they are extremely rare – I have never come across such a case personally, nor have most of the parapsychologists and healers I have worked with) in the most professional manner, using the services of experienced people with a mature ability to diagnose, as well as a great deal of in-depth experience in the extrasensory realm and in esoteric sciences. It is important to be careful of people who claim that they have the power to perform "long-distance exorcism," since long-distance exorcism is an extremely dangerous business both to the person who is suffering from some kind of disturbance that resembles an evil spirit (it is important to know that this disturbance can even derive from some kind of psychiatric illness, such as paranoid schizophrenia and so on!), and to the people in the vicinity of the person who claims to be a "long-distance exorcist." In this type of exorcism, the required control properties do not exist, and the situation is liable to deteriorate or endanger other people as well as the person who is suffering from the evil spirit or from what looks like an evil spirit. Not all exorcism ceremonies are dangerous or violent. Sometimes the exorcism can pass fairly quietly and quickly, when the entity understands the spiritual and energetic force it is facing.

Many parapsychologists insist that the carrier of the evil spirit participate in the ceremony, since no other person is capable of bolstering the possessed person's will power, and a strong will is required on his part to get rid of the disturbance. If the possessed person's will power does not become stronger and improve, and therefore his will to live and his emotional and mental state too, the exorcism is liable to succeed only temporarily, and the situation may to return to what it was before, since the possessed individual remains exposed and weak. Together with the action of exorcism, there is a need to purify the residence and the immediate surroundings of the person, as well as his personal possessions, profoundly and powerfully. All this can only be performed by a very powerful, clean and pure healer who possesses stable and strong mental powers.

# Poltergeist

The traditional definition of the poltergeist is a "joking" or "noisy" spirit that settles in a particular home and disturbs the inhabitants by making noises, lifting and dropping objects, producing irritating knocking sounds, hiding objects and making them disappear, and sometimes even bringing objects! There are friendly forms of poltergeists, but most of their forms are annoying and unwanted. There are many different opinions about the reasons for poltergeist activity. The poltergeist may be a hostile and capricious spirit that harasses the members of the household, or the spirit of a relative who is attempting to communicate with the residents of the house. In many cases, the poltergeist may be a "leftover" from a seance or from the use of a Ouija board, or an entity that was summoned by a medium or a wizard and does not want to leave.

Frequently, the activity of the poltergeist focuses on a particular member of the household by trying to attract his attention or harass him. Many parapsychologists do not believe in poltergeist activities in and of themselves, and try to check whether there is the unwitting activity of a very powerful person behind the activities.

Poltergeist activity can be the result of unacknowledged or unexamined extrasensory ability. This does not mean that poltergeist activity is just in the sufferers' minds. There is real supernatural activity that is linked to this form of poltergeist activity. However, it can come from the individual's very powerful brain. For instance, when a person who has powerful extrasensory abilities of this kind but is not aware of his abilities gets into a state of rage, an object may go flying in the room. If that person is sad and wants to "empty his mind," the TV set may suddenly burst into flames. Few people understand that this is their own action, even though in many cases, the action is indeed a result of the person's emotions. Instead of understanding this, many may suppose that the incident is a figment of their imagination only, ignore it, or "blame" it on spirits. The activity is not necessarily violent or malicious. It is simply meant to be a movement of an object in the room toward the individual. Such cases may be the result of natural and powerful telekinesis, and therefore the first thing that must be checked is whether there is a person with these powers in the house. The event prior to the mysterious moving of the object must be checked out, and it is important to see whether one of the people present experienced a strong emotional state before the event.

One of the theories concerning poltergeist activity, which is very similar to the situation described above, is that this activity occurs after a tragic event in the person's life. According to this theory, in a state of collapsing under the pain of a tragedy or trauma, the person is liable to send that traumatic memory out of his body, which creates a thought product without his being aware of it. The memory, of course, cannot really leave the body, but instead of that, hides in the person's ethereal or emotional body. Over time, this thought product takes on a kind of life of its own. It is nourished on the person's energy. This energy serves as what parapsychologists call the "shadow self" until a particular incident becomes a trigger for the release of the shadow self. Often, children who experienced a tragic event and coped with it by "sending" the event outside of them, see an outburst of poltergeist activity when they reach sexual maturity, when their psychosexual energy is very high. Of course, not everyone who undergoes a traumatic or tragic event reacts in this way. Ignoring problems is a common form of coping, and sometimes ignoring helps to get rid of problems temporarily until such time as the mind can deal with it in a better way. Sometimes "shadow selves" emerge. The shadow self is liable to be very powerful. When it obtains sufficient energy, it can take on a life of its own, without its creator's knowledge. Sometimes, the shadow self causes fear and anxiety in the person that is nourishing it energetically. This thought product must preserve and nourish itself energetically, and creating fear is a way of obtaining the energy it needs. Since they begin to exist through their own devices, they no longer need the constant presence of their creator for their survival.

I heard a story of this kind from a channeler who helps purify houses of the presence of poltergeists. In that case, a full and visible "clone" of a boy was present in the house. It could throw things in the house, slam doors, walk through the house at night and even get into bed with other people and mess up the bedclothes. The "producer" of the poltergeist was a sweet, shy child, who was completely non-violent. The way to deal with the problem was to help the boy by using hypnosis technique to raise up the trauma from the depths of his consciousness and release it. After a long process, the boy was liberated from the tiresome shadow self by accepting it.

In cases of poltergeist activity, people's suggestions of expelling the entity from the home should be taken with a grain of salt. If this really is a thought product that has been produced by the person himself, what is the point of trying to destroy something that is the product of that person's thoughts or emotions?

A method that is used by some of the people who deal with such matters is to turn the shadow self into a part of the person after releasing the trauma, so that the person becomes whole again. Part of the treatment is of course coping with the tragedy or the trauma that caused the creation of the shadow self in order to insure that the person does not have to cope with the same situation again.

# The powers of thought

Human beings have two abilities whose importance and power they do not always acknowledge: free will and the ability to create. We create the whole day though, even if we are not always aware of it. We create thoughts, intentions, emotions, actions, and so on. Regrettably, many people do not understand the power of thought and its capacity for truly physical creation.

We create various formations by means of our thoughts and intentions, and these sometimes have a life of their own. What we create begins to take shape in our energy field; in other words, the beginning of its existence is on the spiritual level. The traditional saying, that the person creates ministering angels and angels of destruction out of vain speech, is this very appropriate. When our mind and emotions are focused on something, that thing begins to materialize in the spiritual energy field of our aura. In many cases, the focus is not sufficiently constant and sharp, and what we create with our thoughts, emotions, and intention passes and disappears. When the focus is sufficiently strong and consistent, or has existed for a long time, a thought formation is created.

Thought formations appear in any conceivable form. They can be transient or enduring. If they receive enough power, that is, ongoing focus, they may leave our energetic field (aura) by acquiring the form of the power of thought, of thought energy that can exist in an almost material way. One of the well-known ways in which thought formations are realized is expressed in the various diseases and ailments of the body. Similarly, thought formations can be realized as events in our lives, various situations and cases that are created by the power of our thought and have assumed their own existence. They can exist in the form of relationships with people who are really amazingly suited to the thought formations we created, positive or less positive, and they can sometimes create a situation that frightens the individual or makes him anxious. For instance, if a person constantly worries that his home will be broken into when he is not there, he sparks the idea, which takes on a momentary shape in his aura, on the spiritual level. If he continues to "feed" that fear, give it additional energy, focus on it, or think about it anxiously for a certain amount of time after he leaves his home, he unconsciously creates a certain reality. In that reality, he is liable to come home and find that his house has been broken into. Sometimes, when the universe itself is not interested in "cooperating" in this matter, and the person's thought is not sufficiently focused on the idea of a break-in but rather on the idea of material loss, he may well land up in a situation in which certain possessions inexplicably "disappear," as if someone had stolen them. That same person creates a kind of warning light around his house or possessions, which is liable to attract casual disturbances.

An American clairvoyant describes the situation from the point of view of her extrasensory vision, when she relates to people's fear of accidents: "I see cars driving along the road, and they look absolutely fine physically. However, on the etheric level, they are shattered and damaged. The prophecy that shows the destruction of the car looks like a huge torch. The torch beckons other cars that are attracting a similar event."

The two instances above have been greatly simplified in order to serve as examples. Thought activity tends to be more complex, but works in a very similar way to that described in the examples. Everything first begins to materialize in the etheric aura prior to its occurrence. In our thought, we create different realities all the time. Sometimes, the person does not need to focus strongly on the idea that his house will be broken into. All he has to do is assume a "victim's" awareness. When the person thinks like a victim, he will find himself in situations of being a victim. As we have said, this is expressed on all levels of life. This can be seen clearly in relationships. If you look at your personal relationships, or those of others, you can find cases in which you, or someone close to you, tend to establish relationships with people with disturbing properties or personality traits, in a truly serial fashion. You can find girls who are cheated on by every man they go out with, or always have problems or hostility with the man's mother, or complain that the men they date "never listen to them." Likewise, there are men who are repeatedly dumped by women, or frequently date girls who "only care about how much money the guy has in the bank," and so on. When you listen to complaints of this type from friends and relatives, you can see the pattern that runs like a connecting thread from one relationship to the next. This is the person's thought pattern or belief pattern regarding a particular situation, which is being expressed in a concrete way in his life. This is what these people attract in an etheric manner, and this type of reality will continue being attracted to them until they change their thought and belief pattern, the way they relate to the world and to life, and the way they process their emotions.

It is our free choice to change our reality to our liking, whether we are aware of this or not. Whatever we place in the center of our focus is what we will create and realize.

We can see a strong manifestation of the power of thought formations in the theory that maintains the poltergeist to be the embodiment of emotions that have been "expelled" from the body because of the difficulty in accepting and processing them. As a result, the "shadow of the self," which functions as a poltergeist, is created. In this case, we can see how the "victim" is actually the creator of the "nuisance." All the feelings, angers, and sorrow, as well as the subconscious violent actions with which the "victim" does not permit himself to cope, come to the fore in the shadow of his self.

Thought formations can be created consciously or unconsciously. Unconsciously, the thought pattern may be created by a mother protecting her child. The power of her love and her desire to protect her child are likely to create a thought formation. When the thought formation receives sufficient energy, it can actively receive properties of protection, and may even be felt as a "guardian angel." The power of the mother's thought and her intentions may cause the thought formation to turn into "power of thought" and behave in a protective way toward the child.

Consciously, thought formations are used by people who meditate, pray, and make lists of objectives and target dates to achieve, as well as by healers and wizards. Every time we focus, we create a thought formation. If the thought formation receives enough power, and we do not thwart it with contradictory or opposing thought formations, it will be realized materially, whether it is positive or negative. When a critical mass of people creates a particular thought formation, it will be materialized and manifested in the world, either as a wave of awareness, or as actions and events.

Sometimes, people are liable to create dangerous thought formations that affect their surroundings, especially if the surroundings contain people who are not aware of the non-positive aspect of the power of thought. People with psychological problems occasionally suffer from organic diseases that constitute a trigger for the creation of thought formations that cause supernatural activity.

Wizards and healers often create thought formations that they endow with sufficient energy to turn them into power of thought. The power of thought realizes the will of the healer or wizard if it is correctly formed and transmitted. People who can heal by the touch of their hands generally have such power of thought that is expressed physically. The power of thought that is created by a person with spiritual strength can be used for good or for evil.

Wizards also have the power to create "artificial elements," similar to the way in which priests created various gods and charged them energetically by making sacrifices. The gods that were created in this manner mainly consisted of one element, as opposed to man, who consists of four elements (air, fire, water, and earth).

Today, too, there are people who create artificial elements for various purposes. A clairvoyant, who was in the habit of creating artificial elements in order to protect her home, tells the following story:

"I found the artificial elements to be extremely effective in protecting my home. I created a number of them to protect the main gates, and others to patrol the estate. When we built the house, I created a gate and afterwards I forgot about it by mistake. The artificial element received the instruction to guard the house at any cost. One gloomy night, shortly after we moved into the new house, I was standing in the back yard, barbecuing meat, when a large, awful creature came running up behind me. It scared the living daylights out of me, until I remembered that I was the one who had created the monster! I rechanneled its energies and sent it on its way. Since it is an artificial element originating from water, it tends to be extremely strong when it's raining or when the weather is foggy. It is almost imperceptible energetically on sunny days and in hot dry weather, but in the evening, when it's foggy or rainy, its presence can be strongly felt."

The creation of artificial elements is neither recommended nor desirable, since it is not always possible to control their energies and actions. Moreover, there are already enough supernatural disturbances in the world without us creating more of them. The above clairvoyant created the thought formation consciously, but people who fear the extrasensory and the supernatural are liable to create powerful thought formations unconsciously by focusing on their fears. Often, therefore, when the person senses the presence or disturbance of any kind of "entity," this entity is likely to be his thought formation. For this reason, it is important not to go too far with extrasensory activity when the soul is not strong and pristine enough, since unpleasant things are liable to be created, and the person must know his soul and his limitations. However, when we are aware of thought formations that are created easily by our imagination, we can destroy them just as easily – with our imagination. It is even possible to change them into something innocuous with our power of thought. When the person finds himself troubled or attacked by something that is the fruit of his imagination, he should focus on it and imagine it as something that can be controlled – like a small kitten, for instance. At this point, the artificial elements or bothersome powers of thought usually disappear, since their original intention has been destroyed. If the thought formation objects to being destroyed by the imagination, it is liable to be, in many cases, an artificial element. In these cases, the help of an experienced healer with extremely powerful thought focus should be sought.

# Channeling

What is channeling?

The word "channeling" has become charged. There are many definitions for it, most of which refer to an "external" entity that speaks through a human host. Such a narrow definition is frightening and engenders a negative feeling in many people. In fact, however, channeling takes all kinds of forms, and many of them refer to inner channeling, such as channeling with the soul, with the soul guides, with the superego, and so on, which are not involved in mediumistic activity.

Those are the types of channeling we will relate to further on.

Channeling is not necessarily what people think it is. Millions of people channel on a daily basis – without even being aware that they are doing so, and they take it for granted. They do not identify the origins of their creative ideas, their abilities to charm, or the rest of their exceptional creative abilities. Frequently, lofty creative insights come from channeling!

The throat chakra is one of the ways in which the spiritual fingerprint can be manifested in the physical world. Music, dance, art, love – every expression of the soul can be channeling. Our entire lives in this world constitute a possibility to channel with the soul that we are, whose knowledge and experience are tremendous.

Heeding inner voices is channeling. So is listening to the voices of "the broad I" – the I that is beyond the entity that we know personally – a spiritual entity that is constantly interacting with other spiritual forces in the universe. (Then, in fact, there is no clear delineation between that entity and what is known as "others." All knowledge is open to it!)

All knowledge is already inside us. When we accept ourselves and the voices inside us, we are channeling.

We must not confuse channeling with spiritualism or mediumism. When we channel, our intention is not to channel with "the dead" or seek their help or guidance. Life on the astral plane is not omniscient, and it also contains fears, opinions, properties and characteristics of a soul in a body, just like here. Often, it lacks the superior perspective with which a soul guide from a high level is gifted. The aim of channeling is to attract and channel with the soul guide, a spiritual guide that has reached the peak of his spiritual objective, and supports the person's spiritual development and health on all levels.

A high spiritual guide encourages the person to find personal solutions to problems, and never convinces the person to relinquish his power by compelling or forcing the person to do something, simply because he said so. He does not order the person to perform tasks or missions, does not criticize him – and, conversely, does not flatter his ego. Having said that, he may well congratulate the person on his spiritual development and help him exploit his potential to the full.

Spiritual guides tend to be attracted to people with a clear purpose, people who are interested in fostering peace, abundance, and love in their lives as well as in the lives of the people around them, and people who are sincerely concerned about humanity and the earth. The principle of "birds of a feather flock together" is clearly manifested here.

Channeling can help people who create, healers, and artists. In principle, it can be of assistance in any creative project or project that is based on love and caring. Nevertheless, even if a person does not find a vocation by which to live his life, the very fact that he desires and longs for spirituality can attract a helpful spiritual guide to him.

## Channeling with soul guides

Every one of us gets help and support from entities from other dimensions – guardian angels, soul guides, and twin souls that want to see us accomplish our objective in life.

Channeling of this type is not always clear and obvious. Many channelers do not know the name of the entity that channels with them, nor do they speak to it face to face, but rather simply receive the messages and the visions. Much of the channeling occurs during meditation, and all it takes is being aware, listening attentively, and remembering the message or the vision afterwards. The guides themselves may change according to the person's spiritual development. Every technique of calming the brain (even washing the floor – mindlessly) can cause us to make the transition to the channeling state.

Many channelers relate that they made no effort whatsoever to channel with their soul guide or with the entity that channels with them. It just happened, during meditation, creation, or even while washing the dishes.

While channeling with soul guides or guardian angels can be useful to spiritual development in many ways, opening the spiritual door to channeling is not free of danger. After the experience of channeling with entities from other dimensions, there can also be channeling with less desirable entities that are liable to upset the person's emotional balance, especially when this balance is precarious to begin with. If you do not engage in profound soul and spiritual work, it would be better for you not to try to channel voluntarily and with prior intent.

In addition to a great deal of faith in meditation, the channeler must also watch his diet, his emotional state, and his mental attitude, and he must be prepared to cope with the ego problems that almost invariably crop up during conscious channeling with entities from other dimensions.

If you have the desire to channel, you must learn to display sensitivity toward your inner beliefs and how they tend to serve as a filter for the information that reaches you. You will also have to be aware of your subconscious and your subconscious urges, the forces that motivate you, your fears and anxieties – since they are liable to attract certain types of entities, or sabotage or distort the information that reaches you.

Some people maintain that everyone has on the average five spiritual guides from other dimensions, each of which aims to help us with a particular and specific vocation that we have to realize in our lifetime.

The guides help us discover new aspects of our soul, serve as spiritual protectors and guards, and assist us in our creative endeavors.

The guides may be entities that are linked to us from previous lives, a deceased close friend or family member, entities from other planets, and sometimes even a twin soul that does not exist on the physical plane. Similarly, the spiritual guide may be a spiritual entity with great spiritual power, such as a rabbi, a shaman, and so on.

Certain guides remain with the person his entire life, while others stay for many years and then leave.

The guides speak to the person and channel with him in many ways. They can channel with him via thought – a kind of "little voice" the person hears in his head. Often, they speak to the person either directly or in signs and symbols, via dreams. Meditations and alternative states of consciousness also constitute a broad basis for channeling with guides and with entities. They can channel with us via ostensibly "simple" symbols and signs! My soul guide tends to channel with me via animals. I don't know when this began, but I noticed it when I began to study and receive information about the symbolism of animals. Nowadays, I can tackle a certain question – generally a creative one – and a certain animal will appear in my house (an insect or a bird, for instance), and sometimes even an animal that I would not expect to see in the region where I live. The animal's symbol usually constitutes an astoundingly accurate answer to the question I was grappling with, and sometimes presents me with an exceptional and unique answer that had not occurred to me. Your guide also uses various "coincidences" for channeling. All you have to do is look and listen carefully.

The guides channel powerfully via various artistic expressions, since at those moments we link up to our superego, through which the guide or entity channels with us. Painting, writing, dance, acting, and so on can be accompanied and supported by channeling, or constitute a trigger to channeling. In certain cases, the channeling situation can be so powerful that the person begins to write or paint automatically. The messages that are conveyed via this kind of channeling can be innovative, inventive, and profound, and lead to unique creation that surprises even the channeler himself.

Soul guides move between the dimensions, and at night when we are asleep, they can "teach" us new information and insights. Most of these cannot materialize physically, since they are pure energy, but they can show us some kind of image, to the best of their ability.

## Channeling with crystals

For many years, crystals have served as effective tools for channeling with divine entities, with the "superego," with the soul, and with soul guides in order to receive answers and insights, and achieve growth and personal development. Crystals themselves have many exceptional properties such as releasing blockages, healing various layers, predicting the future, and a large range of other uses. There are numerous types of crystals, but among them are crystals that are especially appropriate for channeling, and contain a wealth of insights and information.

According to popular belief, there was once a large continent, ancient Atlantis. The people of this continent were exceptionally developed in comparison to nowadays, and they were profoundly acquainted with the secrets of the universe and of the crystals. They developed various methods for channeling cosmic power by means of crystals so as to derive benefit for both practical and spiritual purposes from it. Using the crystals, the people of Atlantis communicated telepathically with various higher entities, from whom they received information about this and other worlds. The reason why Atlantis was destroyed was that some of its inhabitants began to use the crystals' information and power for personal, selfish, and distorted purposes, instead of using them for their true purposes – peace, love, health, and spiritual development. According to the belief, before Atlantis was razed, its sages requested that the vast knowledge be preserved – knowledge that was more valuable than gold – in order that it could reach the appropriate people at the right time, many years after the destruction of the continent. However, those same sages knew that if they wrote down or preserved the knowledge overtly, there was a danger that once again it would fall into the hands of the wrong people, who would use it for selfish and exploitative purposes. For this reason, the Atlantis sages developed methods of programming the crystals and storing the ancient knowledge inside them.

Crystals have a tremendous preservative power, and today, many of those programmed crystals, which store portions of this wondrous knowledge, exist among us. Of course, there is no clear or obvious way or method of discovering them or of knowing what knowledge each one contains. This ensures that the appropriate people are the ones to link up to the knowledge-bearing crystals, and receive insights and information from them through spiritual work and channeling. These crystals are special, and the only way to discover if they are the ones in which the unique knowledge was stored is by working with them. However, in principle, by means of any crystal and good, sincere channeling work, it is possible to link up to the crystal and discover many things about ourselves and the world around us. Crystals can be used for developing the intuition, helping create mental and physical equilibrium, and increasing the chances of having prophetic dreams and receiving divine insights. Every person who is attracted to crystals and senses a connection to them can use them to expand his awareness and his spiritual development. However, it must be remembered clearly and explicitly that their use is permitted for pure purposes only, because if anyone uses them for any purpose that is not pure and humane, he risks directing the tremendous power that is stored in them against himself.

In order to begin channeling with crystals, the person must first find a crystal to which he links up intuitively. For channeling purposes, clear quartz generators, amethyst, sodalite, selenite, smithsonite, apatite, and smoky quartz are highly recommended, but each person must be open to sensing which crystal suits his purposes. By means of spiritual openness and luck, the appropriate person may get hold of a crystal that contains various inscriptions from ancient civilizations, or is suitable for tuning in to divine beings. There are also special crystals called "teacher" crystals, and the fortunate person who encounters one of these will have a faithful guide for the rest of his spiritual development. He must know and understand, however, that this kind of crystal – and many crystals in general – has a tendency to move on to another person when it has completed its mission with him, so that it can disseminate and impart its knowledge to many people. For this reason, the person must understand that the crystal does not belong to him, even if he purchased it. He has to know that he must release it at the appropriate time. If he tries to hold on to it after its mission has been completed and after he has received hints that he must release it, there is a great chance that the crystal will simply mysteriously "disappear," get lost, or somehow make its way to another person.

# Tools for spiritual work

## Improving extrasensory abilities

Some people think that only special types are endowed with supernatural abilities, and that these abilities are innate, a cosmic gift granted to exceptional individuals only. In truth, however, we all have various supernatural abilities, and the sixth sense is not only the gift of exceptional people, but is accessible to each one of us. An in-depth look at everyday life is likely to reveal how we use our sixth sense, sometimes incidentally. Those times the phone rings, and you know exactly who is at the other end of the line, are not at all rare. Similarly, there is the widespread experience of thinking of someone – remembering him suddenly – and shortly afterwards receiving a letter or an unexpected call from him.

Telepathy is an "extrasensory" sense that has been satisfactorily preserved in many people. I have known many people who did not use any of their extrasensory senses for a long time, but after they began to develop their awareness and their extrasensory abilities, they managed to discover extrasensory talents within them relatively easily. Each one of us is able to develop the extrasensory senses that are within us – inside the code of our soul – and are not something external. To this day, in my experience, anyone who truly began to live a more aware life and make an effort to develop his awareness and his extrasensory abilities, developed one or more of his extrasensory abilities fully.

Of course, there are people who find it easier than others to develop their extrasensory abilities. Some of them have a natural ability that was not repressed during childhood, and was allowed to develop naturally. Some are people who engaged in profound work on their awareness, sometimes without any conscious effort, but rather because of a need that sprang from a difficult life – a situation that compelled them "to take themselves in hand" and peer into the depths of their soul. By gazing into the depths of their soul, by learning to balance the unharmonious ones, their extrasensory abilities also begin to reveal themselves gradually and naturally.

Because of what we have read in books and seen in movies and on TV, there is a general belief that extrasensory abilities are "mediumistic abilities" that "land" on the person from out of the blue and cause him to become a mouthpiece for the spirits or to switch the chips so that he wins a fortune in a casino, and so forth. In fact, it is true extrasensory ability that helps him know intuitively what is right or not right for him, discover and recognize his vocation in life, and have the ability – that cannot be explained "logically" – to turn his life into an ideal existence filled with the satisfaction and self-realization he dreamed of.

The purpose of the extrasensory abilities that each one of us possesses is not to perform flashy wonders in front of capacity audiences, to exorcise demons, or to solve murder cases by holding an object that belonged to the victim. Of course, those abilities have their place in the world, but they are the objective of the people who are destined to demonstrate them, and not everyone's aim in life is to be Uri Geller. In contrast, everyone has the obligation to be a healer – his own healer, the healer of his body, mind, and spirit – so that he can repair his life in this incarnation and realize his vocation. This vocation can be anything you can think of, from being an activist in an environmental movement to establishing and developing a happy and harmonious domestic life.

To this end, the first step toward using extrasensory abilities, which are an absolutely natural part of the code of our soul, is also the first step leading to their natural development. These two parameters support each other in a perfect circular manner. It is the step toward discovering our vocation, repairing our lives, and realizing ourselves.

The mental processes that the person has to undergo in order to realize his physical, mental, and spiritual potential are the same processes that lead to spiritual enlightenment. The extrasensory abilities that are revealed in the person as he follows the path of his soul in order to realize his vocation differ greatly from person to person. Sometimes, they will not be as "glamorous" as Uri Geller's abilities, for instance, part of whose vocation in the world was to let people see the spiritual potential that exists in them. However, they are specific abilities that support the person while he realizes his vocation in life.

As an example, we can examine the various talents with which people are endowed, and see how extrasensory abilities support them.

If part of a person's vocation in life is to be a writer, for instance, he may discover that when his extrasensory abilities develop, they make him strongly "intuitive," able to receive intuitive messages that turn his written creation into something significant, both for the repair of his soul and for the benefit of mankind. He may, for example, discover channeling abilities, automatic writing abilities, and so on. A person who discovers that his soul yearns to paint may discover that meditative painting, or "channeled creation," is developing in him. Concomitantly, the emphasis is being placed on two crucial things in his life: developing his extrasensory abilities (from which it is not possible to separate the work on the awareness of body, mind, and spirit), and following his path of destiny – investing his energy in his creative talent. A person whose vocation in life is to build a warm and loving family unit, thus increasing mental and spiritual health in the world, and to go on increasing the critical mass of true maternal/paternal and conjugal love, may discover, for instance, that his abilities to be naturally empathetic, as a **....?** have become very strong, because they will support the realization of his vocation. A person whose function is to raise the world's consciousness about the plight of animals, for instance, may well discover, upon developing his extrasensory abilities and his spiritual awareness, that he can channel with animals easily and naturally. (Consciousness-raising does not necessarily mean making speeches in the United Nations, but rather increasing the critical mass of people who are aware of a certain matter by adding "one soul", that of the particular person, to the general awareness of the subject.) And so on.

In other words, our extrasensory abilities are not separate from our entity and our aim in life. They constitute an inseparable part of the realization of our vocation in the world. Similarly, it is impossible to separate the development of the extrasensory ability from the work on balancing mind and body, because only a well-balanced body, mind, and spirit can make correct and superior use of the extrasensory abilities. There are people who do not work on their soul in depth, and instead permit it to be an inhibiting factor (by constantly harboring anger, sadness, negative beliefs in life, and so on). When these people are gifted with extrasensory abilities, they are liable to cause a great deal of damage to themselves and to the world because they are unable to channel their energies correctly. As an example, we can look at the conduct of various mediums who are indeed gifted with a powerful extrasensory ability, but since they exploit it to inflate their ego, they have to create an illusion in which it is far more powerful or eccentric than it really is. They fall into the trap that they themselves have set in order to continue inflating their ego with "I am the great, powerful medium who can make ghosts appear in front of people's eyes." Of course, the damage that is caused to people, to the spiritual awareness in the world, and to the medium himself is enormous.

For this reason, before beginning to develop your extrasensory talents, you must stop and think: What is my aim in developing them? What do I expect to get out of the fact that they are stronger? Do I intend to use them to increase and deepen my spiritual awareness, or to bolster and inflate my unbalanced ego? Will I use them as a helpful tool for discovering my vocation in life and as a support for finding the various ways of repairing my soul and realizing my vocation, or will I use them for creating devious means of achieving aims that do not in the least resemble my basic and vocational aim?

# Finding one's vocation in life

This is undoubtedly an eye-catching title. Who doesn't want to find his vocation in life? We all hope to go to sleep at night and wake up in the morning saying, "That's it! That's my vocation in life. Now I know."

That is certainly possible, but it does not always happen that way. The path to finding our vocation in life pauses at an extremely important point – the **desire** to find our vocation in life. This involves taking personal responsibility for our lives (and that is a serious matter – understanding that we create the reality of our lives, and no longer blaming other people or the universe for things that happen in our lives) and the decision to seek and find the path along which we were meant to realize our existence in this world. The development and use of extrasensory abilities can be extremely powerful in helping us find our vocation in life. However, these insights may not come to us overnight, either, but rather little by little, step by step, just like the realization of our vocation itself occurs in little steps, and not in one day. Even if the person discovers that his vocation in life is to establish a harmonious and love-filled family life, the discovery of his vocation will not lead to his being married and father of three within a week, with no obstacle or deep spiritual work along his path. Having said this, the fact that he has this information will throw open the gates to realizing his vocation. Fortunate people, whose desire to discover their vocation in life is very strong and directs their entire lifestyle, are likely to be successful in this within a few years – if they invest all their energy in the search. Ultimately, however, time is not very significant to them, since what are a few years as compared to the eternity of our souls?

In contrast, developing extrasensory abilities helps us at the various stages of the path to finding our vocation and realizing it. It also helps develop the mental and spiritual harmony we need for the rest of the path. The ways of helping are many and varied, and the fact of being aware of them, and afterwards using them, will lead to far-reaching changes in life. Here are a few examples:

*Dreaming:* Through dreaming, we can receive messages about the situation in life we are in at the moment, about the path we are following, and about the path our soul wishes to follow (these two are not always the same!). Indeed, when the person knows how to make the correct use of dreams, he can really get up one morning and know what his vocation in life is. This must be preceded by a true and sincere desire to discover the path, and a deep commitment to follow it. Even if such an extreme change does not occur, awareness is likely to come gradually by means of in-depth dream work.

*Channeling, meditation with crystals, meditation to discover previous incarnations:* By knowing our soul's past, we can understand our present and receive clues about the "future." The development of channeling abilities and work with crystals as an excellent tool for increasing self-awareness and spiritual awareness will provide us with additional pieces for understanding this puzzle, which is the sum total that constitutes the "I." When we discover one of our incarnations, we can understand why our soul has chosen to undergo certain kinds of experiences in our present incarnation. We can understand some of the components and properties of our personality, as well as the nature of some of the "obstacles" and "inhibitions" that face us in life. Working with crystals and stones helps in as many ways as there are crystals and stones, starting with the ability to discover previous incarnations, and ending with the raising/dissolving of emotional and mental patterns, among them the various traumas from this life and from previous incarnations.

*Telepathy, energy-sensing abilities, and awareness of inner and outer energies:* When telepathy and the various ways of intuitively picking up energies and their significance reach a level at which the person can "sense" the thoughts, intentions, and emotions of another person, they are extremely powerful tools when the person knows how to use them. People who are gifted with a powerful telepathic ability or a high level of energetic sensitivity, occasionally tend to complain. They say, "Just imagine. I walk into a room and I immediately sense what this one or that one is feeling. Those emotions/intentions/thoughts are not always pleasant! Sometimes it makes me want to simply get up and run out of there, away from those people!"

In that example, it is possible to see how the extent of mental and spiritual work the person has done on himself is expressed in his ability to make effective use of the extrasensory ability itself. When this ability comes to the person without a profound insight of the basic laws of the universe, it is liable to seem like a nuisance, and not as a supportive ability. In contrast, when the person has assimilated the laws of the universe properly and lives accordingly, he knows that every person, feeling, emotion, and even energy that is brought to his attention actually serves as a self-mirror that shows him which aspects of his personality are still not balanced. Therefore, when he senses a pattern of rage in a certain person, for example, he will immediately look inside himself to see how that pattern is embodied in his personality. When he is able to do that, he receives an ongoing status report of what repair he himself needs, as if he were in a workshop for developing and balancing the soul hour after hour. After he has found the inner pattern inside himself, he can pay attention to it and begin mental and spiritual work to understand this pattern in his soul, and thus work toward balancing it.

Of course, the ability to balance and repair mental patterns in our personality is invaluable, and is one of the strongest and most genuine ways of attaining spiritual depth and even spiritual enlightenment. The latter are expressed in every aspect of our life; they help us recognize our vocation in life, and assist us along the long path toward realizing it.

There are endless examples – the above are only a tiny fraction. However, to sum up the influence of the extrasensory abilities on the path we follow in order to know ourselves in depth and realize our vocation in life, it can be said that their most significant effect is the ability to understand profoundly and truly the way the world works, and the truth behind the material illusion in which we live. When the person is enlightened by the insight that life in this world is actually a temporary illusion, and nothing that seems to us to be "vital," or an "insurmountable obstacle" is "genuine" or cannot be changed in some way, he is halfway to the discovery and realization of his vocation in life. After this comprehension, the obstacles that people tend to put up for themselves suddenly seem like just an illusion, which, by means of conscious work, will, and effort, can be removed and discarded. (Every person puts up obstacles that block his path to the discovery and realization of his vocation: "I don't have money," "My wife is holding me back," "I don't have time," "It's too difficult/not possible," "I'm not good /clever enough" "I'm too old/fat/tall/short," etc.) The understanding provided by the extrasensory ability – being able to activate abilities that are "beyond nature" (referring to what we were taught about the meaning of "nature" and "natural" at school…) – causes the person to understand that life is much deeper than what it seems on the surface, and that his abilities in every field are much greater than what they seem. No less important is that the person learns in this way to recognize that what he sees with his physical eyes and experiences with his physical senses is not "everything that exists and no more." He learns to understand that there are reasons for things, and even things that can drive him crazy at times are important and contribute to his life. Of course, life with this kind of awareness quickly becomes easier, because a lot of the things that succeeded in eroding our strength and our belief in ourselves are shattered in the face of a strong basic personality and awareness.

## A warning about the use of extrasensory abilities

It is important to point out that your mental state and rational ability to accept or reject exceptional phenomena exert an enormous influence on your ability to increase your extrasensory abilities. However, there is no doubt that with practice, awareness, and confidence, you can increase your abilities. How you use these abilities is your business, but a warning about this is in order. In general, attempts to influence various people to do something that is not right, appropriate for them, or moral, are not successful. Every attempt to misuse extrasensory powers carries a personal price that is sometimes a heavy one.

An interesting thing that happened to me illustrates how "pulling the string too tight" is liable to cause problems. This type of "pulling the string" mainly stems from some kind of personality trait that is not sufficiently balanced, and tempts the person to use his extrasensory abilities in a way that is not absolutely pure. I became aware that by means of the power of thought, I could "invite" certain events into my life. So, often before leaving on a trip, or sometimes even before going out, I would focus my thoughts on the desire to meet someone who could provide me with information on certain things I was involved with, channel with me about a certain topic, or shed light on a topic that I had not understood sufficiently. Over the years, this ability developed and became stronger, until I could declare, before going to a particular place, "Today I'll meet a person who knows a lot about building sets for movies." And indeed, completely "coincidentally," I would land up meeting a person who was knowledgeable about precisely the subject I was interested in. Having said that, I would always start off by requesting the consent and support of the universe, knowing that we are not allowed to use our powers for obtaining things that are not to the universal force's "liking." Once, when I tried to use this power incorrectly, I was taught not to do so again:

Several years ago, I saw a movie on TV. One of the characters reminded me of a person I had not seen since high school.

That boy was an exceptionally talented actor, and out of some kind of egoistic desire, I decided that I wanted to meet him then and there so that he could teach me a few acting techniques that could help me develop my acting ability. I did not have a good feeling about this wish; I felt as if I was trying to change the order of the universe with it, and that the person had no desire to meet me at that time. Despite that, I insisted. I knew that our whole group of friends was supposed to go out to some place I had never been to, and I decided that that would be a good place to meet that guy. I used my powers to invite him to the place and create a reality in which I would meet him there. As opposed to previous times, I did not simply request to meet a person who would help me with a particular matter, but I insisted on meeting that specific person. Obstinately, out of excessive pride ("It always works for me..."), I went on creating the specific reality. I got all dressed up for the evening, and exchanged my eyeglasses for contact lenses so as to put the finishing touches to my appearance.

During the journey, while I was still busy ordering the event, I began to feel discomfort in one eye. Within a short time, the feeling turned into a sharp, penetrating pain, and I realized that one of the lenses had slipped off my pupil. Not pleasant, perhaps, but not terrible. Generally, you can take out the lens and stop the painful sensation easily. Not this time, however. We stopped at a gas station, and I tried to extract the lens – to no avail. I did not manage to extract it or to relocate it over my pupil, and the pain became more and more severe. I have used lenses for many years, but I have never experienced that kind of pain, and so extreme. By the time we reached the city, it was unbearable. My eye was red and swollen, burning and watering, and the pain was piercing and incessant. I have to admit that I even became slightly hysterical because of the severe pain. Concerned, my friends quickly stopped the car in the city center so that I could go into a restaurant and look at my eye in a mirror in a well-lit place. We passed three or four places, and then we came to a pizzeria in which there was a well-lit bathroom. I climbed the stairs to the bathroom and tried to extract the lens. It was almost impossible. I began to cry angrily from pain and frustration. The outing was supposed to be cool and fun, and here I was, being a drag, stuck with a lens that was killing me!

Help came from an unexpected quarter: One of the pizzeria workers, whose entrance I hadn't noticed because I was so stressed out, came upstairs to the floor where the bathrooms were and began to explain what I should do to get the lens out. When I eventually managed to extract it according to his instructions, I washed my face and calmed down a bit. Then I turned to thank the guy. To my surprise, he resembled the guy I had used my powers to meet like two peas in a pod – except for one difference: that guy had red hair, while this one had black hair. Except for that single difference, they were so similar that I immediately understood what was going on – my inflated ego had blinded my eyes to taking the laws of the universe into account. I could have dubbed this event a "coincidence" had I not been given clear intuitive knowledge of what was going to happen before we went out (a feeling about the future that is about to happen, as if in the "past," a second of seeing future events). Even so, I stubbornly ignored the knowledge I had received.

Although this is a "small" example, I learned from a great deal of experience in the use of thought energy for creating various realities that when we try to "impose" our will on reality, knowing deep inside that it is neither right or proper, we are liable to experience some kind of event that will teach us not to do it again. Over the years, it happened that I met a number of people who had abused their powers in order to get other people to do what they wanted them to do. I got away from them as quickly as possible, since their energetic proximity is not healthy. However, when I met all those people several years later, every one of them was suffering from some serious problem or other – physical or mental, as I had intuitively supposed would happen to them if they continued using their powers negatively. Therefore, even when we succeed in developing our extrasensory abilities, it is very important to notice how we use them and to listen to the inner feelings that tell us if a certain use of the powers is wrong or not in line with the will of the universe. Any attempt to impose our will on someone else or to cause a natural occurrence to veer from its course exacts a certain price, either then and there or at a later date.

## Developing the extrasensory abilities – how do we "do" it?

A common question regarding extrasensory abilities is: "How do I do it? How do I develop those abilities by myself?"

Frankly, there is no simple answer. There is no single way, method, or technique that will make you clairvoyant, telepathic, or able to see auras or visions from one day to the next.

Having extrasensory abilities is more a way of life than a talent. This ability depends more on our perception of the world, on the way we relate to our world and communicate with it, than on study, technique, or a set of laws.

Having said that, there are ways to acquire the ability. There are laws, there are techniques – but even then, this ability is the embodiment of the force of the soul inside you, and as such, the whole is greater than its parts.

Certain cosmic laws and principles are true laws felt by every person who is linked to his soul and channels, regardless of what his religion is, which culture he belongs to, or which tools he uses to arouse his extrasensory ability. It is no coincidence that those are exactly the same laws for a holistic and aware life.

In order for the person to be able to realize his full potential, to fulfill his abilities and discover his paths to the world beyond the senses, he must be able to learn to see, feel, and live himself and the world around him holistically.

Learning the cosmic laws and principles will help you not only develop your extrasensory talents, but derive tremendous enjoyment from all strata of life. They will expand and deepen your everyday life, and through them you can discover new insights of your own. When these laws are familiar to you, the insights and messages that await you will arrive.

# Factors that inhibit/disturb the development of extrasensory abilities

## The judgment obstacle

When judgment is not objective, it is liable to be one of the main "enemies" of the extrasensory ability. When I say "judgment," I mean everything you have learned and accumulated over the years – the large amount of information that has been internalized, a great deal of which consists of prejudices, subjective suppositions, superstitions, and so on. Judgment can be a wonderful tool for helping a person who has supernatural powers, but only when he knows how to recognize the basic prejudices that exist in him.

Judgment stems from what we have learned about this world via our senses, at home, in our community. Prejudice regarding extrasensory activity that claims – consciously or unconsciously, and sometimes in a profound and hidden manner – that any experience of this type is impossible, nonsensical, and unscientific, has been shown by researchers to exert a significant influence on the ability to experience extrasensory phenomena. It can also prevent an extrasensory phenomenon that the person experienced spontaneously from being repeated.

The effect of prejudice on the extrasensory ability has been clearly demonstrated in two famous sets of studies. The first is the renowned study known as "The 'Sheep-Goat' Effect," and the second is a multiple-subject study on telekinesis.

The study known as "The 'Sheep-Goat' Effect" was conducted in 1942 by the professor of psychology, Gertrude Schmeidler, from New York University. She devised a questionnaire in order to examine students' beliefs and prejudices regarding extrasensory activity. She used the term "sheep" to indicate the students who were sure of the existence of extrasensory occurrences, and "goats" for those who were skeptical about the possibility of the existence of extrasensory activity in general, as it was presented in the questionnaire. After the questionnaires had been checked, she gave the subjects a classic test of extrasensory abilities, after which they were given a classic test of telepathic abilities and clairvoyant abilities. This was done by means of special cards, where the subjects had to guess card sequences.

Schmeidler compared the results of the questionnaires with those of the extrasensory tests, and the astounding facts showed that in the "sheep" group, there was a far above average deviation toward positive results in the extrasensory and the telepathic-clairvoyant tests, while the results of the "goat" group demonstrated a significant deviation below the curve of the usual chance of success in this type of test.

Following this study, many other studies were performed, some of them in recent years, clearly demonstrating the systematic accumulation of wrong answers in people who do not believe in extrasensory abilities, as opposed to a high proportion of correct answers in tests done by people who believed in them. The studies conclude that people who believe in the existence of extrasensory phenomena systematically achieve an above-average number of correct answers, while the achievement of the "non-believers" is systematically below average. Studies performed with the specific purpose of examining this phenomenon demonstrated that certain individuals are able to reach such a high level of "wrong answers" that this itself is a kind of "extrasensory phenomenon" no less than the above-average ability to guess the correct cards – showing that this is not a matter of poor extrasensory ability in the "goats." On the contrary, it would seem that these people unconsciously use their extrasensory powers to evade the aim of the test, and unconsciously sabotage their results!

We tend to select information that confirms our beliefs and ignore information that is not compatible with them. Selective perception plays an important role in the personal interpretation of what seem to be extrasensory experiences. Skeptics tend to declare that people who believe in extrasensory phenomena are inclined to see "extrasensory phenomena" in everything, even up to the point of confusing their personal interpretations with the real events. In contrast, non-believers tend to refute situations that seem to be extrasensory experiences, and find "rational" reasons for explaining extrasensory experiences, even when they occur in their lives. But the sheep-goat effect shows that this goes beyond the individual's personal interpretation – the attitude of the person toward extrasensory phenomena influences the probability that phenomena of this type will occur at all. The more the person fosters a narrow view of the world, so his chances of such phenomena occurring in his life decrease. The more interested the person is in a holistic view of the world, and the more open to extrasensory experiences he is, the greater the chances are that the universe will "react" to this by creating experiences of this type.

The second set of tests that stressed this principle focused even more on the practical ability of the subjects to repeat an extrasensory activity after an initial incidence of success. In the set of studies that included large groups of people (between 60 and 100), more than 70% of the subjects succeeded, to varying extents and by means of the correct guidance, in using the power of thought to bend metal. Fewer than 30% succeeded in repeating the experiment a second time. After in-depth research, the reason for this phenomenon emerged: after the person succeeded in bending the metal clearly and surprisingly, he experienced a reaction of being unable to explain the phenomena scientifically, and this created an intellectual paradox that prevented him from being able to repeat the phenomenon.

In order to be able to pick up clear, authentic, and clean extrasensory messages, without causing yourself uneasy feelings, you will have to learn how to distance the sometimes almost automatic subjective judgment that springs up in you upon seeing various visions or messages. Your personal opinions, tendencies, past experiences and background are liable to affect both the manner in which you receive the messages and how you decipher and understand them. The greater your ability to accept matters with great openness, without activating your "automatic" judgment and expressing your personal opinion, the broader and more surprising the range of messages that reach you will be. At the same time, along with the activity to improve and develop your intuition, you will begin to discover your prejudices, fears, and subjective opinions and beliefs, and you will know how to neutralize them when they do not support you and your intuitive activities.

## The obstacle of fear

The obstacle of fear is extremely powerful. If we nourish it energetically, it is liable to completely thwart our attempts to experience our extrasensory abilities. The fear can be a mixture of prejudices, guilt feelings, or even the feeling of "doing something bad" regarding dabbling in the world beyond the senses. You should ask yourself the following questions in order to dispel fears and uncomfortable feelings, most of which are unconscious, about dealing with the extrasensory:

Was anyone in your family, or in your close surroundings – especially when you were a child – deeply afraid of any contact with the extrasensory world? Did adults in your surroundings tend, for any reason, to define this practice as "satanic" or "dangerous"? Is supernatural activity linked with "madness" or "insanity" in any part of your consciousness? Did anyone in your close surroundings, or when you were a child, practice black magic (and was hurt at some stage or other)? Does anyone in your close surroundings tend to relate to extrasensory activity as "nonsense"? Were your brought up to believe that "it's forbidden to dabble in those things"?

We live in the world of beliefs that we create. Prejudices play a very powerful part in the formation of our worldview, and our worldview is one of our tools for forming reality, most certainly in the extrasensory world. Fear and anxiety following any extrasensory experience (even a very positive one), resulting from a belief that the world of extrasensory phenomena is dangerous or unclean, are liable to cause a number of phenomena:

1. Inability to repeat the extrasensory experience you had, because of "panic" and surprise at the very fact of your success and what was revealed to you.

2. Soliciting frightening experiences from the extrasensory realm, and increased sensitivity to non-positive energy, vulnerability and sensitivity that stem from a weak aura because of psychological fear, which is liable to cause nightmares, fear of entities, and so on.

3. Linking extrasensory activity with madness is liable to make you unable to channel the extrasensory messages you receive – again, because of anxiety or a paralyzing fear that interferes with the improvement and increase in your extrasensory powers, and because of the unconscious or conscious fear that these things are liable to cause you to lose your mind.

## Fanatic religious faith

Fanatic religious faith, especially the kind that originates in the home, constitutes a very powerful obstacle for many people who experiment with extrasensory phenomena, and makes them anxious about their achievements. This is generally because certain religious groups link extrasensory activities with satanism, idolatory, and so on. The majority of these links are completely baseless. It must be remembered that the religious writings in the various cultures are full of miraculous deeds and extrasensory phenomena! In both the Old and New Testaments, many of the prophets and other figures were gifted with these powers and used them. It was precisely those extrasensory abilities, such as prophetic ability, clairvoyance, channeling, healing by touch, and so on, that turned "religious heroes" into lofty and holy spiritual figures. If this is the case, why do various religious currents deny the existence of extrasensory phenomena and make people fear them? After all, extrasensory abilities, when they are developed, channeled, and used correctly, help the person distinguish between right and wrong, and help him attain a close and direct relationship with his soul. Of course, this would render all these preachers worthless, and is liable to undermine various religious structures whose source lies in the desire to control, and not in the desire to lead people to love God.

In contrast, various spiritual occupations may very well be dangerous – a large percentage of those involved in them come to harm. This has been proved. Among these occupations, we can include all fields of black magic, voodoo, raising the spirits of the dead, and seances. However, these things are not dangerous because the rabbi, the priest, or Mom said so. They are dangerous because they constitute a distorted use of extrasensory powers, which, according to the laws of the universe, is accompanied by pain and suffering, just like insisting on touching a hot iron turns an ostensibly innocent appliance into one that is dangerous and threatening. I sincerely recommend that you not try things of this type because I have seen many dire consequences as well as the energetic distortion they cause. In contrast, when a person heals by means of energies, prior information, prophecy, feeling auras, and so on, and does so with a pure heart, a good intention, and love, he will attract the same kind of energies as he is sending to the cosmos – healing energies, love, and understanding.

Religious faith is liable to create an additional problem when the person attributes information, insights, or messages to a certain figure (among many Christians, it is common to attribute all healing powers to Jesus – even when this is not the case), and this interferes with his objective scrutiny of his abilities. It is not a good idea to "decide" that the powers with which you are blessed derive from a particular religious source, when this is not the case – it is just your subjective impression.

## Coping with fear

It is important to know that every extrasensory experience becomes more powerful if you are afraid of it. Even if the experience is not pleasant, even if you feel a great deal of discomfort, ask yourself: "Can this really hurt me?" It cannot really hurt you unless you really, really want it to…

Negative entities are attracted to fear and terror. The more frightened attention you pay them, the stronger they will seem to you to become. The more you try to flee, the more it will seem to you that they are becoming stronger. When you stop fleeing, they will lose interest in you. Sometimes, certain experiences are liable to be frightening, and you will find that it is not easy to feel confident. Accept your fear, and don't fight it, but don't cling to it either. If you try to fight fear, you may be trying to control an emotion that cannot be controlled at that moment, and you will only stress yourself out more. What you can do in such cases is *to choose not to cling to fear*. Acknowledge your fears and accept them, but remember that any extrasensory attack is extrasensory, that is, it is not physical, and cannot really hurt you. An experience of this kind can hurt by causing fear and anxiety. When you recall this, the fear will pass more quickly, and you can apply suitable techniques for dispelling an extrasensory attack or non-positive energy. Similarly, developing emotions of humility, understanding, and compassion toward those entities, or toward people who emit negative energy, will help you dissipate disturbances of this type very quickly.

# Preparation – work on the "self"

Work on the "self" is the first and most important tool for discovering the extrasensory abilities that exist in us. These abilities do not come to us from the outside; they already exist within us, and we have to discover them. When we cleanse ourselves of all those numerous layers that hold us back and prevent us from discovering the full potential that exists in us, this potential will begin to realize itself naturally.

## *First exercise*
## Old input – get out, new input, come in!

### Work with inhibiting thought patterns

This is one of many exercises that serve to reveal negative thought patterns and get rid of them by replacing them with new and supportive thought "input." This exercise comes in many variations, and you yourself may well discover the variation that suits you the most. In order to illustrate how to work, I will use a simple example that demonstrates the influence of the mental layer on the physical layer – sore feet.

You are advised to do the exercise on paper, with the date.

***First stage:* The problem**

At the first stage, let's address one problem or issue in life that is bothering us. This problem may be physical or emotional, connected with a relationship, with our income, with creativity – or anything else that belongs to our personal world.

Issues we define as "problems" are a very powerful tool for our spiritual development, even though we sometimes tend to moan about them. As Richard Bach wrote in his book, "Illusions": "There is no such thing as a problem that is not presenting you with a gift. You seek problems because you need their gifts." In this exercise, we will isolate one problem and try to discover its gift of awareness to us. The problem I have chosen is sore feet.

***Second stage:*** **What does the problem represent for me?**

At this stage, we will divide the verbal definition of the problem up into factors, and we will try to understand what the essence of the matter symbolizes for us. In the example I have chosen, the question, "What is pain *for me*?", is asked.

When relating to a physical or emotional problem, we can use Louise Haye's tables in her books, "You Can Heal Your Body," or "You Can Heal Your Life," since she uses a description of patterns that speak to most people.

For me, pain is something that bothers, disturbs, prevents action, inhibits. For me, the feet symbolize forward motion, progress – movement as opposed to a lack of mobility.

***Third stage:*** **Why am I experiencing this problem at this particular stage of my life?**

Now we will see when and how the problem occurs, and in relation to which situation in our lives. Nothing "just happens," and every problem, emotional or physical, that we experience, is closely linked to the circumstances of our lives. Now we must ask: "When do I experience the problem? When does it crop up? During which period of my life did it occur for the first time?" and so on.

The example I gave – sore feet – occurred every time I had an appointment with a healer in order to work on inhibiting thought patterns... and yet I derived a great deal of pleasure from the appointment, and I was aware of the tremendous change it made in my life.

Now, let's write down the conclusions in a table with four columns:

*1. The problem* Sore feet

*2. The deep subject the problem represents* Fear of progress

*3. The problem crops up / gets worse when...* I want to create a significant change in my life – I am required to assume deep-seated responsibility for my life.

*4. Conclusion* There is a fear of going forward, of movement, of progress.

* *New thought pattern* I advance with confidence and love, I walk courageously along my physical and spiritual life path, I am happy to take responsibility for my life.

In the last column (*), we will write the new thought pattern we are creating as a substitute for the old thought pattern represented by the subject that is addressed by the problem. Here we actually do "practical" work – exchanging the old subconscious "input" that causes the problem for new healthy and balanced "input" that supports us. However, the very fact of getting to the root of the problem, and even the desire to take responsibility for our lives and understand that we are the ones that cause our problems in order to progress, develop, and understand ourselves and the universe more thoroughly – also make a profound difference in our consciousness.

Thought patterns for creating positive thoughts operate on the subconscious and are very powerful. For that reason, words must be chosen carefully. Positive words must be used, and negative words avoided – such as "I am not afraid of advancing in life," since the subconscious often tends to ignore the word "not" and accepts the sentence without it.

It is important to point out that after working with a table of this type, we begin to think naturally about how thought patterns create emotional and physical realities in our lives. Then the entire process of getting rid of the old input and exchanging it for new input becomes rapid and natural, as does spiritual development.

Now we will move on to the next stage, which is discarding the physical-emotional “clinging” that is linked to the subject of the problem, discardingt the old and bringing in the new. In order to do this, we will prepare a second table with two columns: 1. Positive Thought, and 2. Feeling.

In the first column, we will write the positive thought over and over again. In the parallel column, we will write the feelings the positive thought evokes. These can be emotional or physical. They are the result of the kind of emotion and thought that has sometimes gone on for years – possibly even since childhood. The thought pattern is also active on the cellular layer, and for that reason exerts an influence on the body. Just as we free the thought layer from the unhelpful thought pattern, so we must also free the memories of the emotions and the body. To do that, we have to listen to ourselves carefully, be linked up to ourselves, and detach ourselves from every judgmental thought, so that the feelings can arise by themselves. It is advisable to do this exercise quickly and without thinking so that associations, feelings, and emotions arise naturally.

**Positive thought**
I advance with confidence and love, I walk courageously along my physical and spiritual life path, I am happy to take responsibility for my life.

**Feeling** Stomach-ache.

**Positive thought** I advance with confidence and love, I walk courageously along my physical and spiritual life path, I am happy to take responsibility for my life.

**Feeling** Unpleasant feeling in the stomach.

**Positive thought** I advance with confidence and love, I walk courageously along my physical and spiritual life path, I am happy to take responsibility for my life.

**Feeling** Fear.

**Positive thought** I advance with confidence and love, I walk courageously along my physical and spiritual life path, I am happy to take responsibility for my life.

**Feeling** Feeling resembling hunger.

**Positive thought** I advance with confidence and love, I walk courageously along my physical and spiritual life path, I am happy to take responsibility for my life.

**Feeling** A little pinch inside

**Positive thought** I advance with confidence and love, I walk courageously along my physical and spiritual life path, I am happy to take responsibility for my life.

**Feeling** A memory of a childhood experience of…

**Positive thought** I advance with confidence and love, I walk courageously along my physical and spiritual life path, I am happy to take responsibility for my life.

**Feeling** A memory of an experience of…

**Positive thought** I advance with confidence and love, I walk courageously along my physical and spiritual life path, I am happy to take responsibility for my life.

**Feeling** Joy

We keep on writing down the positive thought while paying attention to the range of emotional feelings, associations, physical feelings, and memories of experiences and events that arise in us – in short, everything that is evoked in us when we write down the positive thought. We continue until no more unpleasant feelings of any kind arise, and a few more times, until we feel a good and natural feeling about the content of the positive thought, that is, until our subconscious accepts the new thought pattern and adopts it. Of course, the table may well be much longer than the sample one shown above…

When it is a question of a deep and distressing problem, or when you do not reach a profound insight after the initial practice, you must continue with the table every day for a week. Afterwards, it is advisable to write down the positive thought you created for yourself in a place where you will see it frequently during the day – on the refrigerator, on the bathroom mirror, next to the computer in the study, and so on. Recite the positive thought several times a day. It is not easy to make comprehensive promises in this sphere, but experience has shown time and again that it works. Insights occur, and "problems" give us the gift of their awareness, and after we receive their gift, we no longer need them – so they disappear.

## *Second exercise*
## **Positive thought and the self-mirror**

This exercise is very enjoyable, stimulating, and illuminating. It is very simple, but what it gives us is one of the basic tools for understanding the mode of action of the universe, which tells us over and over again: There is no such thing as "just because," there is nothing that does not have a reason, and there are no encounters and relationships that are insignificant.

We all know someone with whom we do not get along too well, but circumstances dictate that the person is part of our world in some way. This person may be our employer, a colleague, a relative, a friend, or even the friend of a friend.

As we said before, nothing happens "by chance" in the world. We meet various people for various purposes, in the spiritual layer. Some of the encounters constitute repairs of the mind, the soul, or the spirit, and some of them come from interactions in past lives. Some of them serve as a mirror to teach us and be examples of what is still in need of repair and improvement in ourselves, and for increasing our mental and spiritual development. Some of them show the challenges facing us. We have to learn how to surmount the barrier that separates us from the other person. Understanding the "mirror effect" – when the other person in the interaction with us shows us ourselves – is the mind's great understanding of the material world.

A theory that can be put into practice states that it is in our power to change the intensity of the antagonism that occurs in relationships of this type, and this will create an experience that is beneficial and supportive to both sides. It is relatively easy to do. This exercise will be very enlightening for you, and will enable you to discover how positive thought materializes in the physical world. The exercise is performed in two stages. The first occurs during the actual interaction with the person who sparks antagonism or irksome emotions in you, and the second is done at home, with your notebook of spiritual development.

***First stage***

You are with the person. You make up your mind that today, when you are dealing with him, you are going to think only positive thoughts about him. In your thoughts, tell the person that you know he has a good soul, that he is kind, pleasant, honest – every positive thought you can project to him.

The most important thing is the sincerity of your intention. You must really believe in these positive thoughts, and this means that you may have to make a bit of an effort to see the person's positive traits. During those moments, at least, there must be no conflict in your beliefs. If you have come across the "mirror effect" in the past, and have assimilated the law of polarity well, you will even be able to send him positive thoughts that are the opposite of his current behavior, because you know that every type of behavior contains the full range of balanced and unbalanced possibilities. For instance, if the person comes through as very egoistic, you can send a loving thought, "You are a wonderful, caring person who supports others." If the person is stingy with love or positive reinforcement (an employer, for example), you can send him the thought, "The love in you is overflowing, you are full of love and permit yourself to show it and share it; you enjoy giving love and making people happy."

Perhaps this sounds bombastic and false, but there can never be too much beauty or love. Just avoid "changing" the person or sending him positive thoughts that are somehow linked to you (such as, "You give me positive reinforcement when I do good work"), because they are less effective, and there is something rather manipulative about them. Try to make your thoughts more general; for example, "Your presence and words encourage and support the people around you."

Everyone has good in him, everyone has beauty in him. When we permit ourselves to link up to the channel that enables us to see the person's beauty, we see his beautiful properties on the physical plane as well.

Sometimes, we are so deeply entrenched in anger or hurt that it is not easy to link up to this cosmic channel. In this case, when you cannot find any beautiful property in the person, and it is not easy for you to find the positive pole of his negative behavior, you can send him thoughts such as "I know that deep inside you're good," "The more kindly you behave toward people, the better you'll feel about yourself," "The more you love, the more complete you'll feel." It is well known that many of our behavior problems derive from a lack of self-love (sometimes, from a lack of love for the inner child, who occasionally goes through a small "hell" in his childhood). Therefore, you can send him a thought such as "You love and esteem yourself," "You are learning to love yourself and others," and so on.

However, it is important that you actually believe in your thoughts. For this reason, do not imagine things in which you cannot believe.

The results will surprise you: both the concrete occurrences that occur in front of your eyes in the material world following the projection of positive thoughts – the change in the relationship and in the way the person relates to you (and you to him) – and the inner occurrences of profound insight and spiritual growth to which this line of thinking leads you.

Occasionally, when we begin to project positive thoughts to a particular person, the latter gradually – sometimes even instantaneously –

begins to seem different to us, sometimes even physically so. I remember a case in which I met a person who decided to serve as an extremely sharp "mirror" for me (for him, it was a conscious decision, but I didn't know that!). Moreover, he decided to show me the "black holes" that still existed in me. To this end, sitting in my apartment, late at night, after he had actually "forced" me to invite him home, he began to spout forth a lengthy stream of negative thoughts and fears. To start off with, I was astounded. I still didn't know that he was a professional actor who had taken upon himself the meritorious role of showing me what I was afraid of and what I was trying to repress and hide. I experienced a tremendous mass of emotions. Initially, I was angry. "He knows I'm collapsing with exhaustion, and I just want a bit of peace and quiet. What does he want of me?" Then, because of the weird things he was saying, I was frightened. How much hatred and anger there was! I wanted to get away from those energies – I didn't want to accept them. I wanted to shut him up, but I reckoned that his "confession" was important for him, and if I was around, I had to be with him, not against him, for the sake of both of our mental and spiritual processes. Our being together was no coincidence, I thought to myself. I began to send him loving, reinforcing, and supportive thoughts without uttering a word aloud. Suddenly, the same face that had seemed coarse and frightening to me softened and seemed more and more beautiful to me. I began to feel the inner child in him, a hurting, hurt child, a child who had undergone a great deal of suffering that was – incredibly – almost parallel to the suffering my own "inner child" had experienced. When I began to see his inner child crying out for love and self-acceptance, a huge wave of compassion and love swept over me. I felt the same love for myself and for my "inner child" as I felt for the person whose inner child I had taken into my heart. His fears and angers disappeared, and I encouraged him wordlessly and hugged him like a child. After a few moments of a loving hug that was totally compassionate and accepting, he raised his head and looked at me with a smile that was completely different than the frightening expression his face had worn previously, and asked me to always be "me." From that moment on, he behaved totally differently – illuminated and loving. Afterwards I realized that it had been a game (worthy of an Oscar!) whose aim was to have me face the angers, fears, criticism, and judgment toward myself and others that still existed in me.

This little story leads us to the second part of the exercise, in which we will see how the very things that drive us to distraction in other people are in fact a mirror, direct or inverse, of our own behavior. It is a case of "the pot calling the kettle black." This saying contains a profound cosmic truth. Every time a certain type of behavior upsets our mental or emotional equilibrium, it is because there is a link between that property or form of behavior and something in our character. It may be a direct mirror: exactly the same property exists in our character in another variation, and we have not accepted this aspect of our character. It may be an inverse mirror: the person behaves in a way in which we do not permit ourselves to behave because we have convinced ourselves that it is not right, because that's how we were brought up, because the property exists in us in a latent manner and we are afraid of it, and so on. They may be mirrors from the past – mirrors that remind us of events or experiences from our past that we have not yet come to terms with, and still evoke anger, fears, disquiet, and so on. Do the second stage of the exercise in a quiet place. See that you will not be disturbed, and do it when you are completely calm and full of love and self-acceptance.

***Second stage***

Prepare a table with two or three columns. However, before doing that, you must prepare yourself, since in this exercise you will delve into the essence of the properties that bother you in the other person, and you will find them in yourself in some form. Your starting point will be non-judgment. There is no place for judgment or criticism – not of yourself, and not of the other person. If we were all completely free of shortcomings, we would have nothing to learn or experience in this world. We are in a state of perpetual change, and the "shortcomings" of today are the nucleus of the power of tomorrow, when we understand them. For this reason, the key words for this exercise are *compassion*, *understanding*, and *acceptance* – regarding yourself and the other person.

While you are listing the properties that "irritate" you in the person, remind yourself to try and do this with love. This is very important, since ostensibly this part of the exercise is the opposite of the first stage, because we are listing the person's "shortcomings" and our own. However, everything that is done with understanding, for the sake of learning and spiritual development, is positive – if we refrain from giving vent to the angers that are liable to arise during the attempt to find the "irritating" properties. During the exercise, every time you try to recall the person's "annoying" properties and you experience some kind of unpleasant emotion, say to yourself, "Thank you, I love you," since, as you will see, those properties constitute a direct or inverse mirror of your own properties, or a mirror that reminds you of painful things from the past. In the first column, write down the property that "annoys" you in the person. In the second column, write "Me." In this column, you will see how this property is connected to you, how it appears in you, or if it is lacking in your character. In the third column, write the conclusion and the insight – the reason for the property affecting you and causing your emotional balance to be upset in some way.

I have filled out the table in order to provide an example of how the process can work.

***The person's property*** Speaks about himself a lot.

***Me*** I'm ashamed to speak about myself and praise myself.

***Why the property irritates me*** Inverse mirror – I sometimes want to flatter myself in public, but I'm ashamed to do so.

***The person's property*** Speaks too loudly.

***Me*** Speak softly.

***Why the property irritates me*** As a child, I would speak too loudly, and they always hushed me up. They taught me that it's "forbidden to shout and speak loudly." I'm afraid to make myself heard freely.

***The person's property*** Asks me to do all kinds of things for him.

***Me*** Ask people to do all kinds of things for me.

***Why the property irritates me*** I'm not comfortable with this character trait.

***The person's property*** Speaks obsessively about his love for my friend, speaks about her incessantly whenever we meet.

***Me*** Think obsessively about people I'm in love with, but I'm too shy to share this with others.

***Why the property irritates me*** Jealousy – I'd also like someone to talk about me from morning to night and dream about me like he dreams about my friend.

As we said before, in order for this exercise to be effective, we have to liberate ourselves from judgment and every attempt to justify ourselves. Similarly, we have to be honest with ourselves and fearlessly allow ourselves to expose various traits and imbalances in our character. The idea of the exercise is **discovery**, not criticism or judgment. If you feel a bit confused about the new discoveries you have made about yourself, tell yourself: "Thank you, I love you, I'm progressing and improving more and more each day, I love and value myself at my present standpoint."

Now you certainly see the other person in a different light. You may even thank him for being such an excellent mirror for you, and for contributing to your mental and spiritual development.

## *Third exercise*
## Working with the inner child

Our inner child is the same child we were and still are. Some of us had a happy and carefree childhood – almost a "perfect" childhood. Many others had a childhood in which the inner child was repeatedly hurt. The hurt suffered by the inner child cannot be quantified. In my work, I have often come across the feeling of quantifying experienced by people who have had a particularly traumatic childhood. When they relate to the stories of people whose childhood was "less difficult," they sometimes tend to say things like, "What's she complaining about? So her parents didn't let her express her creativity – so what? Me, with the beatings/humiliation/abuse/(fill in the relevant word) I suffered – I wish I'd had a childhood as easy as hers." This quantifying is sometimes conscious and sometimes unconscious, but whatever the case, there is no real place for it; it is an illusion.

Each of us accepts his emotions, feelings, and experiences subjectively. Sorrow and pain cannot be quantified or compared. It is possible to determine measures for a "difficult" or "easy" childhood in a conscious and objective way, but the personal feelings of the person are his, and what his friend accepts, he may not accept quite as easily.

Our childhood created many of the layers of our personality, and many of the limitations we set for our potential in every sphere derive from that period. In addition, many beliefs pertaining to the world, to the self – self-esteem, self-love, our perception of the "self" in general – stem largely from that period.

There are people who say, "It's over and done with; today I'm an adult, I'm self-aware, I'm a person who takes responsibility for his life." This is certainly a beneficial and healthy attitude when it stems from the recognition of childhood experiences and their effect on the present, but not when it derives from a fear of coping with the pain of the past. From my experience as a therapist, those experiences do not disappear. When they are not treated, when they are not extracted from the depths of the subconscious and brought to the conscious level, examined, and accepted as another experience that our soul chose to undergo in its life in the physical world, these experiences will live on in our subconscious. They will pop up every now and then in different guises, unclearly and unconsciously, because the conscious is still afraid to deal with them.

When we make a conscious decision to look into our childhood pain – which may now seem "childish" to us, but was important and meaningful when we were children – we undertake an important journey into our soul, and choose an open-eyed, understanding, and compassionate life.

It is important to understand that our soul is the one that chose the experiences we had. Why did it sometimes choose such difficult experiences? Why did it choose suffering and pain? It has its reasons, and as we develop spiritually we occasionally uncover them. However, one of the first steps is to acknowledge the existence of the inner child inside us – the same child we were at age one, two, three and five – all the periods of childhood, according to how each one of us defines them personally. This child may be happy, joyful, full of confidence in himself and in the world, or depressed, frightened, and suffering. But if wc do not acknowledge him and do not take him into our heart, restore his lost feeling of confidence, and give him the love and warmth he needs, his pain will go on bothering him. Of course, this is of tremendous importance when dealing with the world beyond the senses. As we said, "birds of a feather flock together," and the extrasensory experiences we have may constitute occasionally painful mirrors of the child's inner world and his repressed experiences.

In the next two exercises, we will take the inner child into our hearts. The two following meditations, too, will help us cope with childhood experiences lovingly. There are many meditations for working with the inner child, and many ways to acknowledge him and give him the feeling of love that he may lack. For some people, the meditations are simple, easy, and pleasant. For others – the ones that need them the most – they can be more difficult. They may extract a lot of material from the subconscious – material that can be so painful that many people simply skip this type of inner work, consciously or unconsciously, so as not to deal with it. Don't be one of them. If you really want to go on to the next exercises, and are reluctant to perform the meditations, stop yourself. Give yourself the opportunity to bestow love, recognition, and warmth on the inner child – he has longed for them for so many years. After the meditations, if you feel that you still have a great deal of work to do in this field, give yourself a month or longer to repeat the meditations several times, and look for books and additional meditations that deal with work on the inner child.

## *First exercise – meditation*
## **Return to childhood days**

Before doing the meditation, read it through from beginning to end. In this meditation, we will focus on the experiences that are linked to your parents. However, after doing it several times, you can focus on experiences that are linked to the teachers of your childhood, your childhood friends (or "enemies"), siblings, and the rest of the figures that affected your childhood.

Sit or lie down in a comfortable, quiet, and pleasant place. See that you are neither too cold nor too hot. Loosen your clothes and wrap a blanket around you if you feel the need. You can play quiet and meditative music in the background if it does not make you fall asleep, but there must not be any distracting lyrics. You can burn rose, benzoin, jasmine, or lavender oil in an essential oil burner in order to create a warm and pleasant feeling. Take three long, deep, and relaxed abdominal breaths. Inhale through your nose, and exhale through your mouth. Hold your breath for a few seconds before exhaling. Relax your body, clear your mind of thoughts that are not connected with the matter at hand, and close your eyes. Say to yourself: "I feel confident and protected. I am prepared to acknowledge my inner child and accept him with love."

Remember your favorite childhood place. You have nothing but happy, secure, and warm memories of this place. It may be your childhood home, your room, a secret place you used as a child, the yard where you played, a corner in the woods near your home, or any other place or corner that you remember as completely pleasant. This place is your safe place. If you feel any uneasy feeling during meditation, remember that you can always go back to that lovely, safe place. If such a place did not exist in your childhood, build a place in which your inner child can feel wonderful, happy and carefree. You can imagine a beautiful and perfect playground, a petting zoo with cute animals running around nearby, a gorgeous flower garden, a nice place at the shore – anything that causes a feeling of warmth and security.

Reconstruct the feeling of being a child. See yourself playing or resting in your favorite place. Feel and reconstruct your traits and feelings. Feel yourself as a small child and feel your parents' presence near you. Don't be afraid. The safe place is with you, always accessible and open to you if anything happens to frighten the little child inside you.

Now go back to a certain period in your childhood that you remember as difficult or unpleasant, a period during which you felt that they didn't understand you properly, or didn't accept you as you were, or didn't let you be who you really were. Of course, there can be different periods like that in your life as a child. It is possible that some of them are buried more deeply in the depths of your consciousness, and contain less pleasant matters from that period. The more you repeat the meditation, the more you will be able to reconstruct, repair, and raise up various periods, and they may pop up in front of your eyes intuitively. In your mind's eye, reconstruct the place – your childhood home – where you were at the time, the clothes you wore, the objects around you, the faces of your parents and relatives when they were around you at that time.

Now you are in that difficult period as a child. Recall the things that were said or done to you. See the hurtful reactions you received to your deeds or behavior. Listen attentively to the words that were spoken.

Let yourself feel the feeling you felt as a child, in the face of those words or your parents' reactions. Don't hold back if you want to be angry, protest, or cry.

Gaze at the child you see – you in your childhood. See your feelings express themselves on your face – sadness, sorrow, anger, or indifference. Look at him carefully and link up to his feelings. What is he feeling? What is he thinking? What would make him feel better in the same situation? Let the image of the child stand in front of your eyes. Feel your own emotions toward that child. What do you feel? Love, compassion? Or perhaps anger, accusation, shame? Don't be afraid of your feelings, even if they echo the adults' feeling toward the child that is you. There is no point judging him – he was what he was at that moment, he acted in the way he knew, in the way he understood; accept his feelings and actions, let those difficult feelings toward the child dissolve by themselves.

Now see yourself as an adult. See yourself, the adult, in the best possible light. If you do not love yourself entirely today – sometimes that's the situation, and you have to admit to it without shame – see yourself in another guise: a clever magician, an enchanted woman, strong and gorgeous. Permit yourself to see yourself, the adult, as a beautiful, strong, and perfect person. See yourself go up to the child and hug him, stroke his hair, wipe his tears, tell him, "I'm with you, I love you, I trust you, to me you are beautiful and perfect." Feel yourself hugging him tightly, showering him with love and compassion, cradling him in your arms until a smile of confidence and calmness appears on his face.

At this stage, you can stop the meditation, or go on to the next stage. If the meditation is not easy for you, and evokes many distressful feelings, do only the first part this time, and later on do the first part again and then the following part:

Now reconstruct the same incident once more. This time, however, change the situation. Change your parents' reaction or the way in which the event occurs so that you cause the child feelings of joy and self-acceptance. See them smiling, forgiving, and accepting.

Continue taking slow, deep breaths. When inhaling, see the pink light of love entering your body, and when exhaling, see the green light of tranquillity and balance being exhaled into space from inside you. Feel compassion toward your parents, who did not know how to act differently at the time, and made their mistakes as a result of the inhibiting material inside them. See the child smile, happy and joyful, and feel himself strong, whole, and self-confident.

Let us create the picture of the smiling child – this child is you. See him calm, happy, and confident in himself and in the world. Look at his image getting smaller, until it is tiny enough for you to place it in your hand. Take the tiny image to yourself, and put it in your heart.

Continue lying or sitting for a few minutes until you feel the meditative state dissipating. If you still feel a bit "spaced out," walk round the room a bit, jump, skip, and rub your knees and calves.

You should write the material that came up during meditation in your notebook for awareness and spiritual work. Write the date and the incident you recalled during meditation, and the feelings that it evoked. Writing down the incident may revive it once more, and may lead to emotional release, crying, or other emotional reactions. Accept them with love and feel the release they cause you. Write them down, too. Look into your awareness – are there still some negative feelings toward the sweet child that you were, or toward the adults who participated in the incident? It's possible. There's no point repressing them. It's better to write them down and be aware of the fact that there is more work to be done. The inner child must receive more warmth and love from you.

During the week, you can work with this material and see how it has influenced you during your entire life, and how it created your beliefs about yourself and the reality in which you live. You must take into account that meditation raises these layers to the surface, and even if you do not continue working on your awareness during the week, they are still liable to pop up. Know that if you are prepared to cope with them at this time, this inner work sometimes demands great mental strength, but the benefit to you is more valuable than gold. If this meditation indeed "got to you" and uncovered deep layers, devote two or three days a week to doing it and other meditations and work with the inner child – preferably at a fixed time, and always try to persevere at it. Always remember to look and see how the material you raised up influences your life in the present, and what its influence on your perception of the world and on your self was.

## *Second exercise – a letter*
## Corresponding with the inner child

Despite the simplicity of the exercise, it may have a profound mental influence. In this exercise, we will write a letter from the inner child to the adult that is you today. Don't bother with all kinds of preparations. All you need is a quiet, undisturbed quarter or half-hour, paper and pencil. In the exercise, the inner child that was you will write a letter to his adult self, and will receive a reply. The inner child will write down his feelings, his emotions, what is hurting him and what he needs. In order to raise repressed material from the subconscious, it is advisable to write the child's letter with the hand you don't write with, that is, if you are left-handed, use your right hand, and vice versa. You can even write the letter in paint or with a felt-tipped pen in order to reinforce the feeling of the child. Don't think and don't deliberate about the words you use. Nobody is standing beside you watching you while you write. Only you and yourself exist here – simply write without thinking.

Let your emotions rise freely, come what may. You are the child of the universe, and no fear, judgment, or shame exist in front of the universe. If you feel the need to cry or be angry – go ahead. Everything is allowed. Begin the letter with these or similar words: "A letter from little [Jake] to big [Jake]." Write whatever comes into your head, everything the little inner child has to say – fears, wishes, anxieties, desires – whatever comes up.

Rest for a few minutes after writing. Don't correct, don't alter anything. After a few minutes, read the letter that the inner child in you wrote you. Look at his feelings. Now take a fresh piece of paper and use your normal writing hand. You can use regular stationery, as if you were writing to an adult. The letter you will write is a response from the big self to the letter from your inner child. Begin it with the words: "A letter from big [Jake] to little [Jake]." Look at this little child as you would look at a little child, sweet and perfect, with abundant love, empathy, and compassion. Don't judge his emotions. Listen to what he needs, what he is asking for, what he is afraid of. In your letter, promise him your full support, your love, the caring and warmth he is asking for, give him what he needs with words full of compassion and love. There is no end or limit to the love you can give to this sweet child, and he is certainly in need of lots of warmth and love, as every one of us is.

# Grounding

Grounding is one of the most widespread spiritual exercises. Put simply, the idea behind grounding is to link us to the earth, something which is essential for people who are interested in the less earthy layers of life. Grounding to the earth enables us to get rid of excess energy and strengthens the link between us and the earth, which is our current place of residence (unless one of our readers happens to be an alien…). We need this link, since without it we cannot exist in the physical layer. When we begin to get involved in the various astral layers, grounding becomes even more important, since we tend to "levitate." In the material world, however, we are allowed to levitate for a certain length of time only, after which we must return to the physical entity in which our soul chose to live in this world.

Grounding helps us have our head in the clouds safely while we pick up divine messages and insights, and if our feet are planted firmly on the ground, we tread firmly in the material world.

## Quick grounding exercise

This is a quick and simple exercise, and after you practice it a few times, you can apply it to every situation and place, even in crowded public places, by means of your visualization ability.

Stand or sit comfortably. Take several deep breaths and relax your body slightly if it is tense. If it is more comfortable for you, close your eyes. Concentrate on the region of your root chakra – the area between the anus and the genitals. See the root chakra as a spinning red wheel. From the chakra, see a thick red ray of light that splits into two thick, stable stripes of red light, each one flowing through one of your legs. The red light flows along your legs to your feet, penetrates the earth, and enters the bowels of the earth. Focus on this sight and on the feeling of the red light that has penetrated the bowels of the earth for a few minutes and say aloud or mentally: "All the energies I no longer need are descending to the bowels of the earth and are turning into positive energies."

When we say "are turning," we mean the earth's transformational ability to convert one form of energy into another, just as it is able to convert one substance into another – substances that are compounded and rot in it subsequently turn into nourishing substances for various plants and organisms. At the end of the meditation, it is also possible to see in the mind's eye a tall, strong tree coming out of the earth somewhere. Incidentally, the understanding of the earth's transformational ability and the tremendous importance of this ability will evoke in every aware person sincere concern for the children of the earth – the trees and the plants – which, regrettably, totally obtuse and unaware people tend to disregard. Awareness of Mother Earth and her children is an inseparable part of conscious awakening, and an important tool for any person who is involved in the occult and the supernatural. When you take care of the earth and its children, they will teach you marvelous secrets of the universe, if only you listen to them. Therefore, it is every enlightened person's cosmic duty to make sure, as far as possible, to raise other people's consciousness and actively fight against the obtuse and ugly exploitation and destruction that are occurring on earth. The very fact of your cerebral objection to the continuation of this exploitation, and your personal prayer for the welfare of the earth, will increase the critical mass that can stop the terrible destruction before it is too late. The destruction of the rainforests of Brazil is a clear example of how the greed for mammon leads to the devastation of our planet; let's hope that the rape of the forests will stop for the sake of Mother Earth's and our own health.

## Contact with the earth

This simple grounding exercise is suitable for many people, and can easily be applied every time you feel a bit ungrounded.

Go outside and bend down to the earth, bending your knees slightly. Touch the bare earth with your hands for a few minutes. If you feel a need for it, dig your fingers deep into it, and be aware that you are releasing all your unneeded excess energies. Sometimes you can clearly feel the breakdown of the excess energy, or a feeling of release. If you want, you can imagine or visualize a line of energy being released from the center of your body deep into the earth.

# Clearing – purification – cleansing the aura

The aura, the electromagnetic field that surrounds us, tends to be easily influenced by various factors. Some of the factors are internal, dependent on us, while others are external, environmental. The action of cleansing the aura, therefore, must not be neglected.

Energetic purification is especially important and significant to anyone who works on his extrasensory abilities, but actually there is no one who does not need it. Sensitive people must pay special attention to this activity as well as to grounding and protection, since without them they are liable to feel ill at ease constantly. Clearing is important mainly when we feel like "human sponges" – we absorb and pick up the energies of other people. On certain levels – especially when the sponge tends to be a person who is highly sensitive to energies – a state of emotional overload is liable to occur for no obvious reason after spending a lot of time in the company of people who are not emotionally balanced. In extreme situations, which are not rare, the person feels an irksome emotional imbalance after such encounters, to the point that he occasionally finds it difficult to distinguish which emotions are his, and which he simply picked up and absorbed from other people.

Holistic therapists who spend a lot of time in the presence of people that frequently suffer from a lack of emotional, physical, or spiritual balance are susceptible to a state of "energetic identification" in every therapeutic interaction. When working with people on releasing their emotions, strong emotions may emerge, and these emotions have unhealthy energetic frequencies that are emitted from the aura of the emotional body. A release of this kind occurs in many healing and alternative medicine techniques, in psychological treatments, and in various mental therapies. These energies are liable to reach the therapist and upset his equilibrium. This situation is extremely obvious when there is any identification – conscious or unconscious – between therapist and patient. Before the treatment, as well as before any extrasensory activity, the aura must be protected and strengthened. After the activity, it must be cleansed of all the non-positive energy that adhered to it.

Other people who must pay a great deal of attention to the matter of cleansing are those who spend a lot of time working with or in the vicinity of machines that emit radiation, such as computers, TV sets, microwaves, X-ray machines, and all the other the radiation-emitting electrical appliances.

As we said, everyone must practice cleansing techniques. However, energetically sensitive people must apply them on a daily basis in order to improve their feeling and purify themselves of non-positive energies.

There are different types of energetic purification. You might find a certain exercise more effective, and link up to it more easily. Having said that, it is advisable to practice the rest of the techniques a bit, so that you have a number of cleansing tools at your disposal in addition to the daily cleansing technique you have chosen. As you gain experience in the strengthening, protecting, and cleansing of the aura, you might find unique exercises that suit you perfectly and fit in with your daily routine.

Before I describe a number of well-known techniques, I will point out two simple cleansing methods that we use daily, without relating them to the cleansing of the aura: showering and washing hands. A cold shower is very effective for balancing the ionic state of the body, and has a soothing and liberating effect. In addition, it cleanses the electromagnetic field, but not always sufficiently. In order to reinforce the shower's effect on the aura, you must consciously direct your thoughts to the cleansing and purification of the aura while you are showering. Soap does not have a purifying effect on our electromagnetic field; on the contrary, it tends to block energy. Therefore, after cleaning yourself physically with soap and shampoo, stand under the running water for a few minutes and let it flow over your body. While doing so, it is advisable to shake your body a bit, relax your muscles, direct your thoughts to cleansing the aura, and pass your hands over the estimated perimeter of the electromagnetic field – at a distance of outstretched arms, similar to the brushing technique I will describe later.

Washing hands, too, with the conscious intention of cleansing and purifying the electromagnetic field and directing your thoughts to this aim, contributes significantly to the cleansing of the aura field. The Jewish hand-washing in the morning, which is accompanied by a special blessing, is not meant for the physical cleansing of the hands, but rather the energetic cleansing. The aim of hand-washing, in which each hand is rinsed three times alternately, is to cleanse the non-positive energy residues that reach the body during the night, when, according to Judaism, the soul rises above the body during sleep, and the body remains exposed and unprotected energetically. This hand-washing is performed directly upon rising in the morning, before touching the body or any food. Some people wash their hands without saying the blessing, go to the toilet for their morning ablutions, and then wash their hands again and say the blessing. The most appropriate tool for washing hands is a two-handled cup. According to tradition, you take the full cup in your right hand and transfer it to your left hand, pour some water over your right hand, transfer the cup to your right hand, and pour water over your left hand, and repeat this procedure twice more – three times in total. Afterwards, the blessing is recited. In addition to washing hands, cleansing must be performed during the day in every situation in which we come into contact with unwanted energies, or after being in an energetically impure place.

I recommend that you try each technique below a few times and select the one you prefer.

## Ritual cleansing – the four elements

As we said, there are many cleansing methods, and as you get to know yourself and your energy field more deeply, you can invent a suitable one for yourself. Ritual cleansing according to the four elements – earth, water, air, and fire – is matched to the person according to the balance of the elements in him. The efficacy of the various techniques that derive from elemental cleansing depends on the strength or weakness of the various elements in the person's nature. People with star signs that are linked to a particular element may find that other techniques are in fact more suitable for them.

**Earth:** People with a weak earth element have a slight tendency toward levitating, sometimes toward slight physical weakness, pallor, intense mental activity as opposed to a lack of physical activity, and sometimes toward a high sensitivity to energies. People who lack the earth element are likely to find the grounding exercises in this book suitable for purification as well. Similarly, people with earth signs – Virgo, Taurus, and Capricorn – may find grounding an effective method of energetic cleansing.

**Water:** Purifiying with water is recommended for people whose water element is unbalanced. This can be expressed in a state of relatively frequent emotional imbalance, mood swings, and emotional instability. Cleansing with water is very suitable for people with water signs – Cancer, Scorpio, and Pisces. It is possible to use purifying techniques in the shower. It is a good idea to focus on the feeling that the water is rinsing off the excess emotional energy. Energetic purification in seawater is also recommended. If you are not near water and feel that you are in need of cleansing, see yourself in your mind's eye standing under a turbulent waterfall, or bathing into a flowing stream. See how the water washes over your entire body, and feel its coolness and purity. Continue with this visualization for a few minutes.

**Air:** Purification with air is very suitable for people with air signs – Gemini, Libra, and Aquarius – especially at times of emotional confusion and a burden of non-supportive emotions. For them, the wind is an effective tool for dispelling excess emotional energies. This is a method of purification that is extremely simple, and can be applied in a number of ways: sitting opposite a fan, traveling in a car with the window open (not when you are driving) so that the wind blows against your face and chest, a fast bicycle-ride in the wind, running into the wind, and so on.

When you do these actions, see the wind blowing all the unwanted energies away from you, and carrying you far away, purifying and aerating you. You can also sit opposite an open window and visualize in your mind's eye the wind blowing on and around you, as it purifies you and blows all the non-positive energies away.

**Fire:** People with fire signs – Aries, Leo, and Sagittarius – often find themselves attracted to fire and warm colors such as gold, red, yellow, and orange. Light and fire exercises are very suitable for them. In order to fill up with energy, these people are advised to do their filling up and protection with golden light. The combination of this process with the aura-cleansing process using the brushing technique is very effective. Similarly, they are advised to visualize themselves in their mind's eye surrounded by a glowing aura of golden light.

Although the tendency is to match the elemental cleansing to the members of the various signs according to the element that belongs to them, I have discovered that people sometimes find one of the other methods to be their appropriate way of purification. If you feel great when you are in water, and your natural instinct is to take a shower when you feel tired or agitated, or you especially revel in the wind blowing in your face, or feel a need to sit close to fire or to dig your toes into the sand at the shore, you can find the purifying method that is suitable for you by experimenting with the different elements. Of course, you can experiment with all the cleansing methods, all the while noting in your awareness notebook the "before" and "after" feelings, and in this way you can know which of the methods are most effective for you when you experience a particular energetic situation.

## The brushing technique

This is a quick and easy purification technique that is excellent to apply after you have been in a place that you felt to be energetically unclean. Sometimes this feeling occurs after a hospital visit because of the energy of pain and sorrow that exists there and in various other institutions. It occurs in pubs where people fill their bodies with alcohol and try to barricade themselves emotionally against the experiences of life. You may feel it after being in a home where energies of quarrels and anger were present. You may feel it after you yourself were immersed in non-positive energies – energies of turbulence, worry, anger, or sorrow.

Stand with your body upright and comfortable. Shake your legs and arms slightly, release them, and relax your body. Take three deep, slow breaths. Direct your thoughts to cleansing your electromagnetic field of all unwanted energies. Using your palm or the back of your hand, begin to rub every part of your body vigorously with brushing movements. Start by running your fingers through your hair, shake it, spread it out, and stroke your whole hand over it, as if you were pulling and extracting all the unwanted energy from it. Shake your hands at your sides in order to get rid of the energy that adhered to them. Pass your palms gently over your face, with the direction of the movement being from the center of your face outward, as if you were "removing dust" from your face. Continue with a light brushing of your neck, from above (below your chin) downward (toward your shoulders). After a few movements, shake your hands and release the energies that adhered to them. Continue to the shoulders. Brush them with more vigorous motions, as if you were dusting off your clothing. If you suffer from a lot of tension in your shoulder region, use a bit of strength when you perform the brushing movements. After you have cleansed your shoulders, go on to brush your arms. Start by brushing your left arm with your right hand. Brush the entire length of your arm with a strong, continuous, pulling motion to your fingertips and shake your right hand (which did the brushing). Repeat the action with the other hand and arm. When shaking your hands free of the energy you brushed, direct your thoughts to moving the unwanted energy downward, to the bowels of the earth. Afterwards, rub your chest and abdomen vigorously using downward brushing movements. Then brush your back (as much as you can; in areas you cannot reach, direct your thoughts to cleanse them!), your buttocks, your inner and outer thighs and calves, with vigorous downward movements, until you reach your feet. There, you must direct your thoughts to shifting the non-positive energies downward, deep into the bowels of the earth. After you have brushed your entire body with vigorous movements, shake your hands well, imagine in your mind's eye a jet of cold water washing them, and "cleanse" them in the purifying jet of water. Afterwards, with slow and gentle motions, and taking a slow and conscious breath, slowly move the palm of your hand at a distance of a few centimeters from your body, trying to feel the aura field. Start above your head, and slowly descend along both sides of your body, not forgetting the inner side of the arms and legs, from the left, the right, front, and back (wherever you cannot reach, imagine that you are moving the non-positive energy downward). Finish next to your feet, and imagine that you are causing the non-positive energy to sink downward, deep into the bowels of the earth.

You can apply the brushing technique to other people, to animals, and to plants as well. Of course, it should be done gently, paying attention to their reactions and emotions. Always remember to shake your hands after brushing off the energy, and to direct the non-positive energy downward into the bowels of the earth. The technique is also very good when you feel exhausted, fatigued, and drained after being in an energetically unclean place, after a treatment, and after a lot of work at a computer.

### Cleansing the aura by means of incense

This is an easy and effective way of cleansing the aura, and it is used mainly after administering a treatment, after a quarrel, argument, or a long, busy day, and when there you feel that non-positive energies have adhered to your aura. The cleansing is done with the help of a partner, who holds the stick of incense. After you do this cleansing with the help of a partner often, you may be able to do it by yourself.

For the cleansing, you can use any stick of natural and high-quality incense. (There are incense sticks that are scented with low-quality artificial perfumes that are used for purifying the air in toilets, walk-in closets, and so on – it is not advisable to use them.) The types of incense that are most highly recommended are sage, which is very strong and effective for purification, frankincense, and jasmine. However, any stick of high-quality, pleasant-smelling incense will do.

Stand erect, feet slightly apart, and close your eyes. Make sure to take deep, slow, and comfortable abdominal breaths. Your partner holds the lit and smoking stick of incense and begins to walk around your body. There are many different ways of moving the incense around, but it should go in a right-to-left direction – clockwise. It is possible to start at the top, and move the incense stick clockwise around the head, at a distance of 20 to 60 centimeters from the body, and gradually descend, in a kind of spiral, to the feet, and then ascend again.

Another way is to start on the right side of the body and descend very slowly to the feet, and then go up the left side of the body, go down the right side again, and go up the left side once more. In this technique, intuition and emotion are very important, and if your partner feels that another slightly different method of moving the incense stick around is appropriate, it is worth trying. This technique is simple, quick, and extremely effective. After the cleansing, you frequently experience a feeling of relief and purification, a feeling of a burden being lifted off your shoulders, greater vitality, and a feeling of significant tranquillity.

# Channeling with animals

*In the most ancient days,*
*When animals and humans too were on the earth,*
*A man could become an animal if he wanted*
*And an animal could become a man.*
*Sometimes they were humans*
*And sometimes animals*
*And there was no difference*
*They all spoke the same language.*

(from a Native American poem)

We can learn a great deal from animals, whether by observing them – the physical animal – or by using them as a "pipeline" to transmit messages. The totem animal, which we will try to get to know in the next exercise, helps us with our spiritual development. Animals that we encounter by chance may also be a sign or teach us something. More than once, I have asked the universe a question and an animal that is rarely found in the region where I live enters my house. By channeling with an animal (as in the next meditation), or by recognizing the message or insight represented by the animal, I received an answer to my question. People who are very in touch with nature and Mother Earth are inclined to receive many messages in this manner, as are people who work to preserve the environment. It would seem that nature "rewards" them with signs and symbols in the form of the animals that cross their paths. Incidentally, the animal does not have to appear physically in front of you: for instance, you might pass a store window or billboard upon which a picture of an animal appears; the insight that it represents will help you at that moment; or you turn on the TV and see the animal whose insight you are waiting for). Channeling with animals is easy and natural; you just have to open your mind to the idea that animals can channel with us in exactly the same way that we, human beings, channel with one another, and channel well telepathically.

## Channeling with an animal via observation

This apparently simple meditation is one of the most ancient forms of observation (meditation). Many of the ancient philosophers, priests, shamans, and spiritual teachers acquired knowledge by means of this observation. There is no need to set a time limit for the meditation, since this may vary from person to person, from one object of observation to another, and mainly from a beginning meditative exercise to the following exercises. You have almost certainly performed this meditation in the past without calling it "meditation," but rather curious observation. Children, like many ancient tribal members, are gifted with an inner trigger to perform this meditation in certain conditions, and they can persist with it for a long time. It is natural and simple for them, except in cases in which the parents instill a fear of animals in them from infancy. As parents, it is important to support this natural activity, and not stop it or create an artificial barrier between the child and nature – a barrier that stems from the parents' own fears. This ancient meditation symbolizes our link with the animal world, a link in which there is no separation, but rather connection and a single whole. In its upper layers, which are reached – after practicing various meditations extensively – as a result of a deep and natural link with the natural world, and as a result of deep spiritual openness, the meditation leads to a feeling of perfect unity with the object of observation. This means being able to feel its feelings, and understanding the way it perceives, its insights, and often even its language.

Animals and plants have a clear and obvious language. The legends about King Solomon and St. Francis of Assisi state that they could understand the language of animals and plants. These claims are not the product of a fertile imagination, nor are they characteristic of only those figures. Every person has this ability, but he has to cross the conceptual barrier that says that the nature of animals and plants is separate and different from that of human beings. When the person crosses this conceptual barrier, he feels a deep love for nature, various fears regarding nature and its creatures disappear, he is sensitive and caring toward nature, and he eschews any action that can damage it, in the same way as he avoids hurting people.

When we set about establishing communication with animals and plants, we must remember that just as various tribes and peoples have different languages, so it is with animals. Their language is not composed of words, but rather of gestures, movements, looks, unique sounds, and telepathic, extrasensory communication. Plants, too, have a unique language. In deep layers, when the person can "hear" his soul, and he channels with it and knows it, he can reach the stage of "hearing" animals' souls, and may even grasp their message via his extrasensory auditory sense (the fine sense of hearing) as actual words. These wonderful experiences of communication with animals and plants are not the privilege of a few exceptional people only, but rather result from a deep love of nature, from the ability to understand that we and everything around us are one, and from spiritual work and the expansion of our awareness. Moreover, many people are granted these abilities as a gift when they show profound respect, appreciation, and love for nature, and are sensitive to Mother Earth and her children, the plants and animals. In cases like these, they get to feel nature's love for them in a unique way. Nature communicates with them through the channel that they themselves have established with their very sensitivity, concern, and appreciation for it and its creatures. This is an astounding and moving love, which is expressed in many different ways – all of which fill these people with wonder and joy.

The essence of this meditation is observing an animal you have chosen, or that will choose you, at a particular moment.

It is a good idea to perform the initial meditation, before you have become accustomed to the feeling, in a place that is as quiet as possible for you and the animal. It should be a tranquil place, preferably in natural surroundings. Sit comfortably at a distance from which you can observe the animal. This animal may be an ant, a beetle, or any other insect, a dove, a cat, a dog, and so on. However, you should be able to look into its eyes, and it should be able to look into your eyes. Moreover, at least at the beginning, it should be an animal that you like or admire from the outset, and that will stay in your line of vision long enough time for you to observe it profoundly. Animals such as horses, cows, sheep, cats, or dogs (yes, your own dog is great for meditation!) are excellent options for the initial meditation.

Perform the meditation with openness and calmness, without expectations, prejudices, or wishes. When you do the meditation the first few times, and the link with nature is still not familiar or immediate, you should do it sitting or standing at some distance from the animal. Having said that, the meditation itself – the observation and the link-up – may also happen tangibly when you are involved in some kind of activity with the animal – touching, playing, stroking, feeding, and so on.

Look at the animal. Look at its unique shape. Look into its eyes as far as possible. Look at its body, concentrating totally on the object of observation. At this moment, only you and the object of observation exist. Look at the structure of its body – its muscles, its bones, its movements – and do so without using your mental layer. In other words, forget about the explanations and chapters on animal behavior that you remember from textbooks; do not relate to them. Look at the unique expressions of the animal. Let your observation of the animal evoke new insights in you. Look at the animal with appreciation, and while you are looking at it, project your awareness to it. The observation itself is the projection of awareness. Feel the connection between you until you can just about feel the animal's feelings – its unique body movement, its expressions, the feelings that it experiences when it is involved in certain activities. Notice every single detail about its body, concentrate totally on your object of observation, and allow yourself to forget yourself while doing so. Devote as much time as you deem necessary to the observation. At the end of it, thank the animal for its part in the experience and for the gifts it gave you, and wish it health, happiness, and self-fulfillment.

The range of insights and feelings evoked during the meditation is broad and unique. Moreover, it also depends on the state of balance of the chakras and on the stimulation of the third eye center, and, as we said before, on the ability to let the self link up completely to the object of observation. In addition to the insights we receive during meditation, the meditation helps us restore our natural reactive and healing abilities as an inseparable part of nature, and causes tremendous vitality to flow into our entire body.

People with a powerful extrasensory visual ability, who tend to see what they do during meditation with their inner eye, who often see clear dreams, or who are able to see content from the imagination in their mind's eye, can perform this meditation without the animal being present. For that, you should lie or sit comfortably, and enter a deep meditative state. In the meditation for observing animals using this technique, the possibilities for observing various animals are broader, since they do not depend on time or place, and you can summon any animal you like to it. You can also meditate without calling on any particular animal, but just let it appear. The animal that appears opposite your eyes may teach you a number of important insights. If the sight of this animal makes you feel somewhat uneasy or frightened, this is the time to make peace with it and remember that you are part of everything that exists, and the separation between the bodies is an illusion that belongs to this world only. Moreover, by meditating in this way (when the person can see the animal clearly in his mind's eye), the illusions stemming from the material world that are attributed to animals are extremely tenuous. This means that it is possible to listen to the animal and channel with it very easily without the limitations that people's perceptions tend to attribute to the animal world. If you hear the animal speaking during the meditation, or you feel as if it wants to talk to you, you can ask it a question. Animals have the ability to teach us many profound things, reveal secrets, instruct, and serve as messengers between us and the source. Various types of birds, especially the dove and the hawk, are excellent messengers, and we can ask them to relay our wishes to the source so that they can be fulfilled.

# The animal of your strength – the totem animal

The concept of an animal of strength, or a totem animal, is widespread in many cultures. In the Jewish culture, there are examples of the use of animals as symbols of a personality or behavior type. Some of the pennants of the tribes of Israel bore pictures of the animal that represented the tribe. The most famous is the Lion of Judah. The writings of one of the sages, in which he suggested that it is preferable to be a lion's tail rather than a fox's head, describes the way in which our animal of strength is supposed to help us. In the Native American culture, every tribe, clan, and nuclear family had a totem. Today, too, in various organizations and companies, animals are used as symbols that represent the group that participates in a particular type of activity, mainly in the USA (such as the "Lions" organization, etc.). Sports teams also adopt totem animals, such as the Chicago Bulls. Christianity adopted two "totem" animals – the lamb, which symbolizes Jesus, and the fish.

As we said, in Judaism, too, every animal represents a particular kind of energy. The fish is a symbol of fertility, the lion is the symbol of power and strength, the deer is a symbol of speed, and so on.

The second type of totem animal is the personal and individual one. These animals are energies, and, according to certain beliefs, spirits that protect and guide us in life. It is interesting that to this day, many parents give their children some kind of fluffy animal – a bear, for instance – to make it easier to fall asleep and help them feel protected. They are not aware of it, generally speaking, but this is also a totem animal.

The signs of the Zodiac also contain animals that attest more than once to the energy that influences the person's life.

Frequently, we unconsciously identify the totem animal of a particular person. We look at him, and he seems to "remind" us of a certain animal. We also use animal descriptions to describe various people.

Animals hold a place of honor among the shamans. The first task of the future shaman is to learn to travel in other worlds and dimensions and discover his own totem animal, his animal of strength. This knowledge is necessary for starting the young shaman's protracted learning process.

Personal animals of strength are generally the reflection of the self, and also represent qualities needed in this world, which are often hidden, concealed, and not yet expressed. Sometimes, people feel somewhat disappointed when they discover that their animal of strength is a "small" animal that seems to lack strength, such as a rabbit or a mouse. This error derives from a lack of understanding that the spirit of the animals, or their energies, is neither "small" nor "big" – it is not limited to the boundaries of this world and the physical reality and size of the animal, or to its strength in the physical world. None of those factors is relevant. Whether your animal of strength is "big" or "small," you will quickly discover that in time of need, it will help you exactly to the extent that you need help.

According to the Native American tradition, the personal totem animal, in contrast to family, clan, or tribal totem animals, may change several times during the person's lifetime, according to his specific needs. At times when you feel weak, exhausted, and depressed, your totem animal is far away from you, and you have to bring it back or find a new one.

We all have a totem animal – an animal of strength, energy that is represented by a certain animal – that is linked to us and protects us. Many animals of strength serve as our guards and protectors, and exist in other dimensions. Certain animals were with us in previous lives, but they may have had a different physical form. Occasionally, a particular animal of strength of ours may appear in our lives in a different form and establish physical contact with us by coming into the world as a cat, a dog, and so on.

In this chapter, I will present a number of ways for discovering personal animals of strength. When you go on the journey to discover your animal of strength, it is almost certain that forces, or certain energies (as we said, according to the Native American tradition, those are the spirits of the animal; I personally prefer to define them as the energy of the animal), will introduce themselves as your animal of strength. If you already know and are familiar with your animal of strength, the animal you meet on your journey will bless you and grant you additional power.

According to the Native American tradition, all birds and mammals are positive totem animals. Any positive totem animal can be your animal of strength. However, not only familiar and well-known animals are our animals of strength. Insects and reptiles can serve as transmitters of messages or give us a certain insight that will support us during the rest of our mental and spiritual development. Sometimes, the animal of strength may be an extinct animal (such as the Australian bird, the dodo), a mythological animal (such as the unicorn or Pegasus, the winged horse), or even a centaur (half man and half horse, one of Sagittarius' symbols). Sometimes, it can be an animal that does not exist in any mythology or in any zoological textbook – a unique animal, or an animal from another world.

## Meeting the animal of strength

The animal of strength you will meet in this meditation may be the animal you expected – or may not be. You are therefore advised not to have expectations. It is important not to think of a particular animal before beginning the meditation, so that you can be open to all possibilities. If the animal that you imagine to be your animal of strength is indeed your animal of strength during this period of your life, it will appear by itself.

Perform the meditation in a quiet, calm place with quiet and clean energies. Clear your mind of all thoughts. Relax your body. (You can use the Jacobson technique – contracting and relaxing all the muscles from your toes upward, or you can project light onto every organ until you feel totally relaxed.)

Close your eyes. Take two deep, slow breaths. Inhale through your nose and hold your breath as long as you can – without feeling uncomfortable – and exhale through your mouth. Ignore any irrelevant thought that may pop into your mind. Behind your closed eyes, see a white screen. Concentrate on it. You may see some pleasant color or shape beginning to emerge in your mind's eye. In your thoughts, ask your animal of strength to show itself on the screen. Concentrate hard on your request.

Wait patiently and don't let any thoughts distract you. Within a certain amount of time, the image of an animal will appear before your eyes. It may advance slowly toward you, or you may see it in a sharp, clear flash. It may reveal itself from behind, the side, or the front. It may even be an animal that you don't like – don't let this bother you. Let the image emerge in your mind's eye.

The moment you see the animal, look at it quietly, and notice what it is doing, if it is performing any actions. Direct your thoughts to picking up messages telepathically from the animal. These could occur as a voice speaking inside you, as other pictures, or as the intuitive knowledge of the animal's words or messages. As we said before, the message may be in a human language that is familiar to you. Sometimes the animal appears as part of an occurrence or event that is familiar to you. Of course, this situation also bears an individual message.

Concentrate as hard as you can. Notice the colors that surround the animal and then open your eyes slowly. In your heart, thank the universal force for letting you channel with your animal of strength, and write down your experiences and sights in your awareness notebook. You can also draw what you saw. Sometimes it happens that you see more than one animal, or an animal that exists in the real world along with some kind of mythological animal. Similarly, another time, a different animal may appear, bearing a different message.

After the meditation, you should think of the following things: Have you ever dreamed of a particular kind of animal? What happened in that dream? You can ask that animal to appear in your dream at night and channel with it. To this end, you can use crystals for channeling and dreaming. After you have seen the animal in the meditation, ask yourself why that particular animal appeared in front of you.

## Messages and insights

There are many animals, each of which has an important message for us. Of course, there are not more important animals or less important animals, but it would take too long to describe the messages of all the animals, so I will present a variety of animals that appear relatively frequently in meditations. If the animal you saw in the meditation does not appear here, you can discover its message very simply – by observation. Get hold of a picture of the animal, or better still, a videotape (by National Geographic, for instance) in which you see the animal in action. Observe it closely, learn its ways, how it copes with problems, how it obtains food, how it raises its young, how it fights or survives, how it walks, its general appearance, its movements – all those are messages that describe the message that the animal wants to convey to you. Another way, no less simple, is just to invite the animal again, but this time ask it to give you the message and describe what it represents.

# The animals and the insights they represent:

***Albatross:*** Patience; stoicism; endurance; understanding of the importance of long-term parental commitment; ability to remain in emotional states for a long time; uncomfortable, strange, but effective, beginnings and ends.

***Ant:*** Patience; endurance, durability; planning; the necessary energy and patience for completing a task or work; communal life; hoarding for the future.

***Anteater:*** Ability to find lost items; link with the insect world; ability to "sniff out" trouble before seeing it; understanding the value of "digging" for finding solutions.

***Antilope:*** Taking a stand; ability to leap over obstacles; strong survival abilities; speed; gentleness; link to the earth.

***Armadillo:*** Understanding personal boundaries; respecting other people's boundaries; carrying your protection with you at all times and in all situations; understanding your vulnerability and weak spots; empathy; ability to discern.

***Baboon:*** Consecrated to the god Thuth (god of wisdom) and to the god Hepi (god of the Nile); protecting the family.

***Badger:*** Guardian of stories; aggression; biting and courageous self-expression; cunning, deceit; passion; vengefulness, vengeance; stubbornness, persistence; control; antidote to passivity or being a victim; persistence in serving a cause; grounding; knowledge of and familiarity with the earth; charm connected to the earth and the wisdom of the earth; guarding and protecting rights and spiritual ideas.

***Bald eagle:*** Rising up above the material in order to see the spiritual; speed; courage; wisdom; strength; sharp vision; creation; healing; spiritual illumination; knowledge of positive spells and witchcraft; ability to recognize spiritual truths; link to upper truths; ability to see the whole picture; link to spiritual teachers and guides and to soul guides; honor, grace, and goodness; creative and intuitive spirit; tremendous strength and balance; grace and goodness that are attained through knowledge and toil; respect for boundaries of fields and sectors.

***Bat:*** Shamanic death and rebirth; initiation; passage, change; beginning of new ideas; seeing previous lives; understanding sorrow; camouflage; ability to see the invisible; use of sound vibrations;

***Bear:*** Looking inward; healing; loneliness/solitude; change; link with the wind; death and rebirth; astral travel; transformation; production of dreams, shamans and mystics; man of vision; protection and vengeance; wisdom.

***Beaver:*** Persistence, industriousness; preserving the ability to be productive in all ways by not limiting one's options; using existing resources; using various methods for accomplishing tasks; master builder of all things; understanding the dynamics of group work; not stopping the flow of experiences in life; achievements stemming from the completion of tasks.

***Bee:*** Prosperity; concentration; understanding the energy of the female fighter; reincarnation; communication with the dead; helping the spirits that are still tied to the earth to move onward to their appropriate place.

***Black panther:*** Astral travel; protective energy; symbol of femininity; understanding death; death and rebirth; ability to acknowledge darkness; restoration of personal forces that were taken away.

***Buffalo/bison:*** Abundance; feminine courage; creativity connected to the earth; knowledge; generosity; hospitality; courage; collaboration; strength; challenge; survival; giving for the good of others; developing beneficial plans.

***Butterfly/caterpillar:*** Strength of the storm and air turbulence; transformation; reincarnation; spell/witchcraft.

***Buzzard:***

Helps in healing the soul; accompanies the soul back to the world of the souls; the study of speed and agility; control of speed and movement; learning the tricks of life; understanding spells.

***Camel:*** Transformation of the loads we carry; ability to save for future use; understanding the open spaces; learning to walk through the shifting sands of time.

***Canary:*** Beautiful voice; use of song for healing; finding the song of the soul; happiness; ability to find happiness in song in times of darkness and shadow.

***Cat:*** Independence; seeing the invisible; protection; enables us to dream our dreams; love; helps in meditations; ability to fight when pushed into a corner.

***Centipede:*** Coordination; balance; ability to survive at times of pressure and hardship; beauty of movement.

***Chameleon:*** Use of the sun as a source of power; ability to climb up high in order to accomplish objectives; patience; use of color for camouflage; pulling things toward you as a means of survival.

***Cheetah:*** Brotherhood; evasiveness; ability to focus on one thing intensely for a short time; agility and speed; self-esteem; hurrying, sense of time; sharpness of vision.

***Chimpanzee:*** Wisdom; linguistic abilities; understanding the complexities of society; link with the spirits of the forest; solution to problems; skill; ability to balance between aggression and compassion.

***Cobra:*** Soul guide; memory of the world of the soul; memories of previous lives; the wisdom of divine female energy; transformation of the soul; freedom from religious persecutions.

***Cockroach:*** Understanding loathing and revulsion in other people; passage through fear; understanding shadows; speed for the sake of escaping injury.

***Coral:*** Providing a living environment for everything; symbiosis; understanding the need for variety; community life, communal life.

***Cormorant:*** Patience; ability to grasp the essentials; use of the sun as a healing power.

***Cow/bull:*** Love; alertness to danger; satisfaction; link to expanses of green grass; ability to share that is expressed in community life; ability to stand up for oneself.

***Crab:*** Understanding the power of dance; ability to escape by moving sideways; ability to pass through water (emotions); finding new uses for what seems unusable; the masculine aspects of the community; protecting the domestic space.

***Crane:*** Symbol of light and spring; astral travel; longevity; new knowledge; elegance; seeks to help others along their path; wisdom; ability to see all the things that are connected to secrets; unique use of the voice.

***Cricket:*** Finding the way out of the dark by following the personal song; good luck; teaches the power of song in times of darkness; understanding the correct timing to jump out of a particular situation; communication; connection with the plant kingdom.

***Crocodile:*** Maternal protection; link to Mother Earth; protection against manipulations; initiation; vengeance through tolerance; ability to spot deception and cunning; understanding the weather; entry into ancient knowledge.

***Crow:*** Rebirth; renewal; recovery; cycle; healing (return and recovery of lost parts of the soul); casting light on shadow; link-up to the source; reflections/mirrors; self-acceptance; introspection; finding consolation in solitude; honoring the ancient fathers; the spells of the elders; prediction of the future; change in awareness; new occurrences; purity of language.

***Cuckoo:*** Efficiency; ability to adapt; new beginnings; meeting with personal destiny.

***Deer:*** Ability to listen; grace and appreciation of beauty and equilibrium; gentleness of touch, speech, and thought; understanding what is required for survival; power; gratitude and giving; ability to sacrifice oneself for lofty objectives; finding alternative routes to the objective.

***Dingo:*** Human soul that was reborn (possibility); tracking and scouting talents; assistance in hunting; finding warmth in cold situations; loyalty; understanding silence; finding the truth; friendship; protection; correct use of intuition.

***Dog:*** Heals emotional wounds in human beings; companionship, friendship; complete loyalty; unconditional love; understanding the duality of belief and doubt; knowledge of all the sensual things and those that are linked to the senses; protection; ability to "sniff out" trouble from afar.

***Dolphin:*** Gift of God; knowledge of the sea; patron of seafarers; change; balance; wisdom; harmony; communicative abilities; freedom; trust; understanding the power of rhythms in personal life; use of the breath to release repressed or oppressive emotions; spells linked to the element of water.

***Donkey:*** Obstinacy; ability to carry out decisions; saying "no" to other people; objection to taking steps that the person knows are not right for him; ignoring other people's opinions.

***Dove / turtledove / wild pigeon:*** Brings peace and love; messenger; communication between two worlds; understanding pleasantness and gentleness.

***Dragonfly:*** Shattering of illusions; life's secrets in flight; the force of flight; understanding dreams; ability to escape in a flash; seeing the truth in situations; agility and speed; change; link to the dragon.

***Duck:*** Water energy (emotional energy); ability to see clearly through emotions; grace in water; helps mystics and visionaries spiritually.

***Eagle (American) / falcon / condor:*** Death and rebirth; prophecy; purifying and self-purification; new vision; love of the spirit of God; knowledge concerning the death of a loved one.

***Eel:*** Power of electricity; camouflage; ability to observe the invisible; fleeing when threatened.

***Elephant:*** Strength; regality; confidence; connection to ancient wisdom; taking advantage of the possibilities to study and enrich one's knowledge; patience; lack of barriers, boundaries, and obstacles.

***Finch:*** Creating balance in relations with various people; understanding the value of change; ability to resolve family conflicts in an effective and healthy way; understanding the power of the voice.

***Firefly:*** Ability to find the light in the darkness; use of light for communication; ability to channel with colors.

***Fish:*** Abundance; fertility; children; harmony; love; renewal; balance between reason and emotion.

***Flamingo:*** Understanding the language of colors; ability to preserve the purpose of the soul in group life; understanding how to preserve equilibrium; ability to sieve the lessons of the soul out of the emotional waters.

***Fox:*** Change of shape; smartness; ability to look out and observe; cunning; stealth, moving secretly; camouflage; feminine courage; ability to be invisible; ability to see the invisible; persistence; gentleness; agility.

***Frog:*** Reminds us of the link that exists with all the life in the universe; cleansing and purification; transformation; singing songs that celebrate the beginning of the ancient water sources; rebirth; understanding emotions.

***Giraffe:*** Intuition; communication; ability to reach things that others cannot reach; ability to look into the distant future; ability to lift oneself and remain above quarrels and friction.

***Goat, billy-goat:*** Abundance; independence; search for new heights; confidence, no stumbling; discarding guilt feelings; understanding the creatures and energies of nature; lightness of movement;

***Goldfish:*** Prophecy; harmony; beauty; peace; balance between reason and emotion.

***Gorilla:*** Wisdom, intelligence; gentleness; maternal instincts; generosity; verbal and oratorial ability.

***Goose:*** Happiness; walking along the path of the soul; understanding the strength of the community; helping others in times of trouble or illness.

***Hare:*** Quick-thinking; receiving hidden and intuitive messages; deception, trickery; paradoxes and contradictions; living according to personal wisdom; humility; the ability to move through fear; strengthening the intuition.

***Hawk:*** Deliverer of spiritual messages; sharp powers of discrimination; ability to be an observer of what is happening; long-term memory; remembering previous lives; wisdom; guardianship; courage; enlightenment; seeing the whole picture; creativity; truth; experience; overcoming problems; ability to make use of opportunities wisely.

***Hedgehog:*** Innocence; confidence; creating one's personal path; ability to let others follow their personal paths without interfering; renewal of the sense of wonder and of the miraculous in life; maintaining boundaries; protecting oneself when threatened; non-disturbance/non-interference.

***Hen / rooster:*** Hearing the inner voice/listening to your inner voice; picking up the answers that others cannot grasp; powers that awake with sunrise; power of the voice; understanding the language; protecting the family and the community.

***Heron:*** Confidence in the self, ability to rely on the self; boundaries; self-esteem; juggling multiple tasks; colorfulness; honor, nobility.

***Hippopotamus:*** Correct use of aggressions; can move gracefully through the emotions; protecting the family; the birth of new ideas; maternal rage when necessary.

***Horse / pony / mustang:*** Power, strength; endurance and tolerance; devotion; awareness of the power that is attained through true cooperation; broadening the potential abilities; dominance and control over the environment; the liberty to gallop freely; hikes and journeys; astral travel; patron of hikers; communication between different species; warning of possible danger; guide to overcoming obstacles.

***Hummingbird:*** Merriment; love; happiness; ability to heal by using light as a laser beam from the mouth; endurance on long journeys; ability to fly to small (hidden) places in order to heal oneself.

***Hyena:*** Knowledge of the secrets of the wild; ability to adapt; understanding how to control epidemics; strength; understanding the value of cooperation; patience; singing the personal song of the soul; persistence in hunting; connection with the vulture; defense of borders; communication in dark regions; understanding the importance of life in the community.

***Ibis:*** Understanding ancient wisdom; contact with the Egyptian gods; wisdom; enlightenment.

***Jackal:*** Astral travel; access to previous lives; understanding the use of opportunities; ability to see in the dark (spiritual darkness, too); link to the Egyptian pyramids; link to the constellation Orion.

***Jaguar:*** Extrasensory vision; moving fearlessly in the dark; seeing the paths in chaos; understanding the patterns of chaos; promoting the soul's work; empowering the self; movement in unknown places; change of shape.

***Kangaroo:***

Protecting the young; creating a safe domestic environment; leaping far from problematic and negative situations; ability to adapt to new situations.

***Kingfisher:*** Peace; happiness and love; link to the pacific seas (and oceans)/emotional tranquillity; bright and clear observation through emotional waters, and extracting your dream from them.

***Kiwi:*** Link to the ancient wisdom of the enlightened; understanding the earth's changes; ability to "scratch" the truth out.

***Koala:*** Ability to climb over obstacles; understanding the value of slow movement; the power of Yoga; gives useful advice; ability to remain aloof from brawls and disagreements.

***Leopard:*** Strength; energetic; marvelous sense of timing; acting without prior analytical thinking; strength and willpower in the face of trouble and hardship.

***Lemur:*** Seeing the invisible; access to knowledge of forests; ability to navigate through forests; understanding the ability to remain above the vicissitudes of life; ability to grasp ideas that are beyond the static nature of life.

***Lion:*** Brotherhood; courage; energy; power and strength; relieving pressure and burdens; strong family ties; self-realization.

***Lizard:*** Separations from the ego; coping with fears; ability to control dreams; movement in other worlds; ability to revive or renew things that have withered or gotten lost.

***Llama / guanaco / vicuna (South American camel):*** Consoling others; passing over hedges; ability to tolerate and survive the cold; overcoming materialism.

***Locust / grasshopper:*** Astral travel; leap of faith; jumping over time and space; jumping without knowing where you'll land; jumping over obstacles; new leaps forward; ability to change professions swiftly.

***Marten:*** Fearlessness in self-defense and attack; stopping people who do evil/fear of people who do injustice; protecting the family; using speed for protection.

***Medusa:*** Sensitivity to the energy of the element of water – emotions; understanding the value of floating while swimming at difficult emotional times and during emotional trials; correct use of softness; ability to disentangle oneself from the web of life's dangers.

***Mole:*** Guards the low places; linked to the energies of the earth; knowledge of plants, roots, minerals, seeds, and hidden rivers and minerals of the earth; the ability to withdraw into oneself; introspection, being blind to everything in the material world by seeing light and dark only; natural love; sensitivity to touch and vibrations; understanding the energies and their ways of flowing.

***Monkey:*** Movement through the ego; understanding success; good health; ability to change one's surroundings; protecting the family; understanding situations of excess and exaggeration.

***Mosquito:*** Use of water for transformation/use of emotions for transformation; directing the energy flow in one direction; pulling energy inward.

***Moth:*** Power of the storm; slow movement in the dark, in the shadows; ability to find light in the darkness; ability to confuse enemies; transformation.

***Mouse / lemming/ rat:*** Understanding fine details; examining the lesson of life; quiet; diffidence; invisibility; seeing the double meaning of things; ability to be stealthy; guide when signing contracts; discovery and revelation; ability to be invisible.

***Nightingale:*** Correct use of song for healing; use of song for passing beyond fears; link with the moon; use of vibratory energy for seeing between the shadows.

***Octopus / squid / ink-fish:*** Wisdom; destruction of negative barriers; fast movement to get away from danger when necessary; correct use of a smokescreen in order to escape from enemies.

***Orang-utan:*** Gentleness; link with the spirits of the forest; movement above quarrels and disagreements; wit and inventiveness when coping with problems.

***Ostrich:*** Help in expelling evil spirits; spiritual truth; understanding all aspects of denial; evasiveness, abstemious behavior; ability to outrun rivals; community life.

***Otter:*** Feminine energy; the feminine healing wisdom; sensitivity and fineness of feelings without suspicions; guide to discovering and removing the masks covering abilities and talents; extrasensory awareness; faith; matters concerning recovery (physical or emotional); understanding the value of play and fun.

***Owl:*** Secrecy; fast and silent movement; ability to be stealthy; ability to see behind the masks; sharp vision; messenger for signs and secrets; change of shape; link between the dark and the invisible world on the one hand, and the world of light on the other; ability to accept the shadows in our personality; spells and witchcraft regarding the moon; freedom.

***Oyster:*** Understanding when to close doors in order to avoid losing energy; ability to filter out the static aspects of life; maintaining strong and enduring external defense; sensitivity to environmental changes.

***Panda:*** Understanding the value of slow motion; balance; ability to adapt; link to Eastern art; link to the plant kingdom.

***Parakeet:*** Love; imitation, mimicry; ability to change direction abruptly; trust; helps with objectives concerning the community.

***Parrot:*** Use of language; relationship between the members of a couple; imitation; brings rain; wisdom and guidance to think before speaking.

***Peacock:*** All the aspects of beauty; immortality; honor; ability to see into the past, present, and future; self-confidence; ability to get up after suffering a heavy blow.

***Pelican:*** Control of the ego; correct use of abundance; ability to float through emotions; recovery from loss; ability to return from being on the verge of extinction.

***Penguin:*** Paternity; understanding the feminine energy in the male; patience; astral travel; daydreams; endurance.

***Pheasant / partridge:*** Movement beyond the ego; use of color for healing purposes; development and broadening of the self-awareness; understanding the use of ceremonies.

***Pig:*** Knowledge of previous lives; strong earth spell/enchantment; wisdom; cunning; becoming invisible when in danger.

***Polar bear:*** Ability to navigate along all the magnetic lines of the earth; solitude/loneliness; introspection; expertise at swimming through the waters of the emotions; ability to find possibilities of a livelihood in desolate expanses; finding the way back from the brink; dreams; death and rebirth; production of dreams, shamans, mystics, and visionaries; transformation; strength in times of trouble; channeling with the spirit; protection and vengeance.

***Porcupine:*** Protection against negativity; fertility; enjoyment of life; the wisdom of old women; understanding weather patterns.

***Prairie wolf / coyote:*** Wisdom, intelligence; ability to laugh at our mistakes; change of shape; learning the balance between safety and risk; understanding that all things are sacred, but, having said that, nothing is sacred; learning that only when all the masks have been removed can we link up to the source; song of praise to the Creation; innocent belief in the truth; teaches us how to raise our young ones (children, the inner child); rainmaker; enlightenment; ability to be stealthy.

***Praying mantis:*** Ability to maneuver time; ability to move between moments; ability to remain motionless and silent; understanding the circular nature of time; feminine fighting energies; attack strategies.

***Puma / cougar / mountain lion:*** Leadership and charisma; wise, use of the power of leadership without ego; equilibrium between strength, intention, and ability; accumulation of self-confidence; liberation from guilt feelings; cunning.

***Quail:*** Life close to the earth; ability to fade into the background; courage to cope with hard labor; finding peaceful solutions to dangerous situations.

***Rat:*** Protection, defense; sign of fertility and wealth; creation of abundance; wisdom and intelligence; ability to be invisible; ability to be stealthy.

***Rhinoceros:*** Learning the ability to console oneself in situations of loneliness; link to ancient wisdom; wise use of ancient wisdom; knowing oneself; confidence in one's instincts.

***Robin:*** Paternity; courting; an understanding of the strength of the blowing wind; finding the song of your soul.

***Salamander:*** Link to the soul's memory of early days on earth; promoting the connection between earth and water; change; encouragement in the dark; ability to put on a disguise in the face of danger.

***Salmon:*** The value of returning home in order to renew one's forces; swimming on top of the current of emotions in order to achieve new insights; rebirth of spiral knowledge; understanding the messages of fortune-telling.

***Scorpion:*** Death and rebirth; transformation (change of form) of poison; returning dark and negative energy to the sender.

***Seagull:*** Spiritual messenger; channeling; friendship; ability to look at the situation from above; responsible behavior.

***Seal:*** Movement through emotions; protection when changes are occurring; lucid dreams; protection against danger; creativity.

***Shark:*** Ability to live in the here and now; self-acceptance and spiritual, emotional, and physical acceptance; ability to move frequently; work/movement in silence; "devours" negative energy; recycling of energy; link to the past; a living fossil – a living organism while the species closest to it have become extinct; cruelty, ruthlessness; never caught unprepared; ability to defend oneself.

***Sheep / ewe / ram:*** New beginnings; maintaining balance in dangerous situations; fertility; confidence in one's abilities; courage needed for maintaining balance; abundance; feeling of confidence in new places and fields.

***Skunk:*** Self-respect; reputation; sensuality; willpower; understanding of how to "do your own thing"; courage; self-confidence.

***Sloth:*** Understanding the spirits of the trees; the value of laziness; the wisdom connected to slow movement; observing the world upside-down; ability to understand when to stick to your guns and not give up.

***Snail:*** Ability to use slow movement as an advantage or for gaining benefit; the importance of being ambulatory; understanding the importance of leaving a trail behind you; understanding the value of humor; protection by means of retreat; sensuality.

***Snake:*** Messenger of the rainbow snake (according to the Native American and Aborigine tradition); slipperiness; revelation of the mysteries of life; activates lightning (according to the Native American tradition); change of shape; ancient and elemental energy; guarding against religious persecutions; extrasensory energy; creative force; immortality; serves the shaman as a magic rope to the world of the souls.

***Sparrow:*** Fertility; passion; discovery of new love in life; ability to use the power of song; understanding the different aspects of race; all the aspects of color.

***Spider:*** Master weaver; weaves the webs of fate; wisdom; creativity; divine inspiration; change of shape; understanding the patterns of illusion; feminine energy for the creative life force.

***Squirrel:*** Quick change of direction; resourcefulness; change;

revelation; ability to solve puzzles and problems; hoarding for the future; balance between giving and receiving; warning; avoiding danger by climbing up to high places.

***Starling:*** Imitation, mimicry; adaptiveness; ability to control crowds; wisdom, intelligence; mental reception and absorption.

***Stork:*** Creativity; new beginnings; protecting the young; fidelity, devotion.

***Swallow:*** Proximity to the legendary thunderbird; strength of life in the community, in a group; understanding the value of family and home; protection; maneuverability; agility, lightness of movement; a sign of spring (emotional).

***Swan:*** Stimulating the inner strength; understanding of dream symbols; looking into the future; predicting the future; pleasantness and grace in relations with others; developing intuitive abilities.

***Tick:*** Patience; disseminating ideas; trickery, sophistication; ability to use warmth and movement in order to see.

***Tit:*** Lack of fear; standing; ability to wear crowns without ego; the power of the voice.

***Toucan:*** Ease of movement, agility; skill; ability to move to and from the world of the souls; correct use of healing colors; ability to find tranquillity in small places.

***Toad:*** Link to different states of awareness; symbol of the earth; change of luck; long life; camouflage of poison.

***Turkey:*** Self-sacrifice for a lofty cause; understanding the gift of giving; respecting Mother Earth; winning prizes.

***Turtle:*** Symbol of the earth; link to the center; patience; ability to navigate; personal boundaries; link to the feminine; development of new ideas; ability to cure feminine diseases; respect for other people's boundaries; ability to protect oneself spiritually; self-reliance; non-violent protection; stubbornness, taking root.

***Wasp:*** Using the energy of feminine warfare; sisterhood; community life; understanding.

***Weasel:*** Ability to be stealthy; power of discernment, and sharp discernment; slyness; vengeance; trickery; ability to see the hidden reasons behind things.

***Whale:*** Guardian of knowledge; all the knowledge concerning the voice; beauty and movement; extrasensory and telepathic ability; all the aspects of the sea.

***Wild boar:*** Courage; protection; use of the mask of rage; ability to sense danger; ability to find the truth.

***Wildcat:*** Developing the extrasensory senses; sharp vision (sensory and extrasensory); predicting the future; keeping all secrets and mysteries; movement through time and space.

***Wild rooster:*** Stands at the opening of the big spiral; understanding the cyclical nature of time; understanding of and work with circles and cycles; knows how to move through the big spiral; dances the sanctified dance of life.

***Woodpecker:*** Link to the earth; ability to discover hidden layers; understanding rhythms, patterns, and cycles; prophecy; drummer of the earth; lined to thunder; warnings.

***Wolf:*** Death and rebirth; facing the end of the personal life cycle with courage and honor; spiritual study; guide in dreaming and meditation; instincts linked to intelligence; social and family values; tricking and defeating enemies; the ability to go without being seen; stability, permanence; ability to protect the self and the family; ability to exploit changes positively.

***Worm / earthworm:*** Regeneration, renewal; purification of the earth; ability to find nutrition in the depths of the earth; camouflage.

***Zebra:*** Balance; confidence in the route; seeing black and white; brightness without filters; strength; maintaining individuality in the herd.

# Automatic writing: A Practical Guide

Automatic writing is a type of channeling. There are people who do not feel comfortable with the thought that "another entity" is writing through them, so don't "force" yourself to do the exercise if, after reading it, you don't feel comfortable. Before doing the exercise, it is advisable to perform cleansing, filling up, and energetic protection, with the emphasis on the protection. There is no "extrasensory danger" in the exercise, but since we have no idea of who we will be channeling with during the initial stages, and to whom we are opening ourselves during the process, it is advisable to protect the aura, if for no other reason than as a psychological act that prevents us from feeling fear (which, as we have said, is the real "danger" in the extrasensory world). Of course, the protection always acts on the metaphysical layer.

Channeling by means of automatic writing does not always turn out well. It is possible that certain channeling abilities – a natural penchant for this field – are necessary in order to succeed. Sometimes, the very fact of wanting to channel in this way can create a situation in which there are no far-reaching results during the exercise, or there are no results at all. Some time later, however, especially when the person is attracted to writing as a creative process, he finds that he is writing things that originated in channeling.

It is not always easy for us to know whether this is our "developed" imagination or channeling with another entity, but sometimes we understand that this is channeling after we have written things that we had no objective way of knowing, things that may appear in the media later on – in the newspaper, in a TV program, etc. – and we see that we already know things that have only just been discovered. In any event, it's a good idea to keep our expectations low.

Since this is a first channeling attempt for many people, and for even more people it is a first attempt at automatic writing, the exercise is presented in stages, an additional stage being performed each day. It is not a good idea to perform all the stages in one day or more than one stage per day.

The following exercise has been especially adapted for automatic writing on the computer, but if you feel more comfortable doing it on paper, do it in writing – only on the paper, and perhaps you'll want to use the hand you don't normally write with. (Right-handed people should use their left hand, and the opposite, although left-handed people already use their right brain, the intuitive brain, so they may prefer the hand they normally use for writing; try both ways.)

Perform energetic protection, and if you feel like it, also cleansing and filling up (before the protection).

Make sure that you will not be disturbed for about 30 minutes. Turn off the phones and see that you don't have any guests or various obligations that are liable to distract you and break your concentration. At the initial stages of experimenting with automatic writing, you must do the exercises alone. Any disturbance is liable to disrupt the process immediately.

Fatigue while doing automatic writing is not a liability; on the contrary – sometimes it is beneficial, since conscious barriers tend to interfere less. The use of drugs of any kind or alcohol on the day of the exercise is most undesirable.

It is a good idea to light a candle beside the computer – a blue, pink, or purple candle, according to your feeling, and place jasmine or frankincense oil in an essential oil burner, or burn pleasant-smelling incense.

Get into a comfortable position opposite the computer. Clean your mind of all clutter. Empty your mind. Relax the muscles of your body. In particular, think about relaxing the muscles of your neck, your shoulders, your arms and your face, until they are completely loose. You can begin to relax your body from the soles of your feet, by contracting them tightly and then releasing them, the calves, the thighs, and so on, from bottom to top, without skipping any contracted muscle.

In the process ahead, you may channel with a certain entity that is known to you or not, and you may even channel with your own soul, with your spiritual guide, or with your superego. Be open and, at least at the initial stages, don't try to define who and what it is, unless you receive powerful intuitive information about the nature of the channeling.

Ask a question. Ask to establish contact with your spiritual guide. Don't allow yourself to concentrate on, read, or think about the information that comes to you. Your thinking and conscious self will only interfere with the process. In order to prevent yourself from reading the information and going into it in depth – which will immediately disrupt the course of the channeling – you can focus your eyes on something near the computer that will occupy your left brain (the analytical brain). The channeling, meanwhile, is performed in the right brain. At the beginning, it may seem to you that your thoughts are the ones that are coming through, but that's fine. Many well-known channelers who performed automatic writing assumed for a long time that they were writing the messages themselves – until they realized at a certain point that those messages were being transmitted to them by spiritual guides and various entities.

Don't despair if you don't receive any clear messages – or any message at all – the first few times. Automatic writing requires a lot of practice.

Now you can begin the channeling:

Place your hands gently on the keyboard. Be calm, and try to be as nonchalant as possible about the things that will be written. Type the date at the top of the screen.

Concentrate on the desire and openness to receive a message. Call your spiritual guide and tell him that you want to channel with him via the computer. Tell him that you can only work with one guide each time. (This point is important, because sometimes we receive messages from a number of guides simultaneously. Choose one of them and ask to channel with him.) The choice may be made for you. Be open. Even if you are in the habit of channeling with a particular spiritual guide, he may not necessarily be the one that will channel with you through automatic writing, since not all spiritual guides use this manner of channeling.

***First stage* – First day of practice – getting acquainted with the guide/entity, and asking questions that are not complex:**

On the first day of practice, your aim is to get to know who the spiritual guide channeling with you is.

Type: "Hello, what's your name?"

After receiving an answer, continue on to questions about the spiritual guide, his connection and relationship with you. You may discover that he has tried to channel with you several times, and in different ways. Sometimes, it will be a person who is familiar to you in some way.

At first, it is a good idea to start with simple questions to which the answers are "yes" or "no." Don't stop to think. Simply place your fingers in a position to type the answer. This is the time to get to know the guide who is working with you and the connection between the two of you, and what the aim of this connection is. Sometimes, the guides want to transmit personal messages to the person about himself. Sometimes they want to tell about themselves, and in certain cases, their messages concern the whole world, as messages to humanity.

After a few minutes, you are likely to find yourself typing faster. Punctuation errors are not rare, and some words may appear without spaces between them. Strange syntax, unknown or foreign words may appear. This is not important – you can go into that more deeply later on and carefully correct the mistakes. (Sometimes, grammatical errors are intentional, and strange words sometimes have a particular meaning, so use your intuition.) Simply continue typing questions and answers and don't stop to punctuate or separate words.

Don't write too much on the first day. Start slowly and feel comfortable. You can continue any time you like. There is no need for a fixed schedule, and you don't have to move on to the second exercise precisely on the next day. Rather, you can do so whenever you feel like it. Every additional experience will make you feel more comfortable and able to channel more easily.

### *Second stage* – Second day of practice – receiving additional details

On the second day of channeling (not necessarily the day following the first day of channeling, but no later than a few days later, in order to preserve the effect of the first experience), you can ask questions beyond "yes" and "no" and receive more extensive details. It is not advisable to ask personal questions, such as matters of family, health, love, and so on, until you feel comfortable with the spiritual guide, know him in greater depth, and understand the essence of his messages. Channeling tends to flow more easily when the questions do not concern you.

On the second day, ask the entity (he may already have a name) questions about your spiritual work, about the connection between you and him, and various other spiritual questions (those are generally easier to get an answer to, and will also help you feel more sure of the messages you receive, since you are likely to receive answers that generally would not have occurred to you).

It is possible that you will discover that you are channeling with your own soul. Our soul has many ways to channel with us, since the majority of people do not channel with it on a daily basis (such a wonderful thing exists inside us, and so many people don't know it!). The soul has tremendous knowledge about ourselves, our previous lives, and our future, as well as a huge store of metaphysical and cosmic knowledge. If you discover that you are channeling with your soul, and not with an entity of some kind, you can pat yourself on the back, since this is a marvelous experience. The moment we begin to channel with the soul with various practice tools, we don't want to stop. The lovely thing about this is that after some time of channeling with the soul via "external" tools and exercises, we get used to it, and we begin to receive messages and be in touch with our soul all the time. If we were all to channel daily with our souls, the world would look completely different. The feeling of the soul that exists inside us can be amazing, and it can change our perception of the world in an instant.

*Third stage* – **Third day of practice – questions about the universe and what happens in it:**

On the third day, ask questions about universal matters. We are now entering the age of Aquarius, and many changes are occurring. You can request information about these changes, or you can ask your guide's opinion of information that you read or heard. If the answers you receive (and sometimes, the questions, too – they themselves occasionally constitute channeling) seem strange or incomprehensible to you, don't worry about it too much. If we link up to a certain kind of information, which is (apparently) new to us, it may seem incomprehensible at first. However, the moment we have created the link-up (which already existed in us previously, but now we're discovering it in a practical and cerebral way), we will receive many different clues concerning that topic, not just via channeling, and not just when we are tuned in to receiving answers. It is not worth becoming obsessive about the topic, or to boast about the information received, nor is it advisable to rush out and disseminate it, since excessive focus on the matter is liable to make it slip out of our hands or cause us to make various assumptions that are not necessarily correct.

*Fourth stage* – **Fourth day of practice – starting to ask questions about personal matters:**

On the fourth day, you can begin to ask questions concerning personal matters. At this point, it is important to point out that you may ask a particular question only once. If you do not receive an answer, it is either not the right time for receiving an answer about that matter or your guide does not want to reply for various reasons. Asking the same question over and over in order to get the desired answer is not right.

The more you practice and experiment with automatic writing, the easier and quicker channeling will become.

Remember that even if you have not been exceptionally successful with these exercises, they are a preparation for channeling. Therefore, they act as a stimulating effect and as a trigger for this ability, as well as a kind of signal to the universe that we are ready and willing to move on to this stage of spiritual development. It is possible that there will be no results during the course of the exercise. However, at a certain moment, channeling information will begin to emerge and appear naturally. In fact, we often channel during the day. Insights, information, and so on sometimes originate from channeling, except that we are not always aware of it, or know with whom or with what we are channeling. Occasionally, channeling attempts by means of automatic writing are fruitless. At different stages of creation, such as painting or sculpting, however, channeling art takes place. This is painting or sculpture etc. that is directed by a particular entity or spiritual guide whose trigger is activated by the practice and the actual desire to channel "via the hand."

In any event, if at any stage you feel uncomfortable, receive messages that seem "unclean" to you, experience any kind of energetic feelings that are unpleasant, or feel that something inside you wants to stop – then stop.